WORKING ENGLISH COURSE BOOK

Working English

Englisch im Beruf

Course Book

LANGENSCHEIDT

BERLIN · MÜNCHEN · LEIPZIG · WIEN · ZÜRICH · NEW YORK

Working English

by

Paul Westlake
Eeva-Liisa Pitkänen
Eero Lehtonen
Kate Moore

Editor: Anita Seppovaara
Illustrations: Pertti Anikari
Photos: Eero Lehtonen, Riina Hyytiä, Paul Westlake
Design: Heikki Kalliomaa
Layout: Timo Lagerkrans, Eeva-Liisa Pitkänen
Editorial assistance: Paul Dillingham, Merja Hyytiäinen

| Auflage: | 5. | 4. | 3. | 2. | 1. | Letzte Zahlen |
| Jahr: | 1997 | 96 | 95 | 94 | 93 | maßgeblich |

How to use **WORKING ENGLISH**

The essence of WORKING ENGLISH lies in clearly defined and carefully selected phrases which allow you to express yourself in work or work-related situations. Unit 1 of the Course Book is introductory and has no related phrases in the Phrase Book. Units 2 – 11 are intended for use with the Phrase Book. The following procedure is recommended:

One: Study the appropriate phrases in the Phrase Book.

Two: Work through the Course Book, referring to your Phrase Book whenever necessary.

Explanation of exercises

Self-study
For people working alone or for homework.

Pair work
For two people. Many pair-work exercises can, however, be used for self-study if students write down the phrases instead of saying them.

Group work
For three or more people. Some of these are also suitable for self-study.

Listening exercises
The gramophone symbol informs you that there is some listening material on the tape. There are five main types of listenings:
1 Phrase practice – react accordingly.
2 Recorded texts – essentially just for enjoyment and comprehension.
3 Model discussions or conversations to help you prepare for an exercise.
4 Authentic interviews – an opportunity to listen to real English and pick up a few hints.
5 Straightforward listening comprehension exercises.

– **Key and tapescripts** The key comprises solutions as well as model answers and tapescripts.

CONTENTS

Unit	Title	Language Area
1	Introducing	Basics
2	Nice to Meet You	Making Contact
3	On Behalf of Our Company	Receiving Visitors
4	The Floor is Yours	Formal Meetings
5	What do you think?	Informal Meetings
6	Be My Guest	Socializing
7	To Be Quite Frank	Negotiations
8	Clearly and Simply	Presentations
9	No Problem!	Dealing with Difficulties
10	Your Attention, Please!	Conferences
11	Thanks for the Information	Fairs
	Key and tapescripts	Solutions, model answers and tapescripts
	Vocabulary	Alphabetical vocabulary

Language Targets		Pages
		1–20
On the phone – introductions – asking to speak to someone – arranging time and place – hotel reservations – ending the conversation	Meeting people – for the first time – acquaintances – introducing yourself and others – agreeing on meeting later – saying goodbye	21–46
At the reception – asking and giving directions – identification – contacting the appropriate person – messages	Presenting your workplace – welcoming visitors – starting a workplace presentation – asking questions – thanking visitors	47–68
– opening a formal meeting – the minutes – the agenda – taking the floor	– motioning – voting – closing a formal meeting	69–90
– opening a meeting – introducing points – adding, giving examples and balancing – generalizing and stating preference	– opinions and suggestions – agreement and disagreement – rounding up a meeting	91–110
– invitations – breaking news and responding – getting a table in a restaurant	– deciding on food – table talk – sending and giving regards	111–126
– making proposals – agreement and disagreement – exchanging information	– compromising – summarizing	127–144
– beginning a presentation – progressing – digressing	– describing graphs and figures – ending a presentation	145–166
– changes in schedule – changes in travel arrangements – checking information	– complaining – apologizing	167–186
– making travel arrangements – registration – introducing and thanking speakers	– asking for and offering assistance – group work – questions	187–206
– asking about companies and products – answering questions – asking for, granting and refusing permission	– finding out identity – saying goodbye formally	207–226
		227–242
		243–261

Introducing...

A look at some basics

THE ENGLISH-SPEAKING WORLD

i.e. the countries where English is used as a mother tongue or first language.

ARCTI

Alaska

Canada

United States

United Kingdom

Eire

ATLANTIC OCEAN

Gibraltar

Bermuda

Bahamas

Anguilla
Antigua and
   Barbuda
Barbados
Dominica
Grenada
Montserrat
St Lucia
St Vincent and
   the Grenadines
Trinidad & Tobago

Senegal

Gambia

Sierra Leone

Liberia

Ghana

Cameroo

Hawaiian Islands

Jamaica
Belize

Caribbean Sea

Guyana
   Surinam

Ascension

St Helena

PACIFIC
OCEAN

Tristan da Cunh

Falkland
Islands

St Georgia

OCEAN

Aleutian Islands

PACIFIC
OCEAN

Malta

Pakistan

Nepal

Bhutan

India

Hong
Kong

Bangla-
desh

Philippines

Caroline
Islands

neroon

Brunei

Sri Lanka

Malaysia

Uganda

Kenya

Singapore

Papua
New Guinea

Nauru

Kiribati

Tanzania

Seychelles

Salomon Islands

Tuvalu

INDIAN

Zambia

Malawi

OCEAN

Vanuatu

Samoa

Namibia

Zimbabwe

Fiji

Botswana

Mauritius

Tonga

Swaziland

Australia

Lesotho

South
Africa

New
Zealand

Tasmania

SOUTHERN

OCEAN

1  RESPONSES

Listen to the tape and respond to the phrases in any way you wish.
You may want to use some of the phrases given below.

Me too.	You too.	I'm sorry to hear that.
I will.	No, thanks.	
Sorry.	Go ahead.	I'm afraid not.
Fine.	Of course.	
Please.	Yes, please.	You're welcome.
Pardon?	Excuse me.	
I'd love to.	Not so bad.	Never mind.

Now you will hear the same phrases but this time with suitable responses.

2 DO IT YOURSELF

Look at the situations below and on the opposite page and
fill in the bubbles with suitable phrases.

3 ENGLISH AS A LINGUA FRANCA*

One of the fundamental* considerations for a rapidly changing Europe is the challenge of cross-cultural understanding and communication. Everywhere, from Iceland to Italy, committees, unions, institutions, businesses, industry, governmental departments and a host of* other official and unofficial organizations
5 are committed* to broadening their horizons and sharing information.

The concept of thinking globally and acting locally has become very much a cliché in international business. Nevertheless, the question still remains as to how tolerant and cooperative Europeans will turn out to be. Obviously the future of a united and potentially all-encompassing* Europe depends on whether or not we
10 can iron out* our differences and hit on some kind of common 'language'.

Languages themselves will therefore be instrumental* in enabling us to achieve such goals. And English as a *lingua franca* would seem to be a natural focal point* for language learning.

English as a global language

15 English is the number one language in the world in terms of usage: seven out of every ten things written down are in English.

It is, however, more difficult to put a figure on* just how many English speakers there are in the world. Should we include as mother-tongue English speakers people who speak pidgins* or creoles*? And how about those who know
20 English as a foreign language? If so, then we are talking about well over a 1,000 million, approximately a quarter of the world's population. Only Guoyu, a form of Mandarin Chinese with somewhere in the region of 800 million Chinese understanding it can claim to be a serious challenger.

Nevertheless, the fact remains that English is the global language. As such, it
25 carries with it a heavy responsibility as a vehicle for cross-cultural communication.

Global English is rapidly becoming a linguistic idea. Loosely defined, it comprises all coherent* forms of English, not just the English used by native speakers. The emphasis is on whether or not it can be understood and not, as it used to be, on how closely it resembles Received Pronunciation* or so-called
30 Oxford English*.

English in Europe

From a European viewpoint it is well worthwhile recognizing that American English and British English share equal status. Many an English language teacher has been caught in two minds* over which of these he or she should encourage. Fortunately,
35 such a consideration would appear to be outdated. In fact, the English language

would seem to be undergoing some streamlining*. Traditionally, Americans said *the line was busy* while the British claimed that *the telephone was engaged*. In today's Europe they have both been superseded* by a European compromise; *the line is occupied.*

40   WORKING ENGLISH aims at giving you an opportunity of becoming acquainted* with such terms as well as practising English orally*. So, whether you're *engaged* or just *busy* we hope you're not too *occupied* to join us on a little trip through the English language.

Explanation of words:

lingua franca	a language used for communication between people of different mother tongues
fundamental	basic
a host of	a lot of
committed	dedicated
all-encompassing	leaving nothing out
to iron out	solve
instrumental	helpful
focal point	central point
to put a figure on	to state how many or how much
pidgin	a language made up from two or more languages for communication
creole	a pidgin that has become the mother tongue of a community
coherent	logical and understandable
Received Pronunciation	the way some people speak in Southern England
Oxford English	a form of Received Pronunciation thought to be typical of the way some people talk at Oxford University
to be caught in two minds	to be unsure
to streamline	make more efficient by simplifying
to supersede	to take the place of something old-fashioned
to become acquainted with	to get to know
orally	spoken

A European joke?

There was an Englishman, Frenchman, Norwegian, Swede and Finn travelling on an airplane. Unfortunately, the airplane began losing height, so the captain asked for a brave volunteer to jump out to help reduce the load. Up stands the Englishman, shouting: "God save the Queen!", and jumps. A few minutes later the plane starts losing height again and another volunteer is asked for. This time it's the Frenchman who stands up, proclaiming: "Vive la France!", and throws himself out. All is well for a while but then the plane begins to lose height once again. Immediately the Finn and the Norwegian spring to their feet, pick up the Swede and throw him out, chanting: "Long live Nordic cooperation!"

4 A SHORT SELF-ASSESSMENT ON CROSS-CULTURAL COMMUNICATION

 The following self-assessment test is designed to give you some idea of just how aware and sensitive you might be when meeting people from other cultures. Mark your answers with a cross (x). You'll find out how you scored on page 18, together with a simple assessment.

		Yes	Perhaps	No
1	I can manage quite well in new situations.			
2	I try to understand people's opinions and feelings when I talk to them.			
3	I don't worry too much if I make a faux pas *(mistake)*.			
4	I like being with all kinds of people.			
5	I have a pretty good idea of what other people think of me.			
6	When I meet people from another culture it's very important that they like me.			
7	If I have to work with very slow people I get impatient.			
8	Giving people a good idea of me is more important than being myself with them.			
9	I make friends easily.			
10	I believe that all cultures have something positive to offer.			
11	I'm not so good at understanding people when they are different from me.			
12	When I am with people from another culture I try to look at them in terms of that culture.			
13	I can manage in unclear situations.			
14	I trust in my ability to communicate in new situations.			
15	I pay attention to body language when I talk to people from other cultures.			

5 YET ANOTHER ONE OF THOSE EUROPEAN JOKES

 Work in groups of three or more.

Step one
Read through the joke below.

> The European dream is where the French are the cooks, the English are the policemen, the Germans are the mechanics, the Swiss are the organizers and the Italians are the lovers.
>
> The European nightmare is where the English are the cooks, the Germans are the policemen, the French are the mechanics, the Italians are the organizers and the Swiss are the lovers.

Step two:
Discuss the prejudices and ideas suggested by the joke.

Step three:
Imagine you had to select a nationality for a specific job, e.g., a Frenchman for a chef or a German for a brewer. What nationalities would you choose for the following occupations? Discuss this in your group, giving the reasons for your decisions. Then compare your group's results with those of other groups in your class.

Occupation	Nationality	Reason
Engineer	_____	_____
Philosopher	_____	_____
Opera singer	_____	_____
Inventor	_____	_____
Gardener	_____	_____
Clothes designer	_____	_____
Diplomat	_____	_____
Scientist	_____	_____
Actor/actress	_____	_____
Psychologist	_____	_____

6 THE ENGLISH ALPHABET

a [eɪ]	h [eɪtʃ]	o [əʊ]	v [viː]
b [biː]	i [aɪ]	p [piː]	w [dʌbljuː]
c [siː]	j [dʒeɪ]	q [kjuː]	x [eks]
d [diː]	k [keɪ]	r [ɑː]	y [waɪ]
e [iː]	l [el]	s [es]	z [zed] *Am.* [ziː]
f [ef]	m [em]	t [tiː]	
g [dʒiː]	n [en]	u [juː]	

Please note:

ö   is often said as "[əʊ] with two dots"
ä   is often said as "[eɪ] with two dots"
å   is said as "[eɪ] with a circle on top"
ü   is said as "[juː] umlaut"
ø   is said as "[əʊ] with a stroke through it"
æ   is said as "[æ]"

 Work with your partner and fill in the missing letters. Partner B's list is on page 17. Partner A should not look at Partner B's list. Partner A should try to guess what the word is. Partner B knows the answers and tries to help by giving a clue, e.g. "A place where you eat." To make sure you have the right answer, partner A should SPELL the word in English, using the phonetics given above.

Partner A:

1   R E   **S T A U R A N T** _____

2   F O   _____

3   P R   _____

4   I N   _____

5   C O   _____

6   N E   _____

7 THE ENGLISH ALPHABET ON THE PHONE

You might find the following alphabet (used by international airlines) useful when trying to spell a word on the telephone.

A	Alpha	['ælfə]	O	Oscar	['ɒskə]
Ä	Alpha-Echo	['ælfə'ekəʊ]	Ö	Oscar-Echo	['ɒskər'ekəʊ]
B	Bravo	['brɑːvəʊ]	P	Papa	['pɑpə]
C	Charlie	['tʃɑːlɪ]	Q	Quebec	[kwɪ'bek]
D	Delta	['deltə]	R	Romeo	['rəʊmɪəʊ]
E	Echo	['ekəʊ]	S	Sierra	[sɪ'erə]
F	Foxtrot	['fɒkstrɒt]	Sch	Sierra Charlie Hotel	
G	Golf	['gɒlf]	T	Tango	['tæŋgəʊ]
H	Hotel	[həʊ'tel]	U	Uniform	['juːnɪfɔːm]
I	India	['ɪndjə]	Ü	Uniform-Echo	['juːnɪfɔːm'ekəʊ]
J	Juliet	['dʒuːljət]	V	Victor	['vɪktə]
K	Kilo	['kiːləʊ]	W	Whiskey	['wɪskɪ]
L	Lima	['liːmə]	X	X-Ray	['eksreɪ]
M	Mike	['maɪk]	Y	Yankee	['jæŋkɪ]
N	November	[nəʊ'vembə]	Z	Zulu	['zuːluː]

Work with your partner and spell out some names of places or people you know. Write down each letter as you hear it, then say the word. Change roles.

8 AN EXPERIMENT IN TIME

There are many different ways of expressing time.

STANDARD SYSTEM

3.00: three o'clock / three a.m. / p.m.
3.05: five (minutes) past three / three oh five
3.15: (a) quarter past* three / three fifteen
3.20: twenty (minutes) past three / three twenty
3.30: half past three / three thirty
3.35: twenty-five (minutes) to** four / three thirty-five
3.45: (a) quarter to four / three forty-five

* 'after' is often used instead of 'past' (US)
** 'of' is sometimes used instead of 'to' (US)

24-HOUR CLOCK

The 24-hour clock is being increasingly used in travel timetables and international communications.

03.00: (oh) three (hundred) hours
11.36: eleven thirty-six
12.00: twelve (hundred) hours / noon
13.45: thirteen forty-five
18.00: eighteen (hundred) hours
21:07: twenty-one (oh) seven
24:00: twenty-four (hundred) hours / midnight

Work with your partner and point to a time from the following timetable. Your partner should then try to say it, first using the standard system and then once again using the 24-hour clock. Change roles.

| 02.18 | 10.30 | 14.20 | 15.27 | 16.42 | 17.07 |
| 20.00 | 23.53 | 24.00 | 00.01 | 00.40 | 01.05 |

9 SHORT FORMS

 Using short forms in English can definitely help you sound more fluent. Look carefully at the following list and then try practising the sentences below with your partner.

© Oxford Advanced Learner's Dictionary of Current English by A. S. Hornby; by permission of 'Oxford University Press'

Personal pronoun + verb

I'm	[aɪm]	I am
I've	[aɪv]	I have
I'll	[aɪl]	I will/shall
I'd	[aɪd]	I would; I had
you're	[jʊə(r)]	you are
you've	[ju:v]	you have
you'll	[ju:l]	you will
you'd	[ju:d]	you would; you had
he's	[hi:z]	he is; he has
he'll	[hi:l]	he will
he'd	[hi:d]	he would
she's	[ʃi:z]	she is; she has

she'll	[ʃi:l]	she will
she'd	[ʃi:d]	she would; she had
it's	[ɪts]	it is; it has
it'll	[ɪtl]	it will
we're	[wɪə(r)]	we are
we've	[wi:v]	we have
we'll	[wi:l]	we will/shall
we'd	[wi:d]	we would; we had
they're	[ðeɪə(r)]	they are
they've	[ðeɪv]	they have
they'll	[ðeɪl]	they will
they'd	[ðeɪd]	they would

Verb + not

aren't	[ɑ:nt]	are not
can't	[kɑ:nt]	cannot
couldn't	[kʊdnt]	could not
daren't	[deənt]	dare not
didn't	[dɪdnt]	did not
doesn't	[dʌznt]	does not
don't	[dəʊnt]	do not
hasn't	[hæznt]	has not
haven't	[hævnt]	have not
hadn't	[hædnt]	had not
isn't	[ɪznt]	is not

mayn't	[meɪnt]	may not
mightn't	[maɪtnt]	might not
mustn't	[mʌsnt]	must not
needn't	[ni:dnt]	need not
oughtn't	[ɔ:tnt]	ought not
shan't	[ʃɑ:nt]	shall not
shouldn't	[ʃʊdnt]	should not
wasn't	[wɒznt]	was not
weren't	[wɜ:nt]	were not
won't	[wəʊnt]	will not
wouldn't	[wʊdnt]	would not

Other common contractions

here's	[hɪəz]	here is
how's	[haʊz]	how is
that'd	[ðætəd]	that would
that'll	[ðætl]	that will
that's	[ðæts]	that is
there's	[ðeəz]	there is
what'll	[wɒtl]	what will

what's	[wɒts]	what is
when's	[wenz]	when is
where's	[weəz]	where is
who'd	[hu:d]	who would
who'll	[hu:l]	who will
who's	[hu:z]	who is

1 I am tired.
2 She would help, I am sure.
3 You will arrive at night.
4 He does not agree.

5 We would not, could not and should not.
6 There is someone who would know.
7 Where is the person who is responsible?
8 They will not know how he is.

TINY TALK

THANK YOU

1   As you give somebody something this is what you could say:
    Here. / There. / There you go. / There you are. / Here you are.

2   What to say after somebody has thanked you:
    OK. / It's OK. / That's OK. / All right. / That's all right.
    and even *Thank **you.***

3   When you have been very helpful and the person has been very
    grateful and has just thanked you, this is what you could say:
    You're welcome. / Don't mention it. / My pleasure. / Not at all.
    The Americans use *You're welcome* in situations 2 and 3.

SORRY / EXCUSE ME / PARDON

1   *Sorry* is used
    a) after you've done something wrong and you want to apologize.
    b) when you don't understand something (with rising intonation).
    c) when you want to explain that you were wrong.

2   *Sorry* is also used at the beginning (or end) of the sentence to
    soften the effect.
    Sorry, I can't help you. / I can't help you. Sorry.

3   *Excuse me* is used
    a) to signal that you want to do something, e.g. leave a meeting for
    a while.
    b) when you don't understand something (with rising intonation).
    c) when you want to get somebody's attention.
    Excuse me, but do you know where room 3038 is?

4   *Pardon* is used when you don't understand something
    (with rising intonation.)

5   *Pardon me* is used when you don't understand something
    (with rising intonation) or when you apologize for doing something.

PLEASE

Please remember that *please* is used
a) when you're asking for something.
    Can I have a glass of milk, please?
b) when you're asking someone to do or not to do something.
    Open the window, please. / Please don't open the window.
c) as an affirmative answer, with or without yes.
    Milk? (Yes.) Please.
Please don't use *Please* as a response to *Thank you* as is the case in
many European languages.

10 GET READY

 Would you manage in the following situations? Write down a suitable phrase.

1   Someone introduces you to someone with the words "I'd like to introduce you to a colleague of mine, Jan Peters." How would you respond?

_____

2   Someone says, "How do you do?" What would you answer?

_____

3   You help an English friend with her luggage. She says, "Thanks a lot." How would you respond?

_____

4   Someone says something you can't understand. You would like him or her to say it again. What do you say?

_____

5   Someone has just passed his/her driving test. What would you say?

_____

6   Someone has just failed an examination. How would you react?

_____

7   You want to get to the door in a crowded room. What would you say?

_____

8   The phone rings. What would you say to your guests before answering it?

_____

9   Someone asks you if you would mind opening the window. What would you say?

_____

10 What would you say as you hand something to someone?

_____

11 What would you say if you had to introduce a colleague to a guest?

_____

12 What words would you use when meeting a customer/business associate? You have only met him or her once or twice before.

_____

13 Send your regards to a) a close friend and b) a business associate.

_____

_____

14 What would you say to someone who asks if it's all right to smoke and it isn't?

_____

15 How would you ask someone if you could look at a confidential report?

_____

16 How would you propose a toast to a visitor to your company?

_____

17 What would you say if you arrived late at a meeting?

_____

18 How would you congratulate a business associate on a) being promoted b) getting married and c) his/her birthday?

_____

_____

_____

19 What would you say to a colleague whose close relative has just died?

_____

20 How would you invite a new business associate of the opposite sex to dinner in a restaurant?

_____

21 How would you turn down such an invitation yourself?

_____

22 How would you accept the invitation?

_____

11 BODY LANGUAGE

 **Work with your partner and explain the following without saying anything. Use gestures to communicate what you feel or see.
Take turns.**

1   Everything's OK.
2   Good luck!
3   I think that person is crazy.
4   There's a telephone call for you.
5   A woman just jumped off that building over there and simply walked away. Unbelievable!
6   He is really big and weighs 170 kilos. He has short hair and a broken nose.
7   There was a giant spider in the hotel room. Before I could do anything it went under the bed. Disgusting!
8   If you want to sell more of your products you will have to be more aggressive.

Partner B   Partner B   Partner B   Partner B   Partner B

From page 10, exercise 6: The English Alphabet

1   **R** **E** S T A U R A N T
2   **F** **O** R E I G N E R
3   **P** **R** **E** S E N T A T I O N
4   **I** **N** T R O D U C E
5   **C** **O** N T R A C T
6   **N** **E** C E S S I T Y

MS

**Ms is a modern form of address for women.
It replaces the traditional forms of Mrs and Miss.
It is pronounced [miz].**

A SHORT SELF-ASSESSMENT ON CROSS-CULTURAL COMMUNICATION

Scoring system for exercise 4 on page 8.

		Yes	Perhaps	No
1	I can manage quite well in new situations.	2	1	0
2	I try to understand people's opinions and feelings when I talk to them.	2	1	0
3	I don't worry too much if I make a faux pas *(mistake)*.	2	1	0
4	I like being with all kinds of people.	2	1	0
5	I have a pretty good idea of what other people think of me.	2	1	0
6	When I meet people from another culture it's very important that they like me.	0	1	2
7	If I have to work with very slow people I get impatient.	0	1	2
8	Giving people a good idea of me is more important than being myself with them.	0	1	2
9	I make friends easily.	2	1	0
10	I believe that all cultures have something positive to offer.	2	1	0
11	I'm not so good at understanding people when they are different from me.	0	1	2
12	When I am with people from another culture I try to look at them in terms of that culture.	2	1	0
13	I can manage in unclear situations.	2	1	0
14	I trust in my ability to communicate in new situations.	2	1	0
15	I pay attention to body language when I talk to people from other cultures.	2	1	0

Your score:

Score assessment:

The more points you scored the more communicative and empathetic you would seem to be (max: 30 points, min: 0 points). If you have scored below 15 points it would seem that there's a whole new world waiting for you out there. Whatever your score we're sure you'll get a lot out of using WORKING ENGLISH.

EUROPEANS

COUNTRY	A PERSON	PEOPLE	ADJECTIVE
Albania	an Albanian	Albanians	Albanian
Austria	an Austrian	Austrians	Austrian
Belgium	a Belgian	Belgians	Belgian
Bulgaria	a Bulgarian	Bulgarians	Bulgarian
Croatia	a Croat	Croats	Croatian, Croat
Czech Republic	a Czech	Czechs	Czech
Denmark	a Dane	Danes	Danish
England	an Englishman/ -woman	Englishmen/ the English	English
Estonia	an Estonian	Estonians	Estonian
Finland	a Finn	Finns	Finnish
France	a Frenchman/ -woman	Frenchmen/ the French	French
Germany	a German	Germans	German
Greece	a Greek	Greeks	Greek
Hungary	a Hungarian	Hungarians	Hungarian
Iceland	an Icelander	Icelanders	Icelandic
Ireland	an Irishman/ -woman	Irishmen/ the Irish	Irish
Italy	an Italian	Italians	Italian
Latvia	a Latvian	Latvians	Latvian
Lithuania	a Lithuanian	Lithuanians	Lithuanian
Luxembourg	a Luxembourger	Luxembourgers	Luxembourg
Malta	a Maltese	the Maltese	Maltese
Netherlands	a Dutchman/ -woman	Dutchmen/ the Dutch	Dutch
Norway	a Norwegian	Norwegians	Norwegian
Poland	a Pole	Poles	Polish
Portugal	a Portuguese	the Portuguese	Portuguese
Romania	a Romanian	Romanians	Romanian
Russia	a Russian	Russians	Russian
Scotland	a Scot/a Scotsman	Scots	Scottish
Serbia	a Serb	Serbs	Serbian, Serb
Slovakia	a Slovak	Slovaks	Slovak
Slovenia	a Slovene	Slovenes	Slovene
Spain	a Spaniard	Spaniards	Spanish
Sweden	a Swede	Swedes	Swedish
Switzerland	a Swiss	the Swiss	Swiss
Turkey	a Turk	Turks	Turkish
Wales	a Welshman/ -woman	Welshmen/ the Welsh	Welsh

HOW TO BE FRIENDLY
IN 20 LANGUAGES

English
Hello!
Goodbye!
Thank you.
You're welcome.
Cheers!
Yes. No.

Norwegian
Hei!
På gjensyn!
Takk.
Ikke noe å takke for.
Skål!
Ja. Nei.

Italian
Ciao!
Arrivederci!
Grazie.
Di niente.
Cin cin!
Sí. No.

Russian
Zdrávstvujte!
Da svidánija!
Spasíba.
Ni stóit.
Váše zdoróvje!
Da. Njet.

Finnish
Hei!
Näkemiin.
Kiitos.
Ei kestä.
Kippis!
Kyllä. Ei.

Icelandic
Sæll!
Bless!
Takk.
Ekkert aðþakka.
Skál!
Já. Nei.

Spanish
¡Hola!
¡Adiós!
Gracias.
De nada.
¡Salud!
Sí. No.

Polish
Cześć!
Do widzenia.
Dziękuję.
Proszę.
Na zdrowie!
Tak. Nie.

Estonian
Tere!
Head aega!
Aitäh.
Pole tänu väärt.
Terviseks!
Jah. Ei.

German
Hallo!
Auf Wiedersehen!
Danke.
Bitte sehr.
Prost!
Ja. Nein.

Romanian
Salut!
La revedere!
Mulţumesc.
Cu plăcere.
Noroc!
Da. Nu.

Greek
Já su!
Hérete.
Efharistó.
Típota.
Já su!
Né. Óhi.

Swedish
Hej!
Adjö!
Tack.
För all del.
Skål!
Ja. Nej.

Dutch
Hallo!
Tot ziens!
Dankuwel.
Tot uw dienst.
Proost!
Ja. Neen.

Portuguese
Olá!
Adeus!
Obrigado.
De nada.
Saúde!
Sim. Não.

Japanese
Konnichiva!
Sayōnara!
Arigatō.
Dō itashimashite.
Kampai!
Hai. Iie.

Danish
Dav!
Farvel!
Tak.
Selv tak.
Skål!
Ja. Nej.

French
Salut!
Au revoir!
Merci.
Pas de quoi.
A votre santé!
Oui. Non.

Hungarian
Szervusz!
Viszontlátásra!
Köszönöm.
Szót sem érdemel.
Egészségére!
Igen. Nem.

Arabic
Marhaba!
Ma salaam!
Shukran.
Ahlan wa sahlan.
—
Na'am. Laam.

Nice to Meet You

The language of making contact

This unit deals with contacting
associates by telephone
and meeting people.

1 SNAPSHOTS

Listen and repeat. You can also enact the situations.

– CCN International.
  Good morning.
  Can I help you?
– Good morning.
  This is Lisa Kohler
  from Berlin. I'm
  trying to contact
  David Andrews.

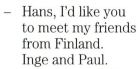

– Hello, Les. Good to see you
  again. How are things?
– Oh, not so bad, you know.
  How about you?
– Pretty good, thanks.

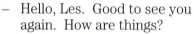

– Hans, I'd like you
  to meet my friends
  from Finland.
  Inge and Paul.
– How do you do?
– Pleased to meet you.
– Nice to meet you,
  too.

– Well, perhaps we can arrange to
  meet later on tonight.
– All right. What time and where?
– How about in the lobby at eight?
– OK. See you then.

– I'm looking forward to
  meeting you.

WISE WORDS ON MAKING CONTACT

Don't tell your friends about indigestion.
"How are you" is a greeting, not a question.

Arthur Guitterman

2 CROSS-CULTURAL CONSIDERATIONS

❏ Throughout Europe, handshakes are frequent and important. Also, in Mediterranean countries, it is not unusual for men to greet each other with a kiss on both cheeks.

❏ The use of correct titles is very important in many cultures, particularly in Europe. In France or Italy, for instance, one does not address business acquaintances by their first names. In Germany, executives are often addressed by their position, such as *Herr Doktor.*

❏ A man is usually introduced to a woman. When introducing two people of the same sex, present the younger to the older.

❏ General tips on meeting people in Europe:

Belgians	Handshakes among business associates. Three kisses on the cheek (alternately) with close friends.
British	Enjoy shaking hands.
Germans	Firm handshakes (usually a quick pumping motion).
Greeks	Handshaking and embracing. Sometimes together with a kiss.
Portuguese	Some handshaking. Men often embrace and slap backs. For women a kiss on both cheeks is considered appropriate.
Russians	Lots of handshaking. The famous Russian "bear hug" and cheek-kissing are still popular.
Spaniards	Some handshaking. Close friends may hug each other.
Scandinavians	Lots of handshaking. They don't feel too comfortable with hugging and kissing.

3 THE FAX OF LIFE

Read the text and do the exercise.

Alexander Graham Bell would have been surprised to hear that you can see on the
telephone. But that's exactly what has happened thanks to the advent of the fax.
Select a number, feed in the information and keep your mouth closed and your
fingers crossed.

5   Let's face facts; the fax has changed the face of communications, particularly
for those who always wanted to be technically-minded but were too afraid to touch
a keyboard. Thanks to the invention of the fax anybody, even executive directors,
can scribble* on a piece of paper and zoom it across the world without having to
ask someone else to do it. There are even three-dimensional faxes available so you
10 can send 3-D plans etc.

    The invention has even given rise to 'faxology', with people being faxed, faxing
others and weird telephone messages which say things like "I've been trying to fax
you all day." And even an updated cliché: "Don't fax us, we'll fax you."

    People no longer ask you if you have a fax. Instead, they ask you for your fax
15 number.

    "Fax now, think later" seems to be the most favoured approach in inter-office
communication. Whatever happened to the good ol' telex? It was such a concise*,
even if a little vague, medium. Perhaps you've heard of the strange telex the actor
Cary Grant received from a journalist enquiring about his age. It read "HOW OLD
20 CARY GRANT?" Cary Grant replied as follows: "OLD CARY GRANT FINE. STOP.
HOW YOU?"

    If the fax continues its present rate of development up-and-coming Cary
Grants will be able to fax themselves to wherever they're wanted.

    "I fax, therefore I am; I am, therefore I fax."

P.W.

Explanation of words

to scribble   to draw or write something which is not clear
concise   short and to the point

....

WISE WORDS ON FAXES

The fax is just right for the contemplative life: it's quick but it's silent.

Sister Scholastique

Understanding faxes very often depends on how clear the message is. Can you understand this hand-written message? Answer the questions below.

The Original Touch OY
Isokaari 6 A 21, 00200 Helsinki, Finland
Tel: (9)0 – 692 2680
Fax: (9)0 – 692 2680

FAX COVER SHEET

To: UTBILDNINGSRADION

Att: Bengt Brattberg

From: Paul Westlake

Date: 20.12.

Pages: (1) + 4

Message: I received your video. Thanks. Unfortunately, it's Beta not VHS. I only have VHS. Please send me one on VHS if possible. I'll return the Beta as soon as poss. I'm also sending you the price list you asked for. Regards

IF NOT CORRECTLY RECEIVED PLEASE INFORM IMMEDIATELY

---

1   Who was the sender of the message?   _____

2   What would Paul like to receive?   _____

3   What should Bengt do?   _____

4   What is Paul faxing?   _____

5   How many pages are being faxed?   _____

4 GET READY

 Can you manage in the following situations? If you have difficulties, turn to Unit 2 of your Phrase Book.

1a   You are supposed to meet Mr Stein at the airport but you don't know what he looks like. You see a person that might be him. How do you approach him?

_____

1b   You meet Mr Stein for the first time. What do you say?

_____

2   You meet an old acquaintance of yours you haven't seen for a long time. What might you say to him?

_____

3   You want to introduce your business colleague to your friend. What do you say?

_____

4   You want to introduce a visitor to your boss. What do you say?

_____

5a   You have had an appointment with Mr Bayer. You want to meet him later on. What do you say?

_____

5b   You settle a time that suits you both. What do you say to show you accept the suggestion?

_____

6   You have had a nice conversation with a group of new business associates but you have another engagement coming up. How do you leave without offending them?

_____

PHRASE PRACTICE (4)

. . . .

This exercise gives you an opportunity to practise English on the telephone. You will hear eight phrases selected from Unit 2 of your Phrase Book. Respond accordingly.

Phrase 1 (receptionist) You respond by asking to speak to someone.
Phrase 2 (receptionist) You respond by giving your name.
Phrase 3 (receptionist) You respond by spelling your name.
Phrase 4 (client) You respond by answering the question.
Phrase 5 (client) You respond by suggesting a day.
Phrase 6 (client) You respond by suggesting a place.
Phrase 7 (client) You respond by suggesting a time.
Phrase 8 (client) You respond in any way you wish.

5 ASKING TO SPEAK TO SOMEONE

. . . .

Work with your partner and act out the following telephone conversation. Before you begin decide on your roles and why you are phoning. You may wish to be yourselves or imaginary characters.
Study sections 2.1 – 2.4 of your Phrase Book.

Caller   **Person receiving the call**

Ask to speak to someone.   Answer the phone.

Give your name.   Ask who is calling.

Spell it.   Ask him or her to spell it.

                                             Thank him or her. Explain that you
                                             are going to put him or her through.

Thank him or her.

6 ARRANGING TIME AND PLACE

 **Work with your partner and act out the conversation.
Study sections 2.1 to 2.13 of your Phrase Book.**

Caller　　　　　　　　　　　　**Person receiving call**

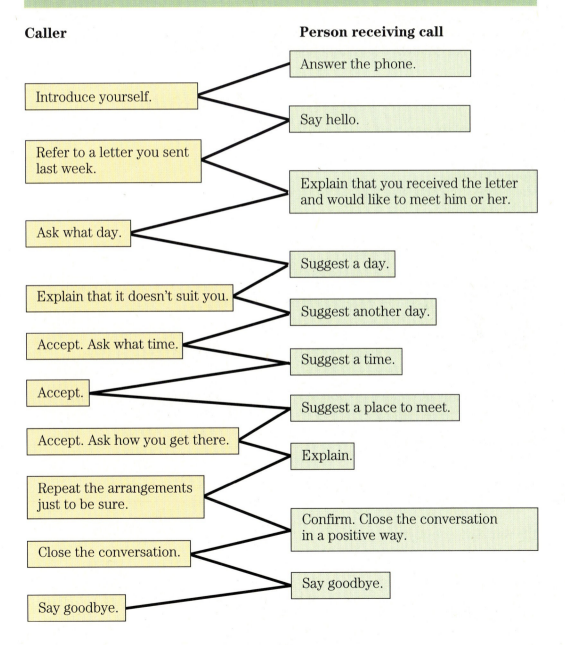

Introduce yourself.

Answer the phone.

Say hello.

Refer to a letter you sent last week.

Explain that you received the letter and would like to meet him or her.

Ask what day.

Suggest a day.

Explain that it doesn't suit you.

Suggest another day.

Accept. Ask what time.

Suggest a time.

Accept.

Suggest a place to meet.

Accept. Ask how you get there.

Explain.

Repeat the arrangements just to be sure.

Confirm. Close the conversation in a positive way.

Close the conversation.

Say goodbye.

Say goodbye.

7 TWELVE POINTS WORTH CONSIDERING

 The following represents our analysis of how to make an effective phone call. Read it through and see if you agree.

One: Prepare yourself
Make a note of what you are going to say or ask about. This saves time during the phone call and can help you sound as if you know what you want.

Two: Greet them
It's important to say *Hello, Good morning* or something to that effect.

Three: Identify yourself
Explain who you are and don't forget who you represent.

Four: Be clear
Make sure you know who you would like to talk to. Ask for the person, department, etc.

Five: Make sure
Make absolutely sure that you are talking to the right person.

Six: Explain briefly
Explain fairly early on the main reason for your call.

Seven: Listen closely
Many of us are too busy talking to listen carefully. Take notes to help you.

Eight: Talk back
It's important to let them know you're still alive and listening. Use words like *I see, Oh, really* or *Yes,* etc. or sounds such as *Mmm, Aah,* etc.

Nine: Give confirmation
Repeat the main details and confirm them.

Ten: Thank them
Be sure to thank them, even if they haven't been of much help.

Eleven: Say goodbye
Don't let them think that the line went dead. Say goodbye.

Twelve: Rapid follow-up
After you have finished the call it's probably a good idea to do whatever you have to do as a result of the call as soon as possible.

Now, following this system, fill in the blank spaces in the "caller" column with words of your own choice.

Person receiving call   **Caller**

Point 2 _____

Point 3 _____

How can I help you?
Point 4 _____

Just one moment, please.
(The person you wanted)
Hello. ...... speaking.
Point 5 _____

Yes, that's right.
How can I help you?
Point 6 _____

_____

_____

(Is talking to you.)
Point 8 _____

Yes, that's it.
Point 10 _____

You're welcome.
Point 11 _____

8 ARRANGING A TIME BY PHONE

 Work in pairs. Use similar phrases and the same format as in exercise 6 but try and find a free hour between 8 a.m. and 6 p.m. for a meeting between the two of you. Partner A's timetable is below. Partner B's timetable is on page 46.
DO NOT LOOK AT EACH OTHER'S TIMETABLES.
Try to find a free hour by referring to your timetable.

IMPORTANT: Sit back to back when doing this role play.

Partner A's timetable

Day/time	8–10	10–12	12–14	14–16	16–18
Monday	meeting	free	business lunch	free	squash
Tuesday	free	free	meeting	free	visiting client
Wednesday	meeting	free	business lunch	free	psychiatrist
Thursday	free	meeting	free	visiting client	free
Friday	business breakfast	free	meeting	free	golf

THE PHONE, so simple to use in theory, can be surprisingly tricky if you're using a foreign language, particularly if you're trying to create a good impression. Knowing suitable phrases and giving appropriate reactions can, however, help you to avoid potentially embarrassing misunderstandings. And whatever your line of work, telephone etiquette is probably well worth working at. After all, in business the telephone is second only to the personal business meeting.

INFO

9 LEAVING A MESSAGE

 Work with your partner.
Study section 2.16 of your Phrase Book.

Caller   **Person receiving call**

Answer the phone.

Introduce yourself and ask for someone.

Explain that you are about to put him or her through. (pause)

(Whistle while you're waiting.)

Now explain that the person he/she wants is talking to someone else on the phone at the moment. Ask if he/she can wait.

Explain that you can't.

Ask if you can take a message.

Say yes and ask for the person to return your call. Give your name and how you can be reached.

Check the information.

Thank him or her for helping you.

Accept the person's thanks. Say goodbye.

Say goodbye.

10 ANSWERPHONES

Answerphones are becoming increasingly more popular for business or households. Being able to leave a clear and efficient message is, however, an art in itself.
Listen to the tape and fill in the information.

Consideration:	Example:
Greet and identify:	Hello, this is .... from ....
Day and time:	Calling at .... on .... the
	.... of ....
Concise reason:	I'm phoning about ....
	....
Give info/ask questions:	....
	....
	....
Give your number and times when you're available.	I can be reached on ....
	until................................. this evening.
Repeat your number:	That's ....
Thank them.	Thanks very much. Bye.

11 GET THE MESSAGE?

Now leave your own message on an answerphone in English. Write it down first. Read it to your partner once at a reasonable speed. Your partner can take notes if he/she wishes. When you have finished your partner should repeat the main points of your message to you IN YOUR NATIVE LANGUAGE AND NOT IN ENGLISH. Change roles.

12 BOOKING YOURSELF A HOTEL ROOM BY TELEPHONE

 Work with your partner. Study sections 2.14 and 2.15 of your Phrase Book.

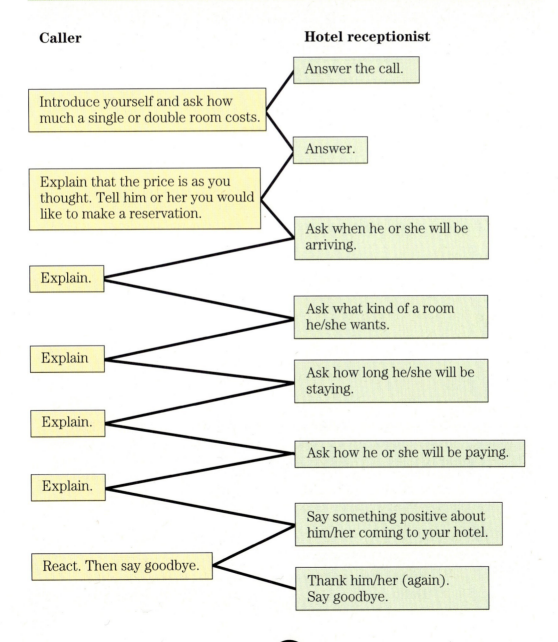

Caller

Hotel receptionist

Answer the call.

Introduce yourself and ask how much a single or double room costs.

Answer.

Explain that the price is as you thought. Tell him or her you would like to make a reservation.

Ask when he or she will be arriving.

Explain.

Ask what kind of a room he/she wants.

Explain

Ask how long he/she will be staying.

Explain.

Ask how he or she will be paying.

Explain.

Say something positive about him/her coming to your hotel.

React. Then say goodbye.

Thank him/her (again). Say goodbye.

13 ARRANGING ACCOMMODATION FOR OTHERS

 Work in pairs. Partner A is trying to make a hotel reservation for two colleagues. Partner B is an enthusiastic receptionist who really needs to study WORKING ENGLISH. Partner A's role is explained below. Partner B's role is on page 46. DO NOT READ EACH OTHER'S ROLES.

IMPORTANT! Sit back to back when doing this role play. You may wish to perform it in front of the class.

Partner A's role:

Fill in the missing details before you start.

Arrange accommodation for two of your colleagues at a festival in

.... You want two single rooms with showers

for four nights. Your colleagues' names are (make them as difficult as you like)

.... and ....

Meeting people either for the first time or otherwise can be a sensitive little ceremony. The *halo effect,* as it is sometimes referred to, is the impression you give to someone the first time you meet via your appearance, smile, handshake, etc. And, although the way you say "hello" would seem to be more important than the actual words themselves, being equipped with the right phrases can certainly help make the whole process go along more smoothly.

When you meet a person for the first time it is not necessary for both of you to use the same phrases.

Person 1: **Pleased to meet you.**	Person 1: **How do you do?**
Person 2: **Hello.**	Person 2: **Nice to meet you.**

14 MEETING PEOPLE FOR THE FIRST TIME

 Act out the following situations. Study sections 2.17–2.19 of your Phrase Book.

Host   **Visitor**

A At an airport

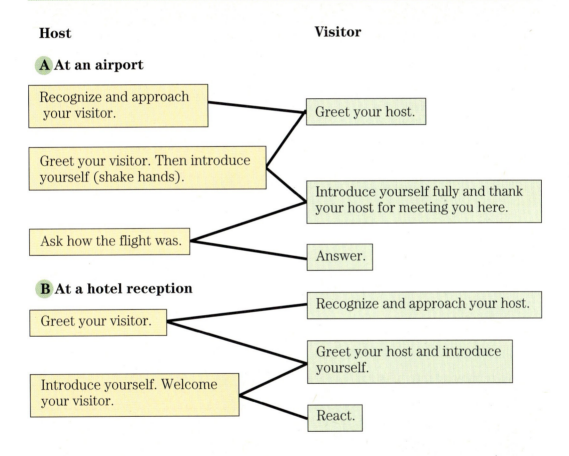

Host	Visitor
Recognize and approach your visitor.	Greet your host.
Greet your visitor. Then introduce yourself (shake hands).	Introduce yourself fully and thank your host for meeting you here.
Ask how the flight was.	Answer.

B At a hotel reception

Host	Visitor
Greet your visitor.	Recognize and approach your host.
Introduce yourself. Welcome your visitor.	Greet your host and introduce yourself.
	React.

Keeping a conversation going can be an important part of meeting people for the first time. Here are some examples of the kind of topics you can rely on when you're involved in those getting-to-know-each-other situations.

The journey   **Mutual acquaintances**   **Places of interest**
The weather   **Cultural differences**   **The programe**
                         The news

15 "MMM..."

 There are many ways of showing that you are actually listening to what a person is saying to you. Facial expressions, nodding, gestures, body language in general, or even sounds such as "Mmm" and "Ah" can all help, but here's a list of short words or phrases that may help you to show that you are listening.

To show you understand:	To show you agree:	To show you disagree:	To show surprise:
I see.	OK.	Well, no.	Oh!
Yes.	Yes.	Not really.	Really?
I got it.	Right.	Actually, no.	You don't say.
Right.	I'm with you.		
Yes, I see.			
OK.			

	To express that something is not so:	To express sympathy:	To show you really want to hear more:
	Of course not.	Oh dear.	Go on.
	No.	What a pity.	Tell me more.
		How boring for you.	Please. Keep going.
		Sorry to hear that.	

Statement   Your response

1   We made an increase in profit of over 20%! _____

2   I had a terrible flight. _____

3   So, I really didn't know what to do next. _____

4   But I'm sure you didn't mean that. _____

5   We're moving into plastics. _____

6   Have you heard enough? _____

7   Is it true you're going bankrupt? _____

8   So, everything's all right? _____

9   I'm not sure if I explained well enough. _____

10   The situation is quite desperate. _____

 Work with your partner. Take turns in reading out the statements and responding.

16 HAVE A PLEASANT TRIP

 Write down suitable responses to the following, using the pictures to help.

1 Did you have a good
   flight?

_____

_____

2 I hope you had a
   pleasant trip?

_____

_____

3 How was the
   journey?

_____

_____

4 Was the crossing
   all right?

_____

_____

5 A good flight,
   I hope?

_____

_____

6 A pleasant trip,
   I hope?

_____

_____

17 AT THE AIRPORT

Partner A: Host
You are receiving a foreign guest at the airport. Greet him / her using the phrases you have already practised but now keep the conversation going by using small talk and pointing out various points of interest while you're driving your guest into the city centre. You can use the topics given to you in the INFO on page 37, if you wish.

Partner B: Visitor
It's your first time in this country. Your host has come and met you at the airport. Greet him/her using the phrases you have already practised but keep the conversation going by using small talk. Everything is new, so why not express interest in the various buildings, museums, sports arenas, housing, natural surroundings, etc. you can see on your trip to the city centre?
Make use of the responses listed in exercise 15 "Mmm...", on page 38.

Before you start, fill in the map together so you will have something concrete to discuss. Things you might like to mark on your route:

A national museum	A sports arena	Your company's
A royal palace	A famous market place	premises etc.
A good shopping area	Parliament House	

AIRPORT:

THE GUEST'S
HOTEL

18 MEETING ACQUAINTANCES

Act out the following situations. But first study section 2.20 of your Phrase Book.

Situation 1: an arranged meeting at an office

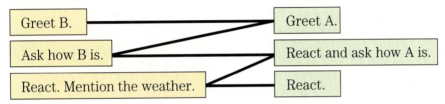

Acquaintance A	Acquaintance B
Greet B.	Greet A.
Ask how B is.	React and ask how A is.
React. Mention the weather.	React.

Situation 2: you run into each other at a conference

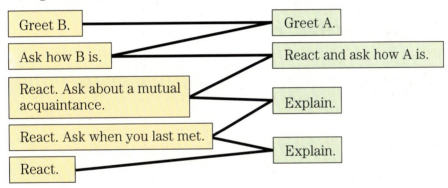

Acquaintance A	Acquaintance B
Greet B.	Greet A.
Ask how B is.	React and ask how A is.
React. Ask about a mutual acquaintance.	Explain.
React. Ask when you last met.	Explain.
React.	

Situation 3: a chance meeting in a restaurant

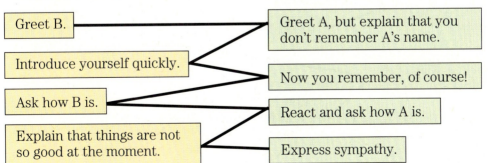

Acquaintance A	Acquaintance B
Greet B.	Greet A, but explain that you don't remember A's name.
Introduce yourself quickly.	Now you remember, of course!
Ask how B is.	React and ask how A is.
Explain that things are not so good at the moment.	Express sympathy.

Introductions

Formal introductions

Allow me to introduce Ken Ross to you.
May I introduce Ken Ross to you?
To the person you are introducing:
This is Lisa Todd.

Examples of what they might then say:
Ken: *How do you do?*
Lisa: *Pleased to meet you.*

Standard introductions

I'd like you to meet Ben Nevis.
I want you to meet Ben Nevis.
Then you might say, referring to the others:
This is … or just the name(s).

Examples of what they might then say:
Ben: *Hello.*
Tom: *Nice to meet you.*

Informal introductions

Sarah. Bob.

Examples of what they might then say:
Hi, Sarah. / Hello, Bob.

19 INTRODUCING OTHERS

Work in threes. Choose one or more of the following situations and act out the meeting with your partners. See section 2.21 of your Phrase Book. Obviously you're now going to have to use a lot more small talk in your conversation. Before you start, decide exactly who you are. You can, of course, be yourselves. Change roles.

Situation 1: Formal (at an official reception)

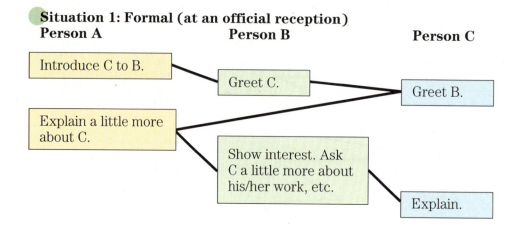

Person A	Person B	Person C
Introduce C to B.	Greet C.	Greet B.
Explain a little more about C.	Show interest. Ask C a little more about his/her work, etc.	Explain.

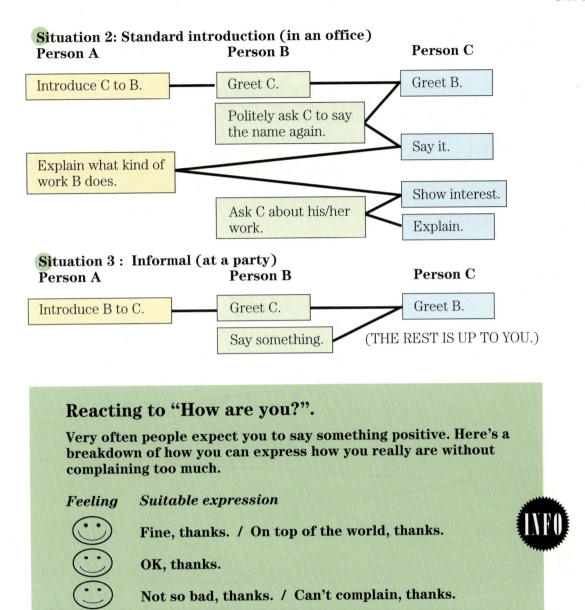

Situation 2: Standard introduction (in an office)

Person A	Person B	Person C

Introduce C to B.

Greet C.

Greet B.

Politely ask C to say the name again.

Say it.

Explain what kind of work B does.

Show interest.

Ask C about his/her work.

Explain.

Situation 3 : Informal (at a party)

Person A	Person B	Person C

Introduce B to C.

Greet C.

Greet B.

Say something.

(THE REST IS UP TO YOU.)

Reacting to "How are you?".

Very often people expect you to say something positive. Here's a breakdown of how you can express how you really are without complaining too much.

Feeling	*Suitable expression*
☺	Fine, thanks. / On top of the world, thanks.
☺	OK, thanks.
☺	Not so bad, thanks. / Can't complain, thanks.
😐	So – so, thanks. / So and so, thanks. / Surviving, thanks.
☹	Not so good, actually.

INFO

Also study the phrases in section 2.20 of your Phrase Book.

20 AGREEING TO MEET UP LATER

Work in threes. Act out the following situations, using the phrases in sections 2.22 – 2.25 of your Phrase Book.

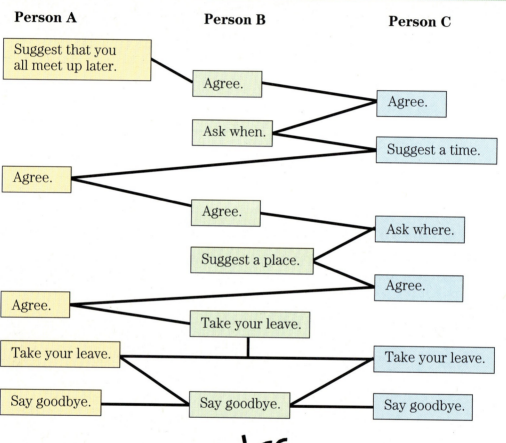

Person A	Person B	Person C

Suggest that you all meet up later.

Agree.

Agree.

Ask when.

Suggest a time.

Agree.

Agree.

Ask where.

Suggest a place.

Agree.

Agree.

Take your leave.

Take your leave.

Take your leave.

Say goodbye.

Say goodbye.

Say goodbye.

Au revoir! *Gracias.* *Egészségére!*

Ja. Nein.

Doo itashimashite.

Da svidánija!

21 INTRODUCING AND MEETING OTHERS

 Work in threes. Act out one or both of the following situations.

Situation one – informal

Person A: older
You are meeting two young students at the harbour. They have had a very bad voyage (rough seas) and they have both been seasick. They have back-packs with them.

Person B: student
Person A is your uncle or aunt. You feel terrible. It was a terrible voyage. You have been seasick and you have a heavy back-pack with you.
All you want to do is rest.

Person C: student
You are travelling with your friend. You have been seasick and you have a heavy back-pack with you.

Situation two – formal

Person A: conference representative
You are meeting two professors at the airport. Unfortunately their flight is late. They only have one suitcase each. They are here to attend a conference on medicine. You only know one of the professors. You are in a hurry to get them to the conference.

Person B: professor
Your flight was late. You should get to the conference as soon as possible, but you are very formal and insist on everything being done correctly. You know the person waiting for you at the airport but your respected colleague does not.

Person C: professor
Your flight was late. You should get to the conference as soon as possible. You don't know the person waiting for you at the airport but your colleague does. Unfortunately, you have problems with your hearing.

22  A WARM RECEPTION

Partner B   Partner B   Partner B   Partner B   Partner B

From page 32, exercise 8: Arranging a time by phone.

Day/time	8–10	10–12	12–14	14–16	16–18
Monday	free	meeting	free	visiting client	free
Tuesday	in Paris	flying back from Paris	free	meeting	free
Wednesday	free	meeting	free	meeting	free
Thursday	business breakfast	free	business lunch	free	body building
Friday	free	visiting client	meeting	free	doctor

From page 36, exercise 13: Arranging accommodation for others

Your English is very weak and you're not exactly sure of what the person on the other end of the phone wants. You don't understand what "single room" means and you certainly don't understand the English alphabet very well. Be polite and friendly but fail to understand what the person wants. Let the caller explain and explain but whatever you do, do not let him or her think that everything is clear and OK. And don't let him or her hang up! Try another language (one he or she doesn't know) if you like.

3

On Behalf of Our Company

The language of receiving visitors

Giving a good impression involves
language and interpersonal skills.
This unit is designed to provide you
with useful vocabulary and phrases
that will help you to be either a
gracious visitor or a confident
guide.

1  SNAPSHOTS

Listen and repeat. You can also enact the situations.

- My name is Les Dunn. I have an appointment with Mr Kaasch at 3.30.
- Just one moment, please. I'll give him a call.

- Excuse me, can you tell me where conference room 3A is?
- Take the lift to the third floor, go straight ahead, and it's at the end of the corridor.

- We're very pleased to have you here with us today.

– First I'd like to say a few words about the basic aims of our organization.

– Sorry to interrupt, but I didn't quite catch what you said about aims.

– Thank you for your attention, everyone.

WISE WORDS ON VISITING

When in Rome, do as the Romans do.   *Proverb*

Do you suppose I could buy back my introduction to you?   *Groucho Marx*

2 CROSS-CULTURAL CONSIDERATIONS

Punctuality and appointments

Austrians	- punctual
Belgians	- look for punctuality
British	- punctuality important
Bulgarians	- very punctual; make appointments in good time
Czechs and Slovaks	- punctual
Danes	- look for punctuality
Dutch	- expect punctuality
Finns	- punctual; seem to prefer appointments in advance
French	- punctuality appreciated; prior appointments preferred
Germans	- punctuality extremely important; make appointments in good time
Greeks	- tend not to be very punctual; prior appointments appreciated
Icelanders	- punctuality not considered important
Irish	- not very punctual; make appointments in advance
Italians	- punctuality would not seem to be important
Luxembourgers	- punctuality important
Norwegians	- punctuality very important; appointments in advance.
Poles	- punctuality not considered important; appointments in advance
Portuguese	- punctuality appreciated; prior appointments necessary
Romanians	- punctuality very important; prior appointments necessary
Russians	- punctuality appreciated; appointments in advance
Spaniards	- punctuality not considered important
Swedes	- punctuality very important
Swiss	- punctuality highly important
Turks	- punctuality appreciated; appointments well in advance

3 DEMONSTRATIONS

Read the text and do the exercises.

A company tour may be the first glimpse* that visiting colleagues, prospective* employees or interested clients may have of your workplace. Their first, and perhaps lasting, impression depends on how interesting, informative and pleasant the whole experience is. Clarity*, ease and comfort should be the main objectives
5 so that the new person feels free to ask questions.

I remember a tour that I went on at a national archive. It was a big deal* that foreign guests had arrived. Our host appeared to be nervous and over-excited. During the tour he spoke faster and faster, throwing out information at lightning speed. He was trying to be conscientious* and thorough. But ten minutes into the
10 tour he could see from our bewildered* expressions that we weren't following him. This made him even more agitated*. He began to dash madly to and fro, pulling dozens of books from shelves, shouting out enthusiastic remarks like "Oh, this one is really good!"

We sat there in disbelief as the tour became a spectator sport. Finally, as the
15 inevitable* finale, he sprinted across the room, stumbled* and fell. As he looked up from the floor, his desperate eyes said it all: "What happened?!"

Another time a foreign scholar was invited to our university. As a gracious gesture*, one professor volunteered to give us a demonstration of the department's computer system. We sat next to a graduate student who operated the machine as
20 the professor narrated. Soon the student noticed that the professor actually had it all wrong, and began gently correcting some of the misinformation. The professor, too proud to admit ignorance, began to argue with him. The verbal battle rose to a frenzy*, and we were left with the sick feeling of eavesdropping* on a family quarrel. Our visitor became so angry that he exploded with the words, "That's
25 enough, please!" This tour has ever since been known as "The Demonstration from Hell".

K.M.

Explanation of words

glimpse	a brief look	**agitated**	nervous
prospective	potential	**inevitable**	cannot be avoided
clarity	clearness	**to stumble**	to fall over
a big deal	important	**gracious gesture**	special favour
conscientious	very careful	**frenzy**	madness
bewildered	confused	**to eavesdrop**	to listen secretly

Explain briefly...

1   what was wrong with the first DEMONstration.

    _____

    _____

    _____

2   what was wrong with the second DEMONstration.

    _____

    _____

    _____

3   what you would have done if you had been the professor in the second situation.

    _____

    _____

    _____

 Now go on and discuss your own experiences of guided tours, company presentations, etc.

 # NICE TO HAVE YOU HERE

Listen to these short extracts from people presenting their workplaces.

5 GET READY

 Would you manage in the following situations? If you have difficulties, turn to Unit 3 of your Phrase Book.

What would you say

1 when you need to stop someone in the street to ask for directions?

_____

2 when a stranger walks into your office?

_____

3 when the receptionist asks you if she can help you?

_____

4 when a visitor shows up, but the person he/she is scheduled to visit is still out to lunch?

_____

5 when you are late for a meeting; you dash into the building but do not know where room 1038 is?

_____

6 to the receptionist if you wanted Mr Smith to contact you later?

_____

7 if you had to welcome visitors to your workplace?

_____

8 when you're about to take a group of visitors on a tour of your workplace?

_____

9 when you want to interrupt the speaker and ask for an explanation?

_____

10 when you don't understand something and you want the person to repeat it?

_____

PHRASE PRACTICE (5)

You will hear seven phrases taken from Unit 3 of your Phrase Book. Mark any phrase from the alternatives given which would be suitable as a response.

1 a) Yes, it's quite near.
   b) No, it's five minutes from here.
   c) Take the first turning right.

2 a) I have an appointment with Mr Brown.
   b) I'm here from ICI.
   c) My name is Anderson. I'm from CNN.

3 a) Can I have your name, please?
   b) What can I do for you?
   c) Oh, yes. She's expecting you.

4 a) No, thank you.
   b) I'm afraid not.
   c) How can I help you?

5 a) Glad to be here.
   b) You're welcome.
   c) Thank you.

6 a) Thanks very much indeed.
   b) Don't mention it.
   c) Sure. I'd be glad to.

7 a) Sorry, but I didn't quite catch what you said.
   b) Would you mind repeating that, please?
   c) I wonder if you could repeat that, please.

6 THE SEVEN DWARFS LTD.

 Work in pairs and carry out the following situation. Before you start decide who you have an appointment with. Study sections 3.3 – 3.7 of your Phrase Book. Your roles are Ms White and Mr Disney.

THE SEVEN DWARFS LTD

3rd floor	**Mr Sneezy**	**Mr Bashful**	**Doc Holiday**
2nd floor	**Mr Grumpy**	**Mr Happy**	**Mr Sleepy**
1st floor	**Mr Dopey**	**Lobby**	**Ms White Receptionist**

Lift

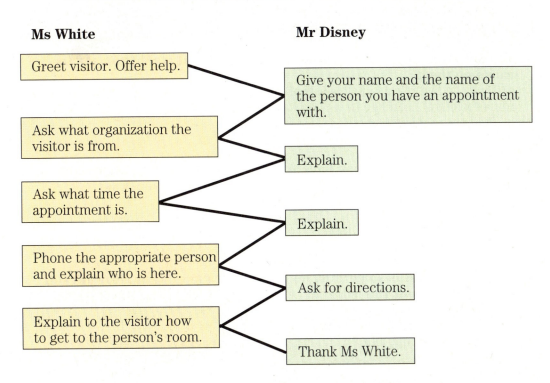

Ms White

Greet visitor. Offer help.

Ask what organization the visitor is from.

Ask what time the appointment is.

Phone the appropriate person and explain who is here.

Explain to the visitor how to get to the person's room.

Mr Disney

Give your name and the name of the person you have an appointment with.

Explain.

Explain.

Ask for directions.

Thank Ms White.

7 PRESENTING YOUR WORKPLACE

The most successful tours are designed with the guest's schedule and objectives in mind. Below you'll find a general outline of the components of a company tour.

1 Welcoming visitors
2 Introductions
3 Stating the purpose of the visit

4 Presenting your workplace
5 Opportunity for asking questions
6 Thanking the visitors

A Match the phrase with the correct stage of presentation.

1 Mr/Ms ... is in charge of our accounting.
2 Thank you for your attention, everyone!
3 To go back to what you were saying about ...
4 Next I'd like you to look at ...
5 I shall be dealing with ...
6 My name is ... I'm ...
7 Glad you could join us.

A Thanking the visitors ☐
B Changing the subject ☐
C Starting presentation ☐
D Asking for clarification ☐
E Introductions ☐
F Introducing yourself ☐
G Welcoming visitors ☐

B Study the phrases in sections 3.11 – 3.15 of your Phrase Book and then select the most suitable alternative.

1 **You are standing before a group of visitors. What would you say to welcome them?**
    a) First, I'd like to say a few words about ...
    b) On behalf of ... I'd like to welcome you here today.
    c) I'm here to tell you about ...
    d) Well, here we are!

2 **When you realise that you have forgotten to mention an important point, or you would like to change the subject, you would say**
    a) I am here to tell you about ...
    b) On behalf of ...
    c) Oh, how stupid of me, I forgot ...
    d) While I remember ...

3 **Your host explains something and you don't understand. How do you politely ask about this matter?**
    a) What?
    b) Sorry, you were not clear about ...
    c) Sorry to interrupt, but I wonder if you could review ...
    d) Say that again.

8 ASKING FOR AND GIVING DIRECTIONS

 Work with your partner and act out the following conversation. Look at the phrases in sections 3.1 and 3.2 of your Phrase Book.

Visitor   **Local Resident**

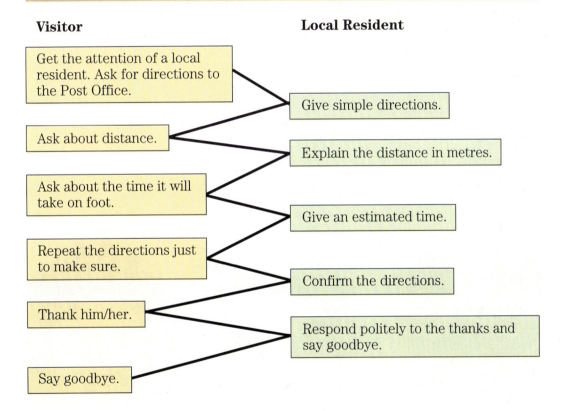

Get the attention of a local resident. Ask for directions to the Post Office.

Give simple directions.

Ask about distance.

Explain the distance in metres.

Ask about the time it will take on foot.

Give an estimated time.

Repeat the directions just to make sure.

Confirm the directions.

Thank him/her.

Respond politely to the thanks and say goodbye.

Say goodbye.

9 COMMUTING

 Take turns in explaining how you got to work this morning. Describe how (by car, on foot, etc.) and where your journey began (your departure point). Give your partner a step-by-step account of the route you took.

10 PUB CRAWL

 You're planning a pub crawl. Take turns with your partner in explaining how to get from one pub to another. Look at the map on the opposite page.

Start at the *Dog and Fox*

Partner 1: Describe the way to the *Queen's Legs*.

Partner 2: Tell your partner how to get from the *Queen's Legs* to the *Pig and Whistle*.

Partner 1: Give directions from the *Pig and Whistle* to *Ye Olde Alehouse*.

Partner 2: Describe the route from *Ye Olde Alehouse* to the *Halfway House*.

Partner 1: Direct your partner from the *Halfway House* to the *Outside Inn*.

Partner 2: Tell your partner how to get from the *Outside Inn* to the *Drunken Sailor*.

Partner 1: Describe the way from the *Drunken Sailor* to the Police Station!

Cheers! You've earned it!

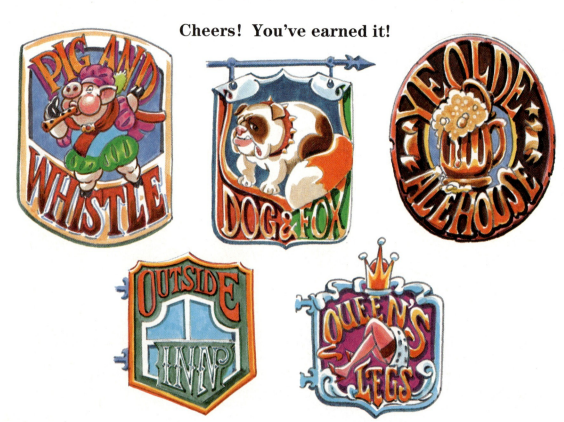

11 LEAVING MESSAGES

 Work with your partner and take turns in being a receptionist and a caller. During the conversation the receptionist should write down the information on the form provided on the opposite page.

Remember to sit back to back.

Receptionist   **Caller**

Answer the phone (remember the name of your company, etc.)

Introduce yourself and your company and ask for Mr Whitney.

Try to contact Mr Whitney. He's speaking on another line.

Explain this to the caller. Ask if the caller can wait.

Decline. Leave a message.

Confirm message (name, telephone number, etc.) and ask if Mr Whitney can phone back.

Confirm and give convenient time.

Explain that you will give the message to Mr Whitney.

Thank the receptionist.

React to thanks. Say goodbye.

Say goodbye.

When I asked my accountant if anything could get me out of the mess I am in now, he thought for a long time. "Yes," he said, "death would help".

Receptionist's Form

To ....

Date .... Time ....

While you were out

Mr / Ms ....

of . ...

Phone ....

☐ TELEPHONED   ☐ PLEASE CALL

☐ CALLED TO SEE YOU   ☐ WILL CALL AGAIN

☐ WANTS TO SEE YOU   ☐ RETURNED YOUR CALL

Message ....

....

....

....

....

....

....

....

SIGNED ....

12  TAKING DOWN MESSAGES

 Listen to the following four messages. Write down the basic information. The first one has been done for you.

 Then take turns in explaining the messages to your partner.

M E M O 1

Jim Porter cannot find
Mr Robinson's fax.
Will he please fax the
information again.
Jim's fax: 6780230.

M E M O 2

M E M O 3

M E M O 4

13 LET'S FACE IT

Decide on the basis of the photos what positions the following people might hold. Select the appropriate title from the list below.

assistant director	managing director	marketing manager
sales manager	company president	technical manager
art director	purchasing officer	information officer
PR officer	personnel manager	chairman of the board
export secretary	shop steward	department supervisor
financial director	secretary	receptionist
clerk	planner	
cashier	graphic designer	

Now go on and compare your selection with your partner's. Give reasons.

14 GET ORGANIZED

Look at this organization chart. Draw an organization chart of your own department, office or company. Write down the job titles in English. You may have to make up some job titles. OR imagine you are setting up your own company and need to make an organization chart.

Present your chart to the rest of the class.

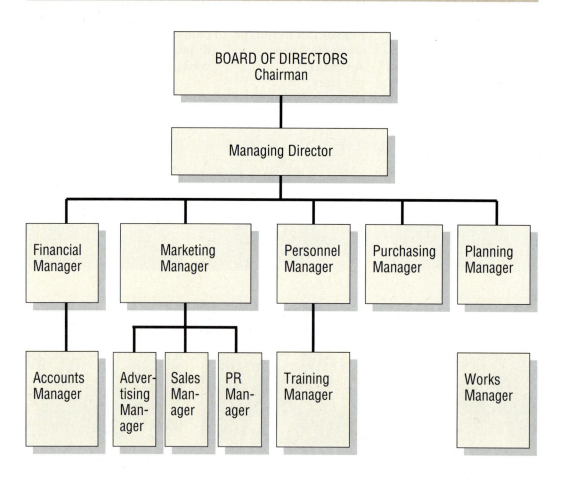

15 DESCRIBING HOUSEHOLD MACHINES

Work with your partner. Study the phrases in section 3.14 of your Phrase Book. Partner A chooses a machine from the list below and describes it to Partner B. Partner B pretends to be a "techno-idiot" who does not understand anything about machines.
Partner A describes step by step how to use the machine.
Partner B asks for clarification of each step.
Partner A must explain in simple terms.

LIST OF MACHINES

Walkman
Coffee maker
Electric kettle
Pop-up toaster
Electric steam iron
Automatic can opener
Alarm clock
Hairdryer
Electric toothbrush
Humidifier
etc.

NOUNS	VERBS
a plug	to turn on/off
an electric cord	to switch on/off
a control button	to put on/off
a socket	to turn up/down
a handle	to warm up
on/off switch	to turn
a spout	to wind
earphones	to plug in/to unplug
	to press
	to insert
	to remove

Example:
A: First you take the plug?
B: A plug?
A: Yes. The thing that goes into the socket.
You take the plug and
put it in the socket.
B: I see...

16 DESCRIBING PROCESSES

Study the car production picture below. The stages of production are in the picture.

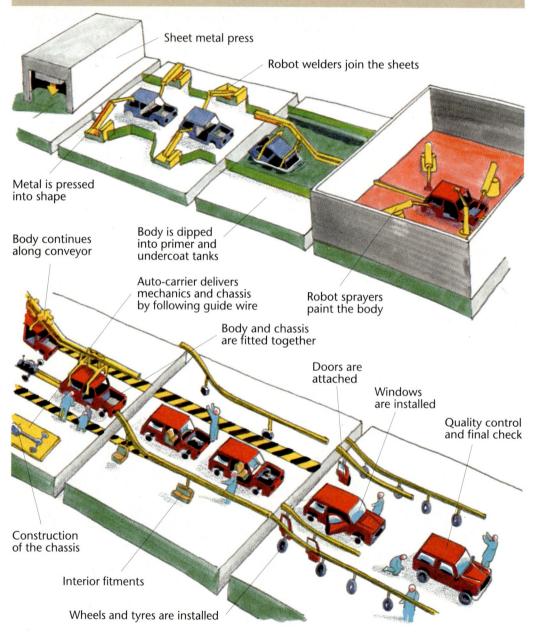

Sheet metal press

Robot welders join the sheets

Metal is pressed into shape

Body is dipped into primer and undercoat tanks

Robot sprayers paint the body

Body continues along conveyor

Auto-carrier delivers mechanics and chassis by following guide wire

Body and chassis are fitted together

Doors are attached

Windows are installed

Quality control and final check

Construction of the chassis

Interior fitments

Wheels and tyres are installed

Read the sentences below. In what order do these steps occur in the car production line?

Order

A   The car body is dipped in paint.

B   A check is made for quality control.

C   The windows are installed.

D   Welders join the sheets.

E   The body is painted.

F   The auto carrier delivers the chassis and mechanics.

Work with your partner.

Partner A   is the "host" and describes the step-by-step process of car assembly by pointing to the picture, using phrases from section 3.13 and the useful phrases given below.

Partner B   is the guest and does not understand each step, forming questions from section 3.14 of the Phrase Book.

Beginning:	First, ... / To begin with ... / To start off ...
Transitions:	Next ... / The next stage is ... / Secondly ... / Thirdly ... / Then the ... travels through ... / After that, it continues ...
Cause and effect:	Due to ... / Because of ... / As a consequence of ... This enables the ... to ... / This creates ... which ... The result is ... / This produces ... / That's why ...
Substance and use:	This material is made (up) of ... / It consists of ...
Size and dimension:	The length / width / height / weight is ... It is ... long / wide / high. / It weighs ...
Final process:	And finally ... / The end result is ...
Useful verbs:	to flow / to contain / to reach / to switch / to draw/ to load / to pass (The temperature reaches ... / Hot air is drawn ... / The thermostat switches off ... / The paper passes through ...)

17 PRESENTING YOUR WORKPLACE

 Prepare a presentation on your workplace, department or job. We strongly advise you to write notes first. Key words or information will do. You may find the tables below of help.

Tips for workplace presentation:

Services / products
Location: factory, office, etc.
Main customers / targets
Number of employees
Turnover
History
Current products / activities
Strong points
Future plans

Tips for department presentation:

Function
Location
Main customers / targets
Number of colleagues
Turnover
Current products / activities
Strong points
Future plans

Tips for job presentation:

Title
Qualifications
Duties
Previous work experience
Likes / Dislikes
Motivation
Current projects / tasks
Future plans

 Now go ahead and prepare a short presentation on your workplace, department or job. Use the organization chart in exercise 14 on page 64 to help you, if you wish. Rehearse it in front of your partner or a small group before you present it to the whole class.

The Floor Is Yours

The language of formal meetings

Formal meetings very often
involve formal procedure and more
often than not demand a Chair. But they
also demand a certain knowledge of
stylized language.

1 SNAPSHOTS

– Let's get down to business, everyone. Our purpose here this morning is to decide on next year's budget.

– Could we move on to item four on the agenda?

– Mr Chairman, could I make a suggestion?
– Go ahead.

– With the Chair's permission I move that we set up a special committee.
– Would anyone like to second the motion?
– Seconded.
– Seconded by Ms Johansen.

– All those for the motion, please raise their hands.
– The motion is carried unanimously.

– The motion has been defeated by seven votes to four.

WISE WORDS ON FORMAL MEETINGS

A committee is twelve men doing the work of one.

2 CROSS-CULTURAL CONSIDERATIONS

❑ Business relations are formal in most countries. Common courtesy is very important. But most important of all is knowledge or lack of knowledge of business protocol. Appropriate dress is an integral part of such protocol. Here are a few tips for dressing and protocol in some European countries.

❑ In Britain avoid wearing striped ties, because universities, regiments, and all kinds of clubs very often have their own striped ties.

❑ Formality and protocol reign in Germany. The business traveller should never make the mistake of becoming familiar or casual with his German hosts or moving to a first name basis without invitation.

❑ In Belgium, it is important to dress well and stylishly. Men should wear dark suits, shirts and ties. For women, trousers are usually unacceptable. Tights or stockings should be worn, even in summer.

❑ Business dress in Denmark is less formal than in other countries in Europe. Blazers, suits and sweatshirts are all acceptable modes of dress.

❑ Style is the key characteristic of Italians, and their dress is no exception. The Italians are proud of their fashion designers and men are exceptionally well-groomed on almost all occasions. Conservative, well-cut suits, shirts and ties should be chosen.

3 🔊 FURNITURE

Read the text and do the exercises.

The language of formal meetings can sound rather like someone talking about antiques. First and foremost* there's *the chair*, then there are people who want *to table* matters or *chair* meetings and last, but not least, there's an endless supply of people who want *to take the floor*. But let's start with *the chair*.

5 Years ago *chairman* was the generally accepted title for the person who held *the chair*. If the position happened to be occupied by a woman then the forms *lady chairman* and *woman chairman* and the form of address *Madam Chairman* were used. However, it did sound rather strange: clearly the man had to go – hence the invention of the word *chairwoman*.

10 But still people were not sure how to refer to the person holding *the chair* when his or her sex was unknown, unsure or of no consequence*. In some cases the neutral term *chairperson* was used and even the ancient word *chair* was brought back. But it sounds rather silly to say things like *"Madam Chair, I have a proposal"* or *"What does the Chair think?"*

15 So, where are we? A feminist will probably object to the use of *chairman* and a traditionalist will object to the word *chairperson*. Although *chairperson* is somewhat favoured in the United States *chairman* is still the favourite term, probably because there are so many men who are *chairmen*. Another problem with the word *chairperson* is its plural form: is it *chairpersons* or *chairpeople*?

20 For the time being, *chairman* is the recommended form, but beware.
The verb *to chair* refers to the act of presiding over* a meeting. And hopefully, there are no problems there any more. (There used to be.)
In British English the verb *to table* means to submit something for consideration but in American English it means to postpone or even shelve*

25 something. In other words the verb has two opposite meanings. We think you'll be better off not trying *to table* anything.
Taking the floor may not sound that inviting either but that's what you'll have to do if you want to voice your opinion at a formal meeting. And *"May I have the floor?"* is the formal way of asking for permission to speak in a formal meeting.

30 Confused by all this furniture talk? Don't worry; in Britain they even have *cabinet* meetings,* but that's another matter.

P.W.

Explanations of words:

foremost	the most important
consequence	relevance
to preside over	to be in charge of
to shelve	to reject for the time being
cabinet	an official, policy-making body of a country; it is also a piece of furniture

A Replace the underlined words with words of your own. The meaning should stay about the same.

1 talking about <u>antiques</u>   *old things* _____
   (line 2)

2 happened to be <u>occupied</u>   _____
   (line 6)

3 <u>of no consequence</u>   _____
   (line 11)

4 I have <u>a proposal</u>   _____
   (line 14)

5 is <u>somewhat favoured</u>   _____
   (line 17)

6 <u>to submit for consideration</u> _____
   (line 23)

7 it means <u>to postpone</u>   _____
   (line 24)

8 taking <u>the floor</u>   _____
   (line 27)

9 <u>to voice your opinion</u>   _____
   (line 28)

B Give explanations in English for the following words.

10 a feminist   *a person who supports women's rights*
    _____

11 a chairman   _____

12 a traditionalist _____

> Seeking his first job, a young man wrote this question on his application form: "Are the salary increases here automatic or do you have to work to earn them?"

4 GET READY

Would you manage in the following situations? If you have difficulties, turn to Unit 4 of your Phrase Book.

If you were the chairperson, what would you say

1   if you had to open a formal meeting?

2   just before you read the minutes?

3   if you wanted to make sure everyone has read the agenda?

4   if you wanted to let someone speak?

5   if the conversation was getting away from the point?

6   if you wanted to move on to a new point?

7   if you thought it was time to vote?

If you were attending a formal meeting, what would you say

8   if you wanted to speak?

9   if you wanted to make a formal proposal?

10 if you wanted to second a motion?

PHRASE PRACTICE (4)

Open your Phrase Book (4.2 – 4.19). Listen to the phrases and repeat them. You will hear the first phrase in each section.

5 MANNERISMS

If you saw someone doing any of the following things during an official meeting, what do you think it might signify?

Mannerism   **Possible meaning**

1 Cleaning/varnishing his/her nails.   *He's bored.* _____

2 Playing with his/her ring.   _____

3 Scratching his/her head.   _____

4 Chewing gum.   _____

5 Biting his/her nails.   _____

6 Rolling his/her eyes.   _____

7 Sitting with his/her eyes closed.   _____

8 Riding his/her chair.   _____

9 Fiddling with his/her glasses.   _____

10 Banging the table with
   his/her hands at certain times.   _____

Discuss your suggestions with a partner or the rest of the class.

MEETINGS

– Prepare the agenda and circulate it well in advance. It should include the purpose of the meeting, a list of the participants, the date and location and times of starting and ending. Also include a list of topics and the approximate length of time dedicated to each.
– Start and finish meetings punctually.
– Minutes should summarize decisions and specify them.
– Minutes should be distributed within two days of the meetings.

6 THE STYLIZED LANGUAGE OF FORMAL MEETINGS

 Study the following:

the minutes:	a concise list of what happens during a meeting
the agenda:	a list of the items to be discussed
to second:	to support a motion proposed by someone else
a motion:	the name given to a proposal while it's being discussed
unanimously:	an adverb used when everybody votes in the same way
an item:	an official matter for discussion
to adjourn:	the verb used when a meeting breaks off before all business has been attended to
the casting vote:	an extra vote cast by the Chair in case of a tie
to resume:	to restart a meeting

Now fill in the blank spaces with the appropriate words from the list above.

After _____ had been read the chairman announced

the first _____ on the _____ . After long discussion

Ms Schwartz put forward a concrete proposal which was _____

by Mr Megwurst. The _____ was eventually passed

_____ . The second motion resulted

in a tie and the chairman was forced to use his _____

_____ , resulting in it being rejected by six votes to five. The meeting

was _____ at 11.00 p.m. because of the lateness of the hour.

7 GESTURES

In meetings, body language can communicate a great deal about the way a person feels. How would you demonstrate the following ideas without saying anything? Work with your partner. In other words, use gestures and/or facial expressions.

1 O.K.
2 Don't know.
3 Sit down, please.
4 Take it easy!
5 Excellent.
6 Be quiet!

7 Yes!
8 No!
9 I'm angry.
10 I really don't agree.
11 Rubbish!

12 You're so right.
13 I'm bored.
14 I don't understand.
15 Look at the time!

8 STARTING A MEETING

Work in threes. Fill in points 2, 4, 5, 6 and 8 on the agenda below. Points 4, 5 and 6 should be matters for discussion, e.g. "Painting the roof".

POINTS

AGENDA

1 Apologies for absence.

2 Minutes of meeting held on _____
(in a nutshell)
 – agreed on new canteen
 – a sub-committee on work safety to be set up
 – more parking spaces for workers
 – increased opportunity of unpaid holidays

3 Matters arising from minutes.

4 _____

5 _____

6 _____

7 Any other business _____

8 Date of next meeting: _____

Go on working in threes and practise being a chairman. Study sections
4.1 – 4.9 of your Phrase Book. Take turns in being chairman, referring
to your group agenda.

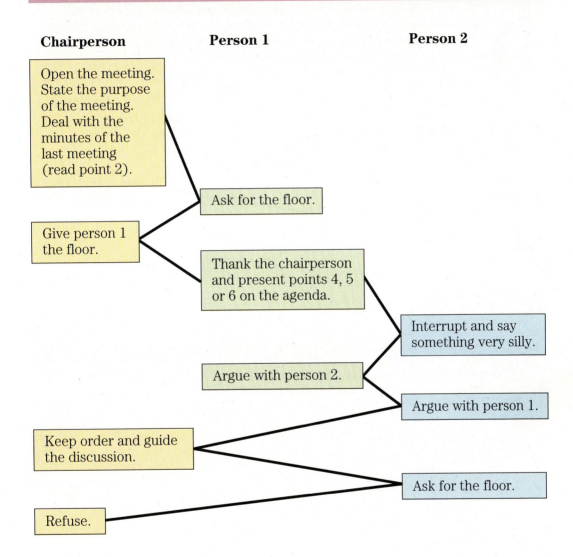

Chairperson

Open the meeting.
State the purpose
of the meeting.
Deal with the
minutes of the
last meeting
(read point 2).

Give person 1
the floor.

Keep order and guide
the discussion.

Refuse.

Person 1

Ask for the floor.

Thank the chairperson
and present points 4, 5
or 6 on the agenda.

Argue with person 2.

Person 2

Interrupt and say
something very silly.

Argue with person 1.

Ask for the floor.

9 MOTIONING

Work in threes and carry on with the meeting in exercise 8. First study sections 4.9, 4.14, 4.15 and 4.18 of your Phrase Book. Before you start, decide exactly what it is you are going to propose. Change roles.

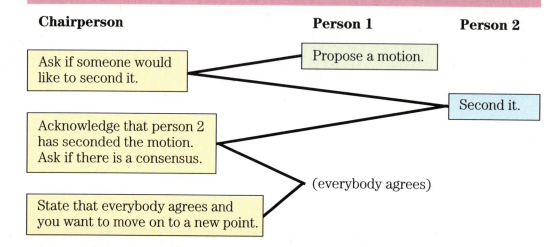

Chairperson   **Person 1**   **Person 2**

Ask if someone would like to second it.

Propose a motion.

Second it.

Acknowledge that person 2 has seconded the motion. Ask if there is a consensus.

(everybody agrees)

State that everybody agrees and you want to move on to a new point.

The language of voting is particularly stylized.

- ❑ The chairman asks, for example: *"All those for the motion that there should be a special committee set up on the subject, please raise their hands."*
- ❑ People in support of the motion raise their hands.
- ❑ The chairman counts (he might say the number).
- ❑ The chairman continues: *"Those against?"* People against the motion raise their hands.
- ❑ The chairman counts (he might say the number).
- ❑ The chairman goes on, if some people have not voted, and asks: *"Abstentions?"*
- ❑ 'Abstentions' refer to those people who don't want to vote for one reason or another.
- ❑ Then, if there are more people 'for' than 'against', the chairman will say, e.g.: *"The motion is carried by four votes to three."*
- ❑ If there are more people 'against' than 'for' he will say, e.g.: *"The motion is defeated by two votes to seven."*
- ❑ If everybody votes in the same way, he might say or add, e.g.: *"The motion was defeated / carried unanimously."*
- ❑ In the event of a tie the chairman might say, e.g.: *"The Chair has the casting vote and I vote for / against the motion."*

10 VOTING

This is either for large groups or with the whole class. Study the phrases on the opposite page as well as the ones in sections 4.16 – 4.19 of your Phrase Book.

Possible motions:

1   Everyone should go on an English language course in Great Britain.
2   You should all go for a cup of coffee as soon as possible.
(Please feel free to make up your own motion.)

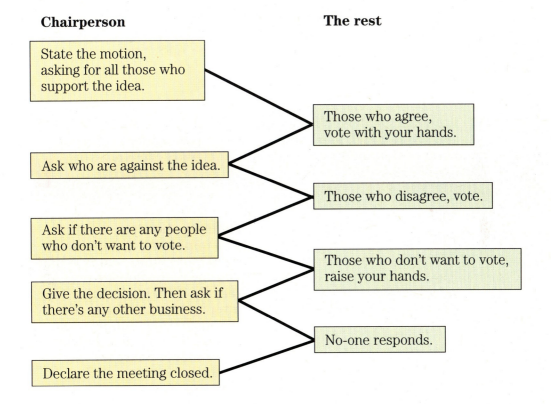

Chairperson

The rest

State the motion, asking for all those who support the idea.

Those who agree, vote with your hands.

Ask who are against the idea.

Those who disagree, vote.

Ask if there are any people who don't want to vote.

Those who don't want to vote, raise your hands.

Give the decision. Then ask if there's any other business.

No-one responds.

Declare the meeting closed.

"Well, I did say that the floor was open!"

11 INTERRUPTING

Interrupting during a meeting is a necessary impoliteness if you are to block ideas or clarify a situation. Here are a few phrases that might or might not help. Mark the ones you consider polite.

1   Wait a minute.
2   Just a moment.
3   Hold on a moment.
4   Sorry to interrupt, but ...
5   How about this?
6   Might I make a point here?
7   Yes, but ...
8   Stop!
9   This is what I think.
10 Could I come in here for a second?

Naturally, how you say it is also important. But perhaps even more important is WHEN you say it. If someone is talking, it's fairly impolite to interrupt in the middle of a sentence so we suggest you choose the end of a sentence or a suitable pause for interruption.

Now, practise interrupting your partner, using polite phrases. Possible topics for your partner to talk about: pornography, violence, rap music, religion, royalty, etc. Change roles.

12 UM'S THE WORD

The sound "um" is very – um – useful in conversation to – um – express certain ideas. It can soften disagreement, reveal embarrassment, signal that you're giving a lot of thought to something or simply help you hesitate.

Look at the examples:
"I think we could – um – accept that proposal."
"It – um – seems to me that – um – some sort of – um – compromise could be worked out."

These examples, particularly if they were said with a frown, would give out a message of doubt or uncertainty. If they were said without "ums" together with a friendly facial expression, they would convey a feeling of acceptance or promise.
"I think we could accept that proposal."
"It seems to me that some sort of compromise could be worked out."

Now look at the phrases below. Work in pairs. One partner says the sentence just as it is, without any "ums" and with certainty. Then the other partner says it WITH an "um" or "ums", showing some kind of awkwardness. Change roles.

1   I'm sure we can reach agreement on this.

2   Has anyone anything further to add?

3   The motion has been defeated by six votes to five.

4   Well, it looks as if we're basically in agreement on this.

5   I object to the whole thing.

6   Well, I propose to defer this matter until the next meeting.

7   I really can't agree with you on this.

8   I really can't understand why a decision has to be made now.

13  PUTTING IT ALL TOGETHER

 Here's your chance to practise most of the language of formal meetings. But first listen to the model discussion on the tape. Then work in groups of FOUR.

Possible topics: refugees, drugs, taxation, car phones for everyone ...

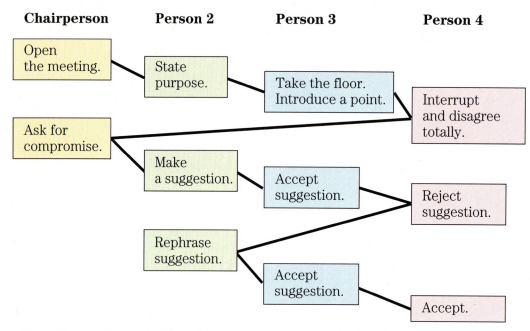

Chairperson	Person 2	Person 3	Person 4
Open the meeting.	State purpose.	Take the floor. Introduce a point.	Interrupt and disagree totally.
Ask for compromise.	Make a suggestion.	Accept suggestion.	Reject suggestion.
	Rephrase suggestion.	Accept suggestion.	Accept.

Now discuss the topic formally.

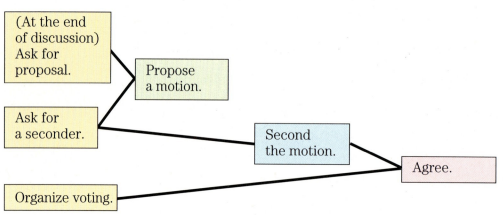

(At the end of discussion) Ask for proposal.	Propose a motion.		
Ask for a seconder.		Second the motion.	Agree.
Organize voting.			

14 THE PUBLISHING COMMITTEE

 Number of roles – unlimited (works best with 4 – 6 people). You are an editorial committee for a large international publisher. You receive hundreds of manuscripts every week by would-be authors. However, with your vast experience you can tell a bestseller simply by its title. You are only interested in accepting ten new titles for publication from the following list.

STEP ONE:
Before you start the committee meeting, read through the list by yourself and select your own ten favourite titles.

Titles for consideration:

I was a Teenage Student

The Sex Life of Frogs

The Life Story of Salman Rushdie

The Filthy Book of Dirty Jokes

Grow Your Own Hashish

How to Lose a Million Dollars in Less than a Day

UFOs in Luxembourg

Madonna's Book of Bedtime Stories

How to Live Forever and Ever

The Truth about Banking

Hang-gliding for the Over-Sixties

Women in Sport

A Pictorial History of Toilets

Is There a Life before Death?

THE SECRET DIARY OF PRESIDENT KENNEDY

Babies as Substitutes for Dogs

Exciting Stories about Scandinavian Libraries

A Complete Guide to Albanian Stamps

Basil, the Invisible Hedgehog

WORKING ENGLISH

STEP TWO:
Choose a chairperson and consider each title in turn and explain why you believe it would sell well or badly. You should arrive at a group decision as to which ten titles you take.
If you have time, you can also rank the ten your committee selects, i.e. 1: the best, 2: the second best, etc.

15 UP AND DOWN LTD

 Ideally for five people.

Up and Down Ltd is a small company making plastic items in your country. It is owned by Up and Down International, based in London. Believe it or not, things have been going quite well for them. So, the parent company has decided to reward Up and Down Ltd by awarding them 100,000 ecus. However, Up and Down Ltd's board of directors have asked the various department heads to suggest ways of using the money. Therefore, a short, extraordinary general meeting has been called to decide how to spend the money.

The Board of Up and Down Ltd.

Chairman

Managing Director **Company Secretary**

| Personnel Manager | Production Manager | Financial Manager | Marketing Manager |

Explanation of roles:

1 Marketing Manager

As head of marketing, you have done a great deal to maintain the company's position. You have five travelling sales representatives under you, all of whom rely on cars for their jobs. However, they have all been complaining about the quality, age and performance of their cars. They have even threatened to leave if they don't get better and newer cars. You feel that the 100,000 ecus could go towards purchasing your team better quality cars, thereby maintaining your effectiveness and solving your personal problem. Fight for the money!

2 Production Manager

You have thirty-five employees under you as head of production. You have had great problems recently meeting the demands promised by the marketing department. What you need is three new machines. You feel the 100,000 ecus would just about cover the cost of purchasing such vital, up-to-date technology. Otherwise, you simply won't be able to meet production quotas. Fight for your money!

3 Personnel Manager

You look after the welfare, employment and training of Up and Down's personnel. There is no canteen in the company, neither are there any sports or social facilities available. The company has relied a great deal on the morale of its work force. In times like these, you see trouble unless people are rewarded somehow. You believe that the 100,000 ecus should be used for the benefit of all the company, not just for a few.

Fight for better facilities and rewards!

4 Financial Manager

You're in charge of the money. But, despite reasonable profits, the company has never wanted to invest in adequate computer systems. Your book-keeping system is out-of-date, everything takes too long. You desperately need modern computer technology. The cost of getting an ideal computer system which would network with the parent company, would be about 50,000 ecus. You don't need 100,000 ecus!

Fight for what you believe to be a reasonable sum.

5 Chairman

Your job is simply to control the meeting and make sure everybody's point of view is heard. However, the decision on how to spend the money should satisfy the parent company, Up and Down International, that you are investing the 100,000 ecus wisely. In the end, you would have to get the board to agree on how the money is to be distributed. Good luck!

EXTRA ROLES FOR LARGER GROUPS OF SIX OR SEVEN

6 Managing Director

As member of the board your job would be to ask questions and help the chairman to make a decision.

7 Company Secretary

Your job would be to take notes, i.e. the minutes, on what was said and on any decision reached and read them out at the end.

16 GREEN ISLAND

 Minimum 4, maximum 7 people.

Roles:

– Chairman
– Minister for Wind
– Minister for Nuclear Energy
– Minister for Hydro-electric Power

– Minister for Solar Energy
– Minister for Oil
– Member of the Greens

Purpose of meeting: to decide upon a minimum of one and a maximum of two energy plans.

Map of Green Island

mountains

winds

Population: 1 million
Location: to the south-west of Iceland
Length: 500 kilometres
Width: 250 kilometres

Explanation of roles

Ⓐ Chairman:

1 Open the meeting. Explain the purpose, then state the facts about Green Island, i.e. location, population and the fact that there is high unemployment.
2 Introduce each minister. Then allow each person to present his / her arguments.
3 Open the debate. Remember to keep order. Make sure everyone has a chance to say what he / she feels.
4 Try and reach a decision.
   Alternative one:
   YOU decide alone, basing your decision on the points you have heard discussed.
   Alternative two:
   Organize a vote, with you having the casting vote in the event of a tie.
5 Close the meeting. Thank everyone for coming. Set a date for the next meeting, if you wish.

Ⓑ Minister for Wind:

1 You would like to build windmills on the west coast. Plenty of good winds hit that coast.
2 Wind power is cheap, clean and technologically advanced nowadays. Great success in Denmark, for example.
3 You will probably need about 1,000 windmills to supply GREYTON with its domestic energy needs – houses, shops, restaurants, etc.
4 Wind power alone is not enough. You will need another energy source to provide energy for industry.
5 You're against nuclear power and oil power because of the risk to the environment.

Ⓒ Minister for Nuclear Power:

1 You would like to build at least one nuclear power station somewhere along the River Blue, away from the cities.
2 It's fairly cheap and long-lasting. It's not so dangerous here. You also believe it's clean.
3 You are against a new oil port in Blix because the nuclear power station needs clean water and oil tankers would pollute the River Blue.
4 Nuclear power would provide new jobs in the area.

D   **Minister for Oil:**

1   Oil is the most realistic energy source in your opinion. The deep harbour at Greyton can be used for unloading the oil tankers.

2   It will also help create new jobs.

3   You think that wind power and solar power are silly, unrealistic solutions.

E   **Minister for Hydro-electric Power:**

1   You would like to build a hydro-electric dam at River Blue's highest point in the mountains.

2   Hydro-electricity would solve all the energy problems. It's not so expensive.

3   You're against solar energy because it's impractical up here in the north. You're also against the Minister for Oil because oil might pollute the River Blue.

4   You might have to cooperate with another energy supply.

F   **Minister for Solar Energy:**

1   You have five good months of sunlight on Green Island. A solar energy station could at least solve the energy problem in the summer. In the future solar technology could help you store the energy, too.

2   Obviously, you need to cooperate with another major energy supply.

3   You are totally against nuclear power.

G   **Member of the Greens:**

1   All you want is a clean and happy island.

2   Obviously, you are against dirty or dangerous energy sources.

3   The oil refineries in Greyton would pollute the River Blue. Not only that but the sea would also be at risk.

4   The River Blue often freezes over in winter. So, would hydro-electricity really be practical?

5

What Do You Think?

The language of informal meetings

This unit concentrates on the
language of meetings in general.
It covers most of the aspects
needed for effective
communication in all kinds
of meetings.

1 SNAPSHOTS

– I'd like to bring up the point about working hours.

– I'd like to hear your views on these investments.

– I agree with you completely.

– I'm sorry, but that's really out of the question.

– Why don't we have a break?

– I was wondering if you'd thought about the final price?
– Well, it's rather difficult to say at present.

– If there's nothing else,
I suggest we finish.

....

WISE WORDS ON MEETINGS

I listen a lot and talk less. You can't learn anything when you're talking.

Bing Crosby

2 CROSS-CULTURAL CONSIDERATIONS

❏ In southern Europe people tend to stand closer, have more face-to-face contact, touch more often and speak louder. In northern Europe people tend to be more conservative with touching. This also applies in Great Britain.

❏ Generally speaking, conventional gestures, such as pointing, shrugging shoulders, patting people on the back, head nodding, thumbs down, clapping, waving and beckoning, are found all over Europe.

❏ Head-shaking in most European countries means "no". However, in many Balkan countries, people toss their head when they mean "no".

❏ Silence is golden, at least in Japan. In that culture it is used as a means of communication. Likewise, in some Nordic countries people tend to be less talkative in communicative situations.

❏ Nodding occasionally, maintaining eye contact, smiling when appropriate, saying "I understand", and so on can act as a good substitute for verbal communication.

❏ Remember to use your guest's name in conversation. People like to hear their names mentioned.

❏ There is one universal form of communication that is recognised and understood by every culture, no matter how remote. It can help you in any situation – business or personal. It is – the smile.

3 A WORD IN YOUR EAR

Effective participation in meetings would seem to demand a keen eye, an attentive*
ear, a smooth tongue and an awareness of one's own body language. If, on top of all
this, the participant then has to communicate in a foreign language, the demands
can become overwhelming*. So, here are a few helpful language hints on how to get
5 by in meetings without developing an ulcer.

First of all, the use of introductory phrases or words can help prepare the
listener for what he or she is about to hear. Phrases like *To be honest* can be used
as a warning that you are about to disagree or give out some bad news. So, *to put it
bluntly*, don't forget introductory phrases!

10 One of the most common introductory phrases, if not THE most common, is
I'm afraid. It's most frequently used as a response. When used in this way it not
only warns the speaker of some bad news or disagreement, but also suggests that
the reaction is quite clearly the most logical or best under the circumstances, e.g.:
All right if I smoke? I'm afraid it's not allowed.

15 Using questions instead of statements can also help to soften the effect.
Would that be too dangerous? sounds less threatening than *It's too dangerous.*
And, if you want to make it sound even more reasonable, you could always change
it into a negative question, i.e. *Wouldn't that be too dangerous?* or by using a
question tag: *That would be too dangerous, wouldn't it?*

20 Generally speaking, the use of *would, could* or *might* takes away the feeling
of inflexibility or impoliteness. Compare the following:
I don't want to go there – I wouldn't like to go there.
I can't accept that – I couldn't accept that.
Perhaps it will happen – I suppose it might happen.

25 And the use of such words can still enable you to get your point across
convincingly*. *In fact, we're positive that this is something you might like to
consider.*

Phrases and words such as *a bit of*, or *slightly*, can help you sound more
specific or certain. For example, on an aircraft, *There will be a short delay* sounds
30 less off-putting than *There will be a delay.* Which would you prefer to hear?

Another aspect of the English language is its aversion* to negative adjectives.
For some reason, British people definitely prefer *It wasn't a very nice city* to *It
was a horrible city* or *The outlook is not so good* to *The outlook is bad.* In other
words they prefer to use the negative form of the verb with a positive adjective.
35 Whatever you say, the right choice of words and accurate pronunciation should
get you through*.

Very rarely do language mistakes really cause a breakdown in communication. We have only once witnessed a serious development caused through an error in language, when, after a long hard week of successful meetings, a Scandinavian boss
40 mistakenly said to some German visitors: *"After this week I can safely say that we are tired of you"*.

The Germans were ready to rip up the contract.

The speaker had meant to say *tied to you*, but mispronounced the verb and said the wrong preposition. Fortunately, the matter was resolved* but only after a
45 lot of explanation.

Clearly, the use of English in meetings between different nationalities can present many challenges. In such circumstances we sincerely hope that you will feel neither *tied to* nor *tired of* the English language.

Explanation of words:

attentive	listening carefully	**aversion**	strong dislike
overwhelming	overpowering	**get you through**	help you succeed
convincingly	believably	**resolve**	settle

 A Look at the following introductory phrases and mark the ones which are NOT warnings.

1   In fact,   _____   4   Actually,   _____

2   To put it bluntly, _____   5   As a matter of fact,   _____

3   To be honest,   _____   6   With respect,   _____

B   Reply to these statements beginning with the introduction "I'm afraid ..."

1   How about that for an idea?

_____

2   Well, where is the agreement?

_____

3   Do you happen to have the figures with you?

_____

4   Is there any way you could get it to us by the end of this month?

_____

5   Wouldn't it be better if we had another meeting?

_____

C   Make these statements sound more flexible by changing them into questions.

1   Leaving right now could help.

   _____

2   We have to change the contract.

   _____

3   You ask him!

   _____

4   It would be a good opportunity.

   _____

5   November the 5th would be suitable.

   _____

D   Now, in much the same way, introduce "would" to the following statements so they sound more open and less dogmatic.

1   That is too little.

   _____

2   Money is no problem.

   _____

3   I prefer the other alternative.

   _____

4   I can't accept that.

   _____

5   KLM is easier.

   _____

6   I'm really not able to say at present.

   _____

E   **Now, by introducing the words below, make the following statements more diplomatic.**

SLIGHT	SOME	A BIT OF A	(A) LITTLE

1   That might present us with a problem.

_____

2   We would need more time to think it over.

_____

3   We have run into difficulties.

_____

4   Obviously, changes will have to be made.

_____

5   There seems to have been a misunderstanding.

_____

F   **Change the verbs into their negative forms and replace the negative adjectives with positive ones.**

e.g. It was a horrible city.   It | wasn't | a very | nice | city.

1   That's unsuitable.

_____

2   This is useless.

_____

3   I'm unhappy about that suggestion.

_____

4   In my opinion, that's a stupid thing to say.

_____

5   It's an insensitive proposal.

_____

4 GET READY

 Would you manage in the following situations? If you have difficulties, turn to Unit 5 of your Phrase Book.

What would you say ...

1   if you had to start an informal meeting?

_____

2   if you would like to make clear that you are about to introduce a point?

_____

3   if you wanted to explain that you were about to give an example?

_____

4   if you wanted to ask someone for his/her opinion?

_____

5   if you completely agreed with something?

_____

6   if you completely disagreed with something?

_____

7   if you wanted to suggest something nicely?

_____

8   if you accepted a suggestion?

_____

9   if you rejected a suggestion?

_____

10 if you wanted to avoid a question?

_____

11 if you wanted to finish off a meeting?

_____

PHRASE PRACTICE (4)

> You will hear ten introductory phrases. Repeat each phrase and then continue in your own way. Remember you are at a meeting. Things you could be discussing: salary, working hours, etc.

1 Let me start by...
2 I'd like to bring up the point about ...
3 I must add that ...
4 But on the whole ...
5 What do you think about ...?

6 It seems to me that ...
7 I can see what you mean but ...
8 I hope you don't mind me asking but ...
9 How about ...?
10 Perhaps we can finish by ...

5 WHEN IN ROME ...

> Body language is very much a part of all kinds of meetings. But different cultures, not to mention different people, behave differently in the same situation. How many of the following relate to you? Work in pairs.

1 **Someone is talking and you want to interrupt. How do you do that?**
a) By raising a finger and waiting for a while.
b) By waiting until he or she has finished.
c) By simply interrupting then and there.
d) By some other means. What?

2 **You're bored and you can't stand it anymore. What do you do?**
a) Show it through a facial expression.
b) Pretend you're not really bored at all.
c) Stop participating.
d) Something else. What?

3 **You're just about to finish talking. How are you going to signal it?**
a) By choosing a suitable phrase.
b) By showing it in your voice.
c) By choosing some kind of a gesture.
d) By some other means. What?

4 **You're talking. What kind of responses do you expect to get from others?**
a) Nodding, shaking of the head.
b) Facial expressions and eye movements.
c) Appropriate sounds or phrases.
d) Something else. What?

6 LANGUAGE CHOICE

 Below you will see some of the language we have already covered in Unit 4 – the language of formal meetings. Make up suitable informal phrases which mean more or less the same thing. Try to do this without looking at your Phrase Book.

FORMAL

INFORMAL

Opening a meeting

Ladies and Gentlemen,
I declare the meeting open.

e.g.: OK, everyone! Let's start.

Stating purpose

Our purpose here
in this meeting is to ...

_____

Introducing a point

Referring to the agenda, ...

_____

Asking for opinions

The floor is open.

_____

Suggesting something

I would like to move that ...

_____

Supporting

I'll second that.

_____

Disagreeing

I oppose this motion.

_____

Closing

Is there any other business?

_____

7 OPINIONS

 Work in pairs and take turns in asking for and giving opinions about the following topics. Begin your sentences in different ways. Study sections 5.8–5.10 of your Phrase Book.

American films   The Eurovision   The Miss World   Equal rights
                          song contest   contest

8 INTONATION

 Intonation can be extremely important when expressing yourself in meetings. You will now hear five sentences on the tape. Mark whether you think the person is angry, excited or bored.

	1	2	3	4	5
angry					
excited					
bored					

 Say the phrases below IN YOUR OWN LANGUAGE as if you were a) angry, b) excited, c) bored.
1 What's your opinion?   3 You must be joking.
2 I don't know.   4 Really?
Now say them IN ENGLISH. Then discuss the differences in INTONATION between your own language and English.

9 DIRECT OR DIPLOMATIC?

Disagreeing with people can be extremely disagreeable. It's therefore important to know whether or not you're being diplomatic. Classify the following as either direct or diplomatic. Look at section 5.12 of your Phrase Book. The first question to ask yourself is whether or not expressing strong disagreement is undiplomatic.

	Direct	Diplomatic

1 I disagree with you.

2 I don't see things that way.

3 There's a lot in what you say, but ...

4 I'm sorry, but I find it difficult to agree with you on this.

5 I'm afraid I can't go along with you on that point.

6 I'm afraid I can't agree with you.

10 DISAGREEING

Now's your chance to disagree strongly with your partner's opinion, giving reasons why. Study the phrases in section 5.12 of your Phrase Book.

Partner 1 **State either alternative** **a) or b).**	**Partner 2** **Disagree (even if it's not your** **real opinion).**
1a Hunting should be banned.	1b Hunting is simply sport.
2a We already have sexual equality in this country.	2b This country is chauvinistic.
3a English is a very easy language to learn.	3b English is a very difficult language to learn.
4a Nuclear power is safe.	4b Nuclear power should be banned.

11 THE PARTY'S OVER

 Work in threes and discuss an office party you have all been to. Try and use as many phrases as you can from sections 5.8 – 5.13 of your Phrase Book.

Person 1

You hated every minute of it. Bad food, warm beer, awful music, boring people.

Person 2

You loved it. Healthy food, enough drinks, great music, interesting people.

Person 3

It was all right. Nothing special but you enjoyed yourself. The music was a bit too loud.

12 DUNNO

 Work in pairs. Each of you has information on three out of the six business ventures 1 – 6. Take turns in asking for information with which you can fill in the empty squares of your table. If your partner asks you for information on a DUNNO* square, use phrases from sections 5.18 – 5.19 of your Phrase Book. Partner B's table is on page 110.
PLEASE DO NOT LOOK AT YOUR PARTNER'S TABLE.

* DUNNO = I don't know.

Partner A

Venture	Company	Location	Turnover (ecus)
1	Mad Ltd	DUNNO	1 million
2			
3	DUNNO	Sweden	0.5 million
4			
5	Different Ltd	Guernsey	DUNNO
6			

13  MINI-MEETING

 Work in threes and carry out the following discussion. Study sections 5.1 – 5.20 of your Phrase Book. Before you start, decide on your topic (e.g., abortion, your political ideas, pop music as opposed to classical music, free health-care, AIDS etc). First listen to the model discussion on tape.

Person 1	Person 2	Person 3

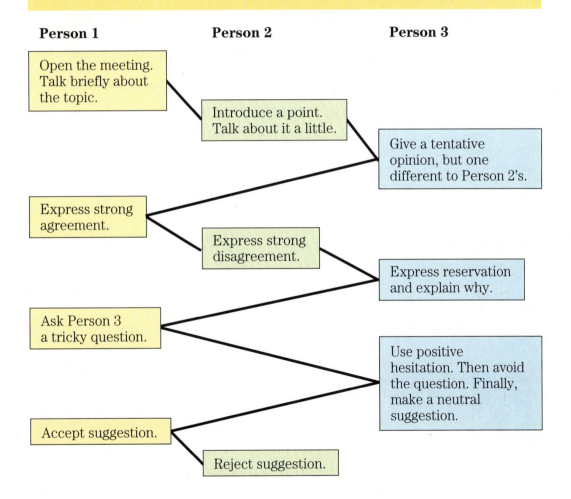

Open the meeting. Talk briefly about the topic.

Introduce a point. Talk about it a little.

Give a tentative opinion, but one different to Person 2's.

Express strong agreement.

Express strong disagreement.

Express reservation and explain why.

Ask Person 3 a tricky question.

Use positive hesitation. Then avoid the question. Finally, make a neutral suggestion.

Accept suggestion.

Reject suggestion.

Now carry on with your discussion.

ROLE PLAYS

The following role plays are designed to give you ample opportunity of practising the language of meetings. Select one which suits your group the best. All the phrases in sections 5.1 – 5.20 of your Phrase Book should be of use to you.

Role play **1** – COMPANY MONEY

Somewhat similar to unit 4 role play, 'Up and Down Limited', on pages 86 – 87. Only this time, whatever the decision, the workers will benefit directly. And this time the discussion should be much less formal. In other words, say what you really feel. Five main roles. (Ideally for five people, but can be used with fewer or more, if no roles are taken.)

Role play **2** – ACADEMIC SELECTION

Here, you have to decide on one candidate from five. The one selected wins a scholarship to a prestigious university abroad. No specific roles. (For any number of people).

Role play **3** – CRIME DOESN'T PAY

You're faced with a list of crimes, some serious, some not. The task of this meeting is to rank them in order of seriousness. This really should generate a lot of discussion. No specific roles. (For any number of people.)

14 COMPANY MONEY

 The organization you work for is releasing 20,000 ecus for staff benefits. How are you going to spend the money?

Options: **A** weekend holiday together

A Christmas bonus

Language training

Renewing the canteen

A gymnasium

Role 1

You believe that your staff need language training.

You are against – a weekend holiday together somewhere
– a Christmas bonus (i.e. 30% more salary for December).
You agree that the canteen needs redoing but somehow you think you can manage without it. You might consider a gymnasium if your idea is rejected.

. . . .

Role 2

You are sure that a gymnasium is exactly what your organization needs. Everyone would benefit from it. 20,000 ecus would be exactly enough to pay for it.

You are against – language training (stupid, waste of money)
– the canteen being redecorated (the one you've got is good enough)
– the Christmas bonus (not worth it, everybody would waste the money).
You might consider the weekend holiday, but only if it were abroad.

. . . .

Role 3

You can't help but feel that a weekend holiday together would be the best way of spending the money. People would enjoy themselves and get to know each other outside the work environment.

You are against – the gymnasium (for macho types only)
– the Christmas bonus
– language training.
You might consider redecorating the canteen since it would benefit everyone.

. . . .

Role 4

A Christmas bonus is the only realistic way of spending the money. Nothing else is of practical help to the workers.

You are against everything else, particulary language training.

. . . .

Role 5

You believe that renewing the canteen would be the fairest way of spending the money. In that way, everybody would feel the long-term benefit on a day-to-day basis.

You are against – the weekend holiday
– the Christmas bonus
You might consider the gymnasium or language training if your idea is not accepted.

15 ACADEMIC SELECTION

 This is an informal but nevertheless crucial meeting. Together you should decide on whom you are going to recommend for a music scholarship to a famous foreign university. Before you begin, decide on the names of the candidates.

THE CANDIDATES:

ONE: Name: _____ **Sex: female Age: 22**

Profile: Single, feminist, and career-oriented. She has run into trouble with the authorities because of her highly-developed social conscience: active member of Greenpeace and Amnesty International, etc. Her parents cannot finance her education, so this is her big chance. She is rather aggressive but very honest and trustworthy.

....

TWO: Name: _____ **Sex: male Age: 40**

Profile: Married with four children. He claims he never had a chance to study after school. At present he works as a bus driver. Nevertheless, he shows amazing insight and promise. This really is his last chance.

....

THREE: Name: _____ **Sex: female Age: 23**

Profile: Hard-working, engaged to a lawyer. She definitely has the ability but her fiancé is not at all keen on her leaving the country. The scholarship is for two years. In many ways she is a typical student. Not outstanding, but reliable. She's also a teetotaller and a regular churchgoer.

....

FOUR: Name: _____ **Sex: male Age: 19**

Profile: Described by many as a genius, but extremely lazy and loves the good life; girls, marijuana, etc. He is also a talented musician. Easily the most able of the candidates, only his ability to apply himself to his studies is at question.

....

FIVE: Name: _____ **Sex: male Age: 27**

Profile: Ex-prisoner who has made great progress since he was released from jail. He has been studying hard and has a steady girlfriend. She is, however, prepared to let him go abroad to study. He is delighted to be considered for such an opportunity. He is by no means the most gifted of the candidates but he's got a lot of guts.

16 CRIME DOESN'T PAY

 Work in groups and decide on the order of seriousness of the following crimes. Rank them starting with 1 – the most serious and ending in 12 – the least serious.

☐ Shoplifting a piece of jewelry.

☐ Causing a death through drinking and driving.

☐ Attempted rape.

☐ Kidnapping a child.

☐ Hijacking an airplane.

☐ Using the drug 'crack'.

☐ Murdering a policeman.

☐ Not declaring the two extra bottles of whisky you happen to have with you at customs.

☐ Spying.

☐ Smuggling heavy drugs.

☐ Tax evasion, i.e. illegally avoiding paying enough tax.

☐ Pick-pocketing somebody's wallet.

If you have time, compare your group's decision with those of the other groups in your class and try and reach a class decision.

17 BODY LANGUAGE

Listen to this interview with an expert on body language.

"I'm afraid I'm not in a position to comment on that."

Partner B   Partner B   Partner B   Partner B   Partner B

From page 104, exercise 12: Dunno.

Venture	Company	Location	Turnover (ecus)
1			
2	DUNNO	Luxembourg	120,000
3			
4	Concourse PLC	Belgium	DUNNO
5			
6	Nuts Inc.	DUNNO	350,000

Be My Guest
The language of socializing

The language of socializing centres very much on small talk and polite remarks. Choosing the right phrase can make all the difference if you are trying to create the right impression. This unit attempts to give you a basic selection of useful phrases and responses, which will help you manage in after-work situations.

1  SNAPSHOTS

– I was wondering if
  you'd like to join me
  for dinner tonight?
– I'd be delighted to.

– I'd love to but I'm afraid I can't.
– All right. Never mind.
  Some other time, then.

– What would you like?
– Well, the Saltimbocca
  alla Romana sounds
  delicious, doesn't it?

– Can I get you a
  drink?
– Thank you. I'll have
  a gin and tonic,
  please.

– Good news! We won the deal!
– That's great. You must be very
  pleased.

– Give my best
  regards to Peter.
– Thanks, I will.

· ·

WISE WORDS ON SOCIALIZING

The world was my oyster, but I used the wrong fork.   *Oscar Wilde*

2 CROSS-CULTURAL CONSIDERATIONS

CONTINENTAL STYLE

❏ *Napkin:* The correct way to handle the napkin is to wait for your host or hostess to take the napkin. Then, using both hands, give the napkin a slight shake under the table and put it on your lap. It should be half open with the fold towards you.

❏ *Cutlery:* Knives should be put on the right of the plate with their blades turned inwards. Forks should be on the left. (The small fish fork is, however, always set on the right.) Spoons should be set to the right of the knives. When selecting cutlery, begin from the outside.

Dessert fork — Dessert spoon
Salad knife
Fish fork
Salad fork   Dinner fork
Dinner knife   Soup spoon

❏ *Eating:* The utensils are held throughout the meal. The diner cuts the food, usually one bite at a time, and uses the fork in the left hand, tines pointing downwards.

❏ *Finishing:* The correct way of showing that you have finished eating is to place your cutlery in a so-called ten to four position. The knife goes first, with the sharp edge facing towards you. Then the fork, tines up.

AMERICAN STYLE

❏ The American standard style calls for cutting a few mouthfuls of food, then laying the knife across the top of the plate, the sharp edge pointing toward the centre. The fork is then switched to the right hand, tines pointing up, and used to bring the food to the mouth. The left hand rests on the lap while the fork is used.

3 🎺 UNDERSTAND?!

While watching television the other day I saw American troops speaking to a group of Somalis. The soldiers spoke in English and instructed the Somalis in a normal tone of voice, "Lie down!" No one moved. The Somalis simply stared at the soldiers, not understanding English. The soldiers raised their voices and shouted loudly, "Lie
5 down!", "Lie down!", again and again. The Somalis were frightened. A newspaper reporter ran up to the soldiers and said, "Hey, why are you shouting at these people"? "Well," the soldiers replied, "the Somalis don't seem to understand when you speak to them in a normal tone of voice!"

   Now, your first reaction to this may be: "O what stupid soldiers." But actually,
10 you would be surprised at the number of people, intelligent human beings all over the world, who raise their voices as a reaction to not being understood.

   Another common reaction to non-native speakers is unnecessary repetition. Often when a non-native speaker disagrees with an opinion of a native speaker, the latter immediately assumes that the foreigner misunderstood, and repeats his
15 position.

   But even when we understand and speak a language fluently, there are those little, invisible differences that occur and cause social misunderstandings. Using English as a *lingua franca* means that everyone is talking the same language, but they are not necessarily communicating on common ground.

20 Dr Raymonde Carroll, a French anthropologist, observes that although the word "conversation" is the same both in French and English, it does not signify the same thing in both cultures. To the French, conversation at its best means being "engaged", "sustained" and "revived", and the French work to keep the conversation nourished by the participants. It is as if conversation were a living
25 creature. To maintain this networking, without "monopolizing" speaking time, is of utmost importance in their culture.

   In contrast to the French, Carroll likens American conversation to a jam session. A jazz musician can bring his musical instrument, join a group of musicians he does not know, play with them and leave, disappearing forever into the night.
30 Likewise, an American can join a conversation if he has something to add, learn from the conversation, and then simply disappear.

   Professor Carroll's position is that in an intercultural situation then, while it may be easier to speak a language without an accent, it is much more difficult to speak without a cultural accent, and it is your own cultural accent that presents
35 problems.

   Keep your eyes and ears open for French-speaking, Somalian jazz musicians.

                                                                    K.M.

A Which alternative fits the meaning of the verb used in the text?

1	INSTRUCT (line 2)	shout	invite	⟨order⟩
2	REPLY (line 7)	request	inquire	answer
3	ASSUME (line 14)	suppose	propose	suggest
4	REPEAT (line 14)	speak up	say again	bring up
5	CAUSE (line 17)	bring up	bring about	bring along
6	OBSERVE (line 20)	throw out	point out	give out
7	SIGNIFY (line 21)	mean	signal	suggest
8	ENGAGE (line 23)	marry	involve	invent
9	SUSTAIN (line 23)	stop doing	keep going	start doing
10	NOURISH (line 24)	feed	eat	consume
11	MAINTAIN (line 25)	give up	sum up	keep up
12	MONOPOLIZE (line 25)	fascinate	nominate	dominate
13	DISAPPEAR (line 31)	punish	vanish	decide

B Explain in simple language the main message(s) of the text.

....

....

....

....

....

....

....

....

4 GET READY

**Would you manage in the following situations? If you have
difficulties, turn to Unit 6 of your Phrase Book.**

What would you say when

1   a guest arrives at your party?

2   someone invites you to a cocktail party you don't want to attend?

3   when a colleague invites you to his/her home for a bubblebath?

4   you have to tell someone some bad news?

5   you are a host/hostess of a dinner party and the food is ready to be served?

6   someone tells you that they have just won the lottery?

7   you are eating dinner and realize that the salt is on the other side of the table?

8   you are at a reception and the host/hostess offers you another glass of wine?
     You've already had one glass, and you are driving.

9   you walk into a restaurant where you have already made a table reservation?

10 you want to send a business acquaintance your regards?

PHRASE PRACTICE (4)

Respond to the following phrases. You will hear ten phrases altogether.

5 INVITING SOMEONE FOR A DRINK

 Work in pairs and act out the following conversation. Study the phrases in sections 6.1 – 6.3 of your Phrase Book. Change roles.

Person 1   **Person 2**

| Invite your partner for a drink. |

| Turn him/her down. |

| Persuade him/her to accept. |

| Give in. Accept the invitation. |

6 COCKTAILS

 Work in pairs. Take turns in being the bartender and the customer. The customer asks what the three cocktails are and the bartender explains. The customer then decides which one he wants and orders it. Partner B's material is on page 122.

STEP ONE: Partner A, customer.

| **Paradise Cocktail** | *Crimson Fizz* | *Blood 'n' Sand Cocktail* |

STEP TWO: Partner A, bartender.

Between the Sheets	*Moscow Mule*	**Old-Fashioned Cocktail**
Juice of 1/2 lemon	2 oz. vodka	1 1/2 oz. whisky
3/4 oz.* Jamaica rum	juice of 1/2 lime	2 dashes angostura bitters
3/4 oz. brandy	1 split ginger beer	1 small lump sugar
3/4 oz. Cointreau	or ale	2 dashes Curacao
*oz.=ounces		dash club soda

7 A NIGHT AT THE OPERA

**Work in pairs and act out the following conversation.
Study sections 6.1 – 6.3 of your Phrase Book.**

Person 1

Person 2

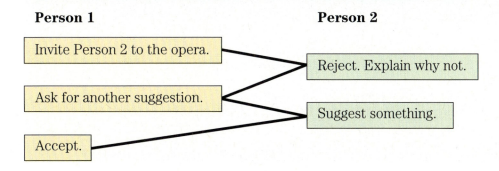

Person 1	Person 2
Invite Person 2 to the opera.	Reject. Explain why not.
Ask for another suggestion.	Suggest something.
Accept.	

8 DECLINING AN INVITATION

 Fill in the invitation to a party.

*You Are Cordially Invited
To A Party*

On ....

At ....

Place ....

Given by ....

R S V P

BUT...

INFO

All the "accepting" phrases can be made into "declining" statements simply by adding "but" immediately after the phrase and giving a suitable reason, or by saying "but I'm afraid I can't". The timing of the "but" is rather important. Say "but" as part of the phrase, without hesitation, otherwise your listener will interpret your phrase as an acceptance and thank you for agreeing before you can get a word in edgewise. You can also begin with a compliment and top it off with an excuse, "That's really very kind of you, but ..."Another polite way of turning someone down is to use one of the declining phrases and then ask to be invited later: "Perhaps another time."

Now work with your partner and respond to the invitation on the opposite page. This is a telephone conversation, so sit back to back. Change roles.

Host/Hostess	Guest

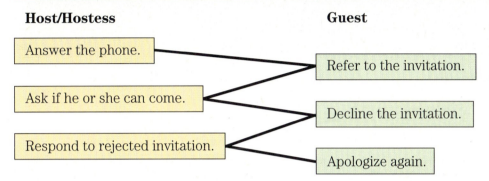

Answer the phone.

Ask if he or she can come.

Respond to rejected invitation.

Refer to the invitation.

Decline the invitation.

Apologize again.

9 GOOD NEWS, BAD NEWS

 Partner A reads the following sentences. Partner B responds accordingly. Study sections 6.8 and 6.10 of your Phrase Book.

1 Our house was burgled last night.
2 They took everything I've got, even the car.
3 Fortunately, I have a very good insurance policy.
4 But not on the car.
5 Anyway, never mind, I've been offered a new job as a travelling salesman.
6 That means a bigger salary.
7 But I'm unable to accept it.
8 I haven't got a car!

A checklist for power (business) lunches

❑ Make reservations.
❑ Be punctual.
❑ Order familiar, easy-to-eat foods.
❑ Don't drink too much.
❑ After opening pleasantries, talk business.
❑ Pay the bill discreetly.
❑ Tip adequately.
❑ If you're the guest, send a thank-you note.

10 GOOD NEWS

 Work in pairs. Study sections 6.5 – 6.8 of your Phrase Book.

Host/Hostess	Guest

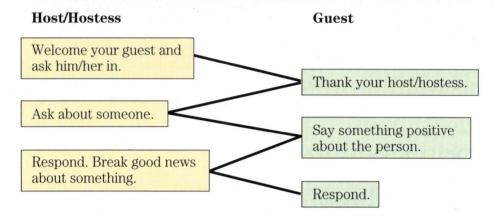

Welcome your guest and ask him/her in.

Ask about someone.

Respond. Break good news about something.

Thank your host/hostess.

Say something positive about the person.

Respond.

Partner B   Partner B   Partner B   Partner B   Partner B

From page 118, exercise 6: Cocktails.

Partner B, bartender.

Paradise Cocktail	*Crimson Fizz*	*Blood 'n' Sand Cocktail*
3/4 oz.* apricot brandy 1 1/2 oz. gin 1/4 oz. lemon juice *oz.=ounces	1/4 t of sugar 6 fresh strawberries mashed 1 1/2 oz. gin juice of 1/2 lemon	1/2 oz. orange juice 1/2 oz. scotch 1/2 oz. cherry brandy 1/2 oz. sweet vermouth

Partner B, customer.

Between the Sheets	*Moscow Mule*	𝕺𝖑𝖉=𝕱𝖆𝖘𝖍𝖎𝖔𝖓𝖊𝖉 𝕮𝖔𝖈𝖐𝖙𝖆𝖎𝖑

11 WOULD YOU LIKE A DRINK?

 These people are being served drinks. What would they answer to this question? Read the situation and write out the response. Study the phrases in sections 6.13 and 6.14 of your Phrase Book.

Lucy Jameson
Six months pregnant.
Can't drink.

_____

_____

....

Matthew Wilson
The village drunk.
Already had six beers.

_____

_____

....

Kim Kristoffsen
Fat.
On a diet.

_____

_____

....

Tim Davies
Just arrived.
He's thirsty.

_____

_____

....

Barbara Cohen
Taking medication for
allergies. Can't drink.

_____

_____

....

James Brinkley
Driving home.
Already had a drink.

_____

_____

....

Charles Williams
Wine lover. Needs to
show off his expertise.

_____

_____

....

Mary Holmes
Gin lover. Just walked
in. Very eager.

_____

_____

12 RESTAURANT SMALL TALK

Sit in groups of four around a table. You're eating in a restaurant with three business colleagues. Work through the situations clockwise starting with A1, B1, etc. and finishing with D4.

IMPORTANT:
The other three should keep on reacting to the one who is talking, e.g. responding to questions, agreeing, disagreeing, commenting, supporting etc.

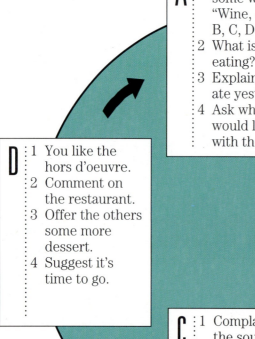

A
1 Offer everybody some wine (e.g. "Wine, everyone?"). B, C, D react.
2 What is it you're eating? Ask.
3 Explain where you ate yesterday.
4 Ask what people would like to drink with their coffee.

B
1 No spoon!
2 Ask for more bread.
3 Tell the rest about your favourite food.
4 Thank everyone for a nice evening.

C
1 Complain about the soup.
2 Ask what people think of the food.
3 Ask the others if they're allergic to any foods.
4 Offer to pay the entire bill.

D
1 You like the hors d'oeuvre.
2 Comment on the restaurant.
3 Offer the others some more dessert.
4 Suggest it's time to go.

13 WHAT'S COOKING?

Study the recipe and explain it to your partner in your own language.

Baked Apples

4 large green apples
honey or brown sugar
raisins, nuts, cinnamon

Wash the apples.
Cut out the cores.

Put the apples in a tin.
Put some water
in the bottom.

Put some honey or brown
sugar in the apples.

Chop the nuts. Put nuts
and raisins in the apples.
Sprinkle sugar and
cinnamon on the apples.

Put the tin in the oven.
Cook for 30 minutes.

Serve with cream or vanilla
sauce.

Now go on and explain in English how you make a typical dish in your own country. Below is a list of verbs to help you.

add	bake	beat	boil	burn	chop	cook
cover	cut	fry	heat	mix	put	serve
simmer	sprinkle	stir	wash	whip		

14 PARTY-GOERS

Working in pairs, discuss the following problem and decide on a solution.

Jim and Susan want to host three dinner parties: one on Friday, one on Saturday and one on Sunday. You are Jim and Susan. You want to invite two couples (four guests) on each evening. There are problems, however, in that many of the guests do not like each other, and most of the people have very busy schedules. Can you arrange a supper party where everyone is happy? Below is a list of the facts that must be kept in mind.

1   John was Linda's first husband. They do not get along.
2   Ed and Dave are business rivals. They never meet socially.
3   Anita has judo classes on Friday evenings.
4   Ed secretly suspects that his wife is interested in John. He becomes very jealous when they all meet.
5   Carol can't stand the Irish. Jeff and Christina are Irish.
6   Kevin was very rude to Anita at the last party.
7   Susan wants to try out her recipe for Tex-Mex food, but Christina and Joe hate Mexican food.
8   Ed works late on Fridays.
9   Kevin smokes cigars. Christina is allergic to smoke.
10   John's mother comes to see her son and daughter-in-law on Sunday evenings.
11   John and Carol visit Carol's parents on Saturday evenings.
12   Jeff and Christina always play tennis on Fridays.
13   Anita and Linda hate the sight of each other.
14   John and Carol lent money to Dave and Anita. They never got it back. Now the two couples are not on speaking terms.
15   Jeff and Christina don't like Ed and Maggie.
16   Jane plays bridge on Saturday nights.
17   Kevin never leaves his house on Saturday evening because he likes to watch his favourite television show.
18   Joe and Linda go away for the weekend and come back on Sunday morning.

Couples	Friday	Saturday	Sunday
John and Carol			
Dave and Anita			
Jeff and Christina			
Ed and Maggie			
Joe and Linda			
Kevin and Jane			

To Be Quite Frank

The language of negotiations

This unit looks at the language of
negotiation, provides you with a
few hints on the subject and gives
you an opportunity of putting some
of your own negotiation skills into
practice. This unit is particularly
suited to business people.

1 SNAPSHOTS

Listen and repeat. You can also enact the situations.

- Well, I strongly recommend that we contact ICI.
- I can see your point but I'm not sure I agree with you.

- Could you be a little more precise?
- Sorry. Let me put it in another way.

- We will do everything in our power to help you.

– Is that acceptable
as a compromise
solution?
– Yes, I think that
would be perfectly
acceptable.

– I'm afraid it just wouldn't be
feasible.

– Well, if I could just
sum up the
discussion.

WISE WORDS ON NEGOTIATION

Negotiation is a process in which both sides win.   *Ideal*

My idea of an agreeable person is a person who agrees with me.   *Reality?*

2 CROSS-CULTURAL CONSIDERATIONS

Safe gifts for them if you are invited to their homes.

Austrians	small flowers or chocolates when visiting their home for the first time
Belgians	avoid giving chrysanthemums as gifts; they symbolize death
British people	flowers or chocolates; beware of giving white lilies – in some households they suggest death
Bulgarians	flowers, chocolates or wine
Czechs and Slovaks	flowers, wine or spirits
Danes	flowers
Dutch people	chocolates or flowers
Finns	flowers
French people	any quality gift
Germans	flowers; avoid red roses – they are usually reserved for lovers or husbands/wives
Greeks	flowers or a cake (for the hostess)
Icelanders	nothing too expensive
Irish people	chocolates, flowers, wine
Italians	chocolates, flowers, wine
Luxemburgers	avoid giving chrysanthemums as gifts; they symbolize death
Norwegians	chocolates or flowers
Poles	avoid red roses; they are usually reserved for lovers or husbands/wives
Portuguese	no gifts expected
Romanians	flowers
Russians	flowers or liquor
Spaniards	flowers or chocolate; avoid dahlias and chrysanthemums – they symbolize death
Swedes	flowers
Swiss people	flowers or chocolates; red roses are reserved for lovers or husbands/wives
Turks	flowers or chocolates

3 NEGOTIATING

Read the text and do the exercises.

Apart from behaving in an acceptable way and remembering what it is you are
supposed to be negotiating, the choice and timing of a suitable phrase can make all
the difference during a negotiation. Understanding exactly what you (and they) are
saying is therefore vital if you are to negotiate successfully. Understanding who you
5 are negotiating with, as well as their cultural etiquette, is probably even more
important. But, if you're a good negotiator you will have already done your cross-
cultural homework and know exactly what, and what not, to do.

Generally speaking, negotiations would seem to go through four main phases:

1 The beginning
10 The negotiators get to know one another so that strategies, reactions and behaviour
can be anticipated. Patient observation is essential.

2 Proposals
This is where the negotiators set out to what extent they should negotiate. It's a
good time for deciding on objectives and suggesting alternatives as well as
15 explaining what they would like. Keeping options open is probably the most
important consideration.

3 Problem-solving
Here, the negotiators attempt to reduce the gap between them. They are prepared
to compromise but more than ready to persuade the 'others' to change their minds.
20 Solutions are vital.

4 The ending
At this phase the negotiators should be looking ahead and agreeing on future
procedure.

 **A At what phase of negotiation, 1, 2, 3 or 4, would you
expect to hear the following statements?**

Phase

1 I suggest that we discuss prices first.
2 Is this your first time here?
3 We've been through all this already.
4 I feel quite confident that we can solve this matter.
5 I propose that we meet in our company next time.
6 Obviously we will have to discuss the after-sales service.

Other considerations include indirectness, friendliness, openness and softness.

25 ◈ **Indirectness**
Try to use an introductory phrase before you actually say anything, e.g.
Well, how about this for an idea?

◈ **Friendliness**
Why not put across your ideas more as a question than a direct statement?
30 Obviously, intonation is the key here.

◈ **Openness**
Certain words suggest flexibility. Instead of saying WILL, why not use WOULD, or
instead of CAN, COULD? This just MIGHT make them feel more free to negotiate.

◈ **Softness**
35 Using little phrases such as *I'm afraid* can soften even the worst news. And even
the biggest problems can be made to sound less unpleasant when watered down
with words such as *a bit, slightly* or *a little*, e.g. *We might have a SLIGHT
problem with the colour but ...*

 **B Read the following phrases to your partner and ask him
or her to say them again in a different way, so they sound
more polite or less direct. Change roles.**

1 That's no good. _____

2 No, we won't. _____

3 I don't agree. _____

4 I can't do that. _____

5 It's going to be a problem. _____

6 You're right. _____

7 She's not here. _____

8 Do you want coffee? _____

9 I don't believe you. _____

10 Where's the toilet? _____

4 GET READY

 Would you manage in the following situations? If you have difficulties, turn to Unit 7 of your Phrase Book.

How would you begin if you wanted

1   to propose something?

2   to agree partially?

3   to show that you disagreed, but not too strongly?

4   to add some information?

5   to make sure you understood correctly?

6   to correct a misunderstanding?

7   to say the same thing again in another way?

8   to reassure someone?

9   to play down a point?

10   to offer a compromise?

11   to accept a compromise?

12   to reject a compromise?

PHRASE PRACTICE (4)

Open your Phrase Book (7.1 – 7.18). Listen to the phrases and repeat them. You will hear the first phrase in each section.

5 EVERYDAY NEGOTIATIONS

 Choose one of the following situations and act it out in front of the class.

You're in a restaurant. You order chicken, but the waiter/waitress brings you pork instead. You tell him/her he/she has made a mistake, but he/she insists that he/she is right.

. . . .

You're at a train station. You have with you several heavy suitcases. You ask a porter to help you carry the suitcases to the taxi. He / She asks for twice the amount of money you had in mind. You argue over the price.

. . . .

You buy a new radio. You take it home, but it doesn't work, so you take it back to the store and complain to the manager. You want your money back but the manager has other ideas.

. . . .

You buy a new coat and leave it in the store by mistake. When you discover it is missing, you return to the store and ask the clerk if he / she has seen it.

. . . .

You go to the bank to withdraw some money from your account. When the cashier asks for your identification, you discover that you've left all means of identification at home.

. . . .

You're in a restaurant. You've just had a good dinner. The waiter is waiting for you to pay the bill. You look for your wallet and discover that you've left it at home.

. . . .

You've bought a plane ticket to New York. You go to the airport only to hear from the airline representative that the flight has been cancelled. You are extremely angry because you absolutely must get to New York as soon as possible.

6 PROPOSALS

 Work in pairs and carry out the following conversation. Before you start, we suggest you decide exactly what it is you're negotiating about. Possible areas for negotiation: price, delivery time, guarantee, quantity, costs, etc. Make sure you are familiar with sections 7.1 – 7.6 of your Phrase Book.

Person 1

Make a proposal which would be good for you.

Make a proposal which is more reasonable.

Give the information. Then add some more information.

Confirm.

Person 2

Express neutral disagreement.

Express partial agreement. Then, ask for further information.

Ask for confirmation.

7 THE TRAVEL AGENCY

 Sit back to back with your partner and perform the following telephone conversation.

CALLER
You work for a travel agency and would like to try and get a good deal for a group of ten business people visiting a European capital. Try and get ten single rooms for five nights at a cost of 60 ecus per person, per night, including continental breakfast. Remember, there are plenty of other hotels to choose from.

PERSON RECEIVING THE CALL
You work as a reservations manager in a hotel. The standard price for five nights in your hotel, excluding continental breakfast, is 70 ecus per person, per night. Including breakfast, the price is 75 ecus per person, per night. Remember, there are plenty of other hotels to choose from.

8 A MISUNDERSTANDING

 There has been a misunderstanding. Write suitable phrases on the lines below. Study sections 7.7 – 7.9 of your Phrase Book.

SITUATION
Your customer has misunderstood your offer.
Your offer was 14 items at 10 ecus each.

Person 1   **Person 2**

(But you said 40 items at 10 ecus each.)

→

_____

_____

(Correct misunderstanding politely.)

(Are you changing your offer?)

←

_____

→

_____

(Oh, I see.)

←

_____

(Rephrase the point.)

→

(I hope this won't create any problems.)

_____   ←

_____   ↙

_____

(Reassure him/her.)   *(React.)*

TELEPHONE TIPS

☐ Smile.
☐ Try to sound positive, avoiding words like *maybe* or *I don't know*.
☐ Avoid eating, smoking, drinking or talking to others at the same time.
☐ Speak more slowly than you usually do, but not too slow.
☐ Make the call as short as possible.

9 TRANSLATION AGENCY

Here's another chance to practise telephone negotiations. Sit back to back with your partner and perform the following conversation.

CALLER
You have received a bill from a translation agency for a brochure. You are satisfied with the work but the bill is too high. The bill was for 1,000 ecus. You are not prepared to pay more than 500 ecus. Try and get them to reduce the bill.

PERSON RECEIVING THE CALL
You just billed a client 1,000 ecus for a translation job. You charged your standard fee. Your client seems reluctant to pay. What are you going to do? Remember, you would like to keep them as your clients.

10 FINDING A COMPROMISE

Here Person 1 should suggest that Person 2 pays the shipping costs. Refer to sections 7.10 – 7.18 of your Phrase Book.

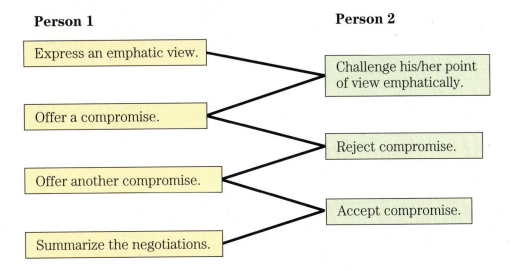

Person 1

- Express an emphatic view.
- Offer a compromise.
- Offer another compromise.
- Summarize the negotiations.

Person 2

- Challenge his/her point of view emphatically.
- Reject compromise.
- Accept compromise.

11 THE DEAL

First listen to a model conversation based on the negotiation below. Then go on working in pairs. Act out this negotiation. Try and do this without your Phrase Book.

SITUATION
The seller is trying to sell 100 tractors to the buyer.
The seller's offer is 10,000 ecus per tractor.

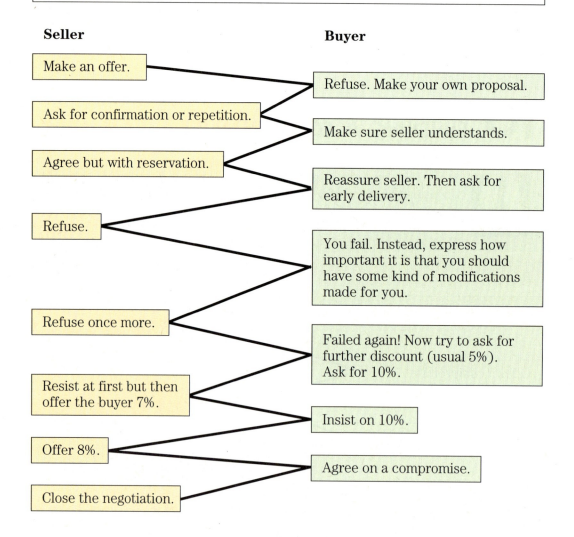

Seller

- Make an offer.
- Ask for confirmation or repetition.
- Agree but with reservation.
- Refuse.
- Refuse once more.
- Resist at first but then offer the buyer 7%.
- Offer 8%.
- Close the negotiation.

Buyer

- Refuse. Make your own proposal.
- Make sure seller understands.
- Reassure seller. Then ask for early delivery.
- You fail. Instead, express how important it is that you should have some kind of modifications made for you.
- Failed again! Now try to ask for further discount (usual 5%). Ask for 10%.
- Insist on 10%.
- Agree on a compromise.

12 THE QUALITIES OF A GOOD NEGOTIATOR

 Rank the following qualities in order of importance in terms of negotiating, i.e. 1 – the most important and 10 – the least important.

Your list   **Joint list**

☐ The ability to express yourself well.   ☐

☐ The ability to read people well (body language, etc).   ☐

☐ The ability to deal with difficult questions.   ☐

☐ The ability not to show your feelings.   ☐

☐ The ability to withstand pressure.   ☐

☐ The ability to ask the right questions at the right time.   ☐

☐ The ability to sound convincing.   ☐

☐ The ability to prepare well.   ☐

☐ The ability to listen carefully.   ☐

☐ The ability to admit you don't understand even if it's embarrassing.   ☐

 Now compare your lists and try and agree on a new joint list. This is a good opportunity to practise some negotiating skills; explaining your position, compromising, bargaining, disagreeing and agreeing, etc.

13 SELLING BOOKS

 You may remember the book committee meeting in Unit 4 on page 85. Now you are going to sell those books to other publishers.

Publisher 1

Titles:
I Was a Teenage Student
The Sex Life of Frogs
The Life Story of Salman Rushdie
The Filthy Book of Dirty Jokes
Grow Your Own Hashish

Publisher 2

Titles:
How to Lose a Million Dollars
    in Less Than a Day
UFOs in Luxembourg
Madonna's Book of Bedtime
    Stories
How to Live Forever and Ever
The Truth about Banking

Publisher 3

Titles:
Hang-gliding for the Over-Sixties
Women in Sport
A Pictorial History of Toilets
Is There a Life before Death?
The Secret Diary of President
    Kennedy

Publisher 4

Titles:
Babies as Substitutes for Dogs
Exciting Stories about
    Scandinavian Libraries
A Complete Guide to Albanian
    Stamps
Basil, the Invisible Hedgehog
Working English

STEP ONE
Form groups and give your company a name.

STEP TWO
In your group decide on what the books are like and why they should interest other publishers. Don't worry about the price etc. You're only supposed to get other publishers interested.

STEP THREE
Each group takes in turns trying to sell their books to the other groups.

STEP FOUR
Who sold the most books?

14 SETTLING A DISPUTE

 For a minimum of four people. **STEP ONE:** Read through both briefs and fill in the spaces together. **STEP TWO:** Divide yourselves into Company A and Company B. Prepare according to the notes given under the title Preparation.

COMPANY A	COMPANY B
BRIEF	**BRIEF**
Last year your company sold a (machine)	You are purchasing officers for Company B. Last year you purchased a (machine)
....	
to Company B in (country)	....
....	from Company A. This year, however, the machine broke down only a few days after the warranty had run out. The other company sent out an engineer to repair the machine. Later, you were sent an invoice to the sum of
The machine broke down only a few days after the warranty had run out. You had to send an engineer there to repair it. Understandably, you invoiced them for her work, but they complained that repairs such as this should be part of your after-sales service. The value of the invoice was	
	....
....	You were surprised since, in your opinion, such repairs should be part of a standard after-sales service.
Situation: YOU ARE NOW VISITING THEM IN THEIR COUNTRY TO SETTLE THE DISPUTE.	**Situation:** THEIR REPRESENTATIVES ARE VISITING YOU TODAY TO SETTLE THE DISPUTE.
Aim: Try to obtain agreement on payment.	**Aim:** Try to get them to take care of all or most of the repair costs.
Points: Legally they are obliged to pay, but you don't want to lose your customer.	**Points:** Legally, you don't have a case. Potentially, you are an important client for them.
PREPARATION	**PREPARATION**
Work out what arguments the other company will use in order to avoid payment. Decide on your strategy and in what order you will introduce your arguments.	Work out their probable point of view. Decide on your arguments and the order in which you would like to present them.

STEP THREE: Now carry out the negotiation.

15 WHICH AGENT?

 For a mimimum of three people. This is a more advanced activity that gives you an opportunity of practising a variety of skills you need in meetings and negotiations.
The situation is as follows: Company 1 is looking for an agent abroad. Company 2 and Company 3 represent potential agents. Which one would you choose?
Fill in the missing details together.

Name of Company 1 (and from what country): ....

....

This company is a successful manufacturer of ....

....

They would now like to concentrate on a new market: (country)

....

In order to do this they would like to sign an agency contract with Company 2,

(name of Company 2): ....
or with Company 3
(name of Company 3): ....

Participants at meeting:
1) representative(s) of Company 1: ....

....

2) representative(s) of Company 2: ....

....

3) representative(s) of Company 3: ....

....

POSSIBLE THINGS TO CONSIDER:

a) the nature of the agreement – exclusive, franchise, what?
b) transportation and delivery details.
c) distribution – wholesale, retail, stores, what?
d) payment responsibility for sales promotion etc.
e) length of agency contract.

Company 1
Representative(s) of Company 1:
Make up a list of the things you are interested in and looking for. Keep an open mind but look for the better deal. Before you actually meet the two other companies, please make sure that they both know exactly what it is you are looking for.

. . . .

Company 2
Representative(s) of Company 2:
Draw up a plan of action for selling Company 1's products as well as some proposals for possible cooperation. During the meeting, please feel free to change your ideas.

. . . .

Company 3
Representative(s) of Company 3:
Draw up a plan of action for selling Company 1's products as well as some proposals for possible cooperation. During the meeting, please feel free to change your ideas.

Please note:
Although this is not a formal meeting, i.e. no chairman, etc. it is official, so try and be as diplomatic as possible.

AIM:
Company 1 should decide, on the basis of the meeting, which of the other companies will be its agent.

16 HOW TO NEGOTIATE

Philip O'Connor is a language trainer and author. In this interview you will hear him talking about eight steps of negotiation. Number the phrases according to the order in which Philip introduces them.

☐ Asking questions

☐ Bargaining

☐ Relationship building

☐ Concluding

☐ Generating options

☐ Agreeing on procedure

☐ Exchanging information

☐ Bidding: putting forward proposals

Clearly and Simply

The language of presentations

Being able to give a presentation

in a foreign language is extremely

challenging, even if you are a "born

speaker". So, this unit tries to deal

with the bare essentials of

presentation whilst giving you the

opportunity of practising the kind

of language involved.

1 SNAPSHOTS

Listen and repeat. You can also enact the situations.

– Good morning, ladies
and gentlemen.
Welcome to our
company.

– I'm here to present our
organization to you.

– I'd now like to draw
your attention to
something else.

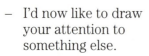

– OK. So much for that. Now I'd like to move on to my next point.

– Let me get back to my main point.

– Well, that's it really. Thank you very much for listening to me.

....

WISE WORDS ON PRESENTATIONS

Friends, Romans, countrymen, lend me your ears.   *Shakespeare*

Empty vessels make most noise.   *Proverb*

2 CROSS-CULTURAL CONSIDERATIONS

Look at the pictures of common gestures and expressions. In different countries they can mean different things. Choose the alternative you think is correct.

1 HEAD TAP
In Argentina:
a) I'm thinking.
b) He's crazy.

2 HEAD NOD
In Greece:
a) Yes.
b) No.

3 FINGERS CIRCLE
In America:
a) Okay.
b) Zero.

4 FINGERS CROSS
In England:
a) Buzz off.
b) Good luck.

5 ONE-FINGER POINT
In the Middle East:
a) impolite
b) polite

6 THUMBS UP
In Australia:
a) rude
b) Good luck!

7 TAPPING THE NOSE
In Scotland:
a) I'll consider it.
b) We've got
a secret.

8 WAVING
In Peru:
a) Come here.
b) Go to hell.

3 ONE MAN'S MEAT IS ANOTHER MAN'S POISON

Read the text and do the exercises.

A good presentation is worth its weight in gold. The least it can do is open the door, and at its best it can clinch* a deal. Look good, sound good, talk good and you're more than half way there. But the question surely should be "What exactly do we mean by 'good'?" One man's meat is another man's poison, as the saying goes. In
5   other words, what may have them stomping* their feet in South Dakota may leave them stone dead in North Korea and vice versa.

      Very often in Scandinavia I've heard comments like *too slick* for my liking* or words to the effect about what was, in my opinion, an extremely polished performance. On the other hand, I've seen North Americans yawning
10 disapprovingly at what some Europeans might consider a 'tidy little performance'.

      Clearly cross-cultural differences come very much to the fore* in a presentation involving a foreign speaker. That's why it really pays to know exactly who you are talking to or 'at'. Audience research can save an awful lot of tears and disappointment, not to mention lost deals.

15   A Dutch friend of mine made the mistake of telling what he considered to be a harmless little joke in the middle of his lecture to commercial students in Nigeria. This was the joke: *Who invented the five-day working week?* Answer: *Robinson Crusoe.* Why? *Because he had all his work done by Friday!*

      This failed to amuse the audience since, although they were indeed familiar
20 with the works of Daniel Defoe, they all happened to share the same skin colour as Crusoe's manservant.

      Another classic faux pas* I know of concerns a British colleague of mine who was lecturing to young Saudi airmen on emergency landing procedures. Being left-handed and rather extrovert, he spent most of the first part of his lecture waving
25 his left hand in the air or directly at his rather uneasy audience.

      During the interval another trainer politely informed him that according to Moslem tradition the left hand was reserved as the toilet hand and should be used with caution. "No wonder they kept on moving back in their chairs every time I pointed at them!" he added.

30   But even being aware of cultural differences is no guarantee that a presentation will go smoothly. It also needs careful planning and sometimes ingenuity* to carry it off. A good case in point concerns a Finnish acquaintance who was faced with the unenviable task of giving a lecture in Japan to an audience

of Japanese and Americans. As he well knew, the American half would be expecting
35 a snappy*, lively or preferably plain 'funny' beginning. The Japanese, on the other
hand with their essentially reserved approach, would feel more at home with an
apologetic beginning expressing humility and respect.

He was faced with a dilemma*. Should he be funny and win the attention of
the Americans and run the risk of losing the respect of the Japanese? Or should he
40 be humble and apologetic and win instant respect from the Japanese but run the
risk of losing the Americans' attention? This is how he began his speech, a
masterstroke* of cross-cultural consideration: "Good morning, everyone. If I were
American I would begin this presentation with a joke. But I'm not American. If I
were Japanese I would begin this presentation with an apology. But I'm not
45 Japanese – I'm a Finn. So, I would like to begin my presentation by apologizing for
not telling a joke."

P.W.

Explanation of words:

clinch	win	**ingenuity**	originality
stomping	stamping	**snappy**	quick and witty
slick	clever	**dilemma**	two-way problem
to the fore	into the picture	**masterstroke**	clever solution
faux pas	a mistake		

 Which of the following agree with the text?

1 In a presentation it is important
   a) to know something about the cultural background of your audience.
   b) to know personally all the people in the audience.
   c) to give a polished performance if you're in Scandinavia.

2 The Dutchman's joke about Robinson Crusoe didn't work in Nigeria
   a) because it was racist.
   b) because the audience had never heard of Robinson Crusoe.
   c) because they don't have a five-day working week in Nigeria.

3 The British lecturer in Saudi Arabia made a big mistake because
   a) he was left-handed.
   b) the toilet was reserved.
   c) he used his left hand too much.

4 Japanese presenters often begin a lecture
   a) with a joke.   b) by apologizing.   c) in silence.

**5 The Finnish presenter who began his presentation by apologizing for
   not telling a joke**
   a) failed.   b) made the Americans angry.   c) succeeded.

4 GET READY

Would you manage in the following situations? If you have difficulties turn to Unit 8 of your Phrase Book.

What phrase would you use if you wanted ...

1   to get attention at the beginning of a presentation?

_____

2   to actually start a presentation?

_____

3   to explain the purpose of a presentation?

_____

4   to draw attention to a point?

_____

5   to finish a point?

_____

6   to start another point?

_____

7   to show that you were going to talk about something else for a while?

_____

8   to indicate that you were ending your presentation?

_____

PHRASE PRACTICE (4)

Open your Phrase Book (sections 8.1 – 8.8). You will hear eight instructions. Select a suitable phrase for each instruction from each section.

5 THE UNPRESENTABLES

Work with your partner and take turns in presenting one of the following products to each other.

HELLO I'M PHIL!

The ladder specially made for the idle.

The hanger specially made for the shoe.

The spectacles specially made for the ears.

The talking name tag specially made for a shy person.

The telephone specially made for the office gossip.

The umbrella specially made for the sun.

The lawn specially made for the garage.

Sun glasses specially made for a person who is happy only behind the steering wheel.

6 ONE-TO-ONE PRESENTATION

Work in pairs and present to your partner one or more of the following. The one who is listening should imagine that he/she knows nothing or very little about the subject being presented.

A   your car

B   your home

C   your education

D   your country's school system

E   your country's transport system

F   your country's political system

7 THE BARE ESSENTIALS

 Analyzed very simply, most presentations would seem to fall into three phases: the introduction, the main body and the conclusion.

THE INTRODUCTION

The introduction can also be divided into phases: a) getting attention b) setting the scene and c) explaining the purpose. (Study sections 8.1– 8.3 of your Phrase Book.)

a) Getting attention

This simply means letting people know you are ready to start. Phrases such as *Right then, everybody* are very useful here. There are, of course, numerous other techniques such as blowing into the microphone or dimming the lights.

b) Setting the scene

Here, it's important to either welcome the audience or thank them for inviting you. It's also an ideal opportunity to tell them about yourself and who you represent. You can also use flowery phrases such as *On behalf of … I'd like to take this opportunity of welcoming you all here this morning* etc.

c) Explaining the purpose

It's a good idea to give your audience some idea of what you're going to be talking about. It's also polite to sequence (to put in order) the topics or matters you will be covering. Here, simple words or phrases such as *To start with, after this, next, then* and *finally* can make sure that you get your message across.

Fill in the spaces with an appropriate word or phrase from the list below:

Good afternoon, everyone. May I [1]_____ this opportunity of [2]_____ you all here today. My name is Peter Van Cleef and I work [3]____ Eurotop [4]_____ a technical adviser. My main [5]_____ is to explain our new product line to you. First, I shall say a few words about our existing products. [6]_____, I'll be looking at our two new models and [7]_____, I will try and give you some information on our future plans. If you have any questions I shall be [8]_____ _____ to answer them later on. However, please feel free to interrupt me [9]_____ any time.

1 make / take / fake
2 thanking / spanking / welcoming
3 at / as / for
4 at / in / as
5 object / objection / objective

6 thereafter / then / therefore
7 final / at last / lastly
8 not only delighted / only too delighted / not too pleased
9 in / on / at

THE MAIN BODY

Keeping things interesting and clear are very important during the main body of a presentation. There are, of course, many language points to consider but we have selected four which we hope will be of help: a) drawing attention, b) paragraphing and proceeding, c) digressing and d) justifying.

a) Drawing attention

If you want to make sure your point gets through, phrases such as *I think it's very significant that* ... can put extra emphasis on what you're saying. Emphasizing your words can also have the same effect. So can leaving a dramatic pause before or after a statement. (Study section 8.4 of your Phrase Book.)

b) Paragraphing and proceeding

When listening to a presentation it's very helpful if the speaker moves clearly from one point to another. This is called paragraphing and proceeding. A particular point or matter can be brought to an end with phrases such as *So much for* ... or *That's all I'm going to say about* ... Signalling the start of another point can be achieved through the use of phrases like *Now I'd like to proceed by* ... or *Next, I'd like to concentrate on* ... Changing pitch can add to the effect.
(Study sections 8.5 and 8.6 of your Phrase Book.)

c) Digressing

Digressing simply means leaving the point. And although there's nothing wrong with digressing (sometimes it can save a situation) it is a good idea to let the audience know about it. Phrases such as *Let me digress for a moment* give the audience adequate warning of a slight change in direction. Phrases such as *To return to my original point* or *Allow me to get back to my main point* actually allow you to get back to your main point. (Study section 8.7 of your Phrase Book.)

d) Justifying

This simply refers to explaining the reason why. This actually comprises very simple words and phrases such as *because, as there is, due to, owing to* etc... But despite their simplicity they are easy to mix up or use incorrectly.

Fill in the blanks with the appropriate words taken from the list below. The result should be logical.

_____ rumours in some European countries there has been some speculation.

_____, the situation is a little unsteady at present. However, _____

the stability of the Deutschmark, _____ wise investment, no long-term trend

is forecast _____ no change whatsoever in German interest rates.

Select from: **due to / so / thanks to / as there was / a result of / that's why**

THE CONCLUSION

The conclusion loosely seems to comprise four elements:
a) summarizing, b) final point, c) inviting questions and d) thanking the audience.

a) Summarizing

This is your last chance to get your points or information across. Here's a chance to repeat yourself if you wish. But it's also an ideal phase to strengthen your argument. You can signal the phase with phrases such as *Let me sum up by saying...* or *To summarize ...*

b) Final point

Not everyone has a final point. Some speakers just fade away or stop suddenly. If you like the idea of a final point a little anecdote or thought-provoking idea can often give your presentation that nice little finishing touch. If you don't like the idea why not finish with an earth-shattering statement like *Well, I think that's just about all I have to say. So, ...*

c) Inviting questions

Asking for questions at the end of your presentation can be a risky but nevertheless necessary formality. Appropriate invitations range from the lengthy *If you have any questions I'll do my best to answer them* to the good old-fashioned, short but sweet *Any questions, please?*

d) Thanking the audience

If there have been no questions, why not go straight into something like *Thank you for listening to me* or *Thank you very much indeed for letting me have the opportunity of talking to you today* or even *Thank you very much.*

If there have been questions but you think (hope) the last one has been asked, you can always finish by saying *If there are no more questions, I think we should finish here* or *No more questions?* And then proceed to thank the audience as previously mentioned.

If there's no more time but it looks like there are still some questions left you can always invite people to discuss matters with you later. Suitable phrases include *I'm afraid we're out of time but, if you wish, we can continue the discussion later.*

8 HOW EFFECTIVE DO YOU THINK YOU ARE AS A PRESENTER?

 Interview your partner and ask each other the following twenty questions. Answer the questions with a YES or a NO.

		YES	NO	points
1	Before you actually planned a presentation would you decide on your basic objective(s)?	....	....	....
2	Would you analyze your audience beforehand?	....	....	....
3	Would your presentation include a preview and a review?	....	....	....
4	Would you try to make your introduction and ending as sensational as possible?	....	....	....
5	Would you make sure that your visual aids were clear, simple, easy to read and useful?	....	....	....
6	Would you try and be as enthusiastic as possible?	....	....	....
7	Would you rehearse thoroughly?	....	....	....
8	Would you rely a great deal on your notes?	....	....	....
9	Would your notes only contain key words or phrases?	....	....	....
10	Would you check out the seating, AV equipment, lighting, etc. beforehand?	....	....	....
11	Would you maintain eye-contact with your audience?	....	....	....
12	Would you use your normal voice?	....	....	....
13	Would you be aware of your own body language?	....	....	....
14	Would you read directly from notes?	....	....	....
15	Would you care about what clothes you had on?	....	....	....
16	Would you use humour ?	....	....	....
17	Would you be worried if your audience looked bored?	....	....	....

	YES	NO	points
18 Would you be constantly worried about making language mistakes?	....	....	....
19 Would you feel safer talking from behind something, e.g. a table?	....	....	....
20 Would you feel that what you were saying was far more important than how you said it?	....	....	....

Your partner's total:

Now turn to page 166 for the grading system.

0 - 5 points:	You may be better off sitting in the audience.
6 - 10 points:	You should get a lot out of this unit.
11 - 15 points:	You are obviously a good presenter.
16 - 20 points:	We'd love to listen to you.

9 PRESENTATION

Imagine you were about to give an extremely short presentation. In what order would you do the following? Number them and then compare your results with your partner's and the rest of the class. Discuss the results.

- ☐ Tell them your position/title.
- ☐ Inform them that you will answer their questions later.
- ☐ Mention your name.
- ☐ Explain what your work basically entails.
- ☐ Thank them for listening.
- ☐ Welcome everybody present.

Now go on and introduce yourself to the rest of the class. Include the elements mentioned above in an appropriate order. You will find suitable phrases in sections 8.2 and 8.8 of your Phrase Book. Remember to keep this presentation very short, i.e. 30 seconds. (You may find the section "Explaining the purpose" in exercise 7 of some help.)

10 PRESENTING INFORMATION

Before we take a look at some of the language needed for presenting information let's take a look at some of the most common forms of charts and graphs.

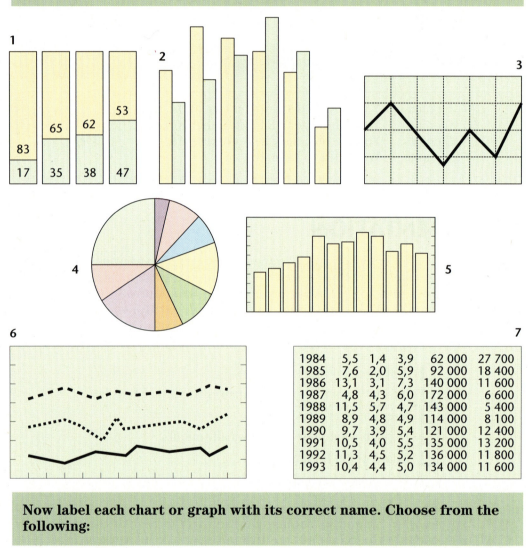

Now label each chart or graph with its correct name. Choose from the following:

☐ A pie chart
☐ A percentage bar chart

☐ A table
☐ A simple bar chart

☐ A multiple bar chart
☐ A multiple line graph
☐ A simple line graph

11 SPEED AND DEGREE

 Describing how much or how fast a change is can be an important part of presenting information.

SPEED
Typical adjectives and adverbs used when describing speed:

SLOW

A   gradual / gradually   _____

B   rapid / rapidly   _____

C   steady / steadily   _____

D   sharp / sharply   _____

FAST

Number them (1 – 4) in terms of speed, starting with THE SLOWEST and ending with THE FASTEST.

DEGREE
Typical adjectives and adverbs used when describing degree:

A LITTLE

A   substantial / substantially   _____

B   slight / slightly   _____

C   dramatic / dramatically   _____

D   insignificant / insignificantly   _____

A LOT

Number them (1 – 4) in terms of degree, starting with A LITTLE and ending with A LOT.

LANGUAGE HINTS

Here are some examples of how to use the language of description in a presentation.

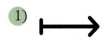

1)

a) to stand at ...
e.g. "Investment stood at 300,000 ecus last year."
b) to remain / stay at ...
e.g. "Losses stayed at 200,000 ecus per month between January and June."

2)

a) to rise / go up / increase by ... to ...
e.g. "Costs rose by 5% to 25%."
b) to rise / go up / increase from ... to ...
e.g. "Profits went up from 20% to 25%."
*Note noun forms: "There was an increase / a rise of 5%."

3)

a) to drop / go down / decrease ... by ... to ...
e.g. "Expenses dropped by 50,000 ecus to 300,000 ecus."
b) to drop / go down / decrease ... from ... to...
e.g. "Interest rates decreased from 18% to 16%."
*Note noun forms: "There was a drop / decrease / fall of 2%."

4)

a) to peak at ...
e.g. "Sales peaked at 6,000 units in January."
b) to reach a peak of ...
e.g. "Sales reached a peak of 6,000 units in January."

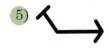

5)

to level off / out ... at ...
e.g. "Figures levelled out at 100,000."

6)

**to bottom out at ... /
to reach their / its lowest at ...**
e.g. "Our market share bottomed out later that year at around 25%."

12 DESCRIBING CONTENTS

**Look at the example and decide which verb group fits which
arrow best. Mark each arrow with the appropriate number.**

VERB GROUP

1. (figures) **stood at ....**
2. (figures) **rose / went up / increased**
3. (figures) **dropped / went down / decreased**
4. (figures) **peaked / reached a peak**
5. (figures) **levelled out / off**
6. (figures) **reached their lowest / bottomed out**
7. (figures) **picked up / began to recover**

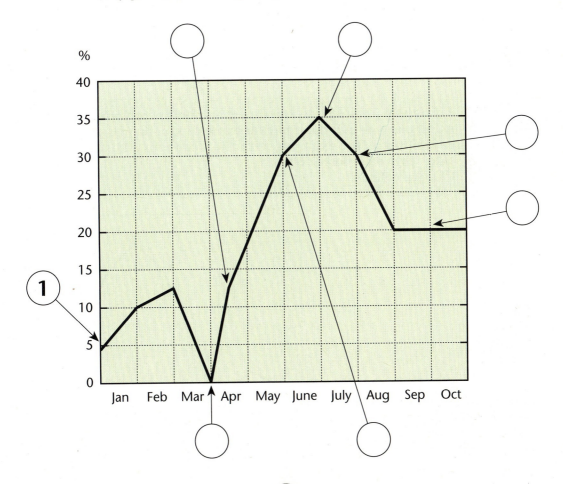

13 TALKING OF FIGURES

Fill in the missing spaces with appropriate verbs.
- **to double / to treble / to quadruple**
- **to increase five-fold, six-fold ...**
- **to be reduced**

1   Food profits .... this year, rising from 200,000 ecus to 400,000 ecus.

2   Profits on drinks ...., increasing from 130,000 ecus to nearly 400,000 ecus.

3   And most amazing of all, profits from the fruit machines went up from 100,000 ecus to 700,000 ecus, representing a .... increase.

4   Nevertheless, our overall profits have been .... by 50% because of increased taxation.

14 UPS AND DOWNS

Now go on and explain the line graph below to your partner, using phrases and information given to you on the previous pages. Begin, for example, with the words: In January the sales figures stood at 5% ...
Change roles.

Now listen to this model presentation based on the same graph.

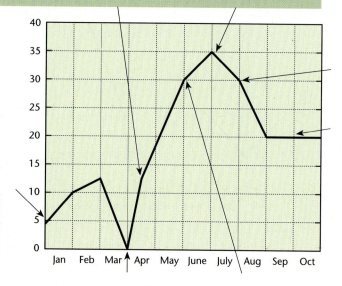

15 DRAW IT YOURSELF

Short phrases can help introduce, explain or develop a graph / chart you have on display.

Introducing
I'm now going to show you ...
I'd like to show this ...
Have a look at this ...

Describing structure
The curve here clearly shows ...
If we look at the vertical axis, we can ...
The horizontal axis represents ...

Labelling
It's a diagram showing ...
It's an organization chart of ...
It's a bar graph demonstrating ...

Describing features
You can clearly see that ...
Its most significant feature is ...
You'll see immediately that ...

Interpreting
This would seem to suggest that ...
Obviously, this implies that ...
It's quite evident that ...

Now, go ahead and prepare a SIMPLE graph of your own. It can be something to do with your workplace, job or hobbies – anything you like. Obviously you will need to decide on what the vertical and horizontal axes represent.

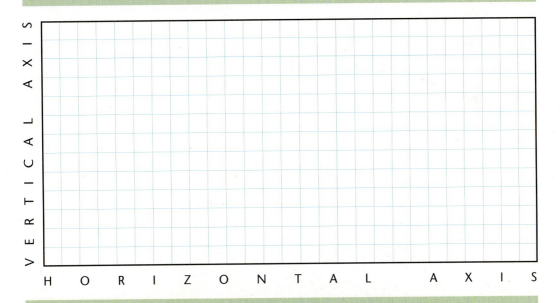

VERTICAL AXIS

HORIZONTAL AXIS

After you have drawn and labelled your graph, copy it onto a transparency and present it to the class. Good luck!

16 THE MOST AMAZING BICYCLE IN THE WORLD

 Work in pairs and design a bicycle of your own. It can be as crazy or conventional as you like.

Step One:
Decide as a class what country you would like to export it to. Then, consider the local conditions and market. (Holland is obviously ideal.)

Step Two:
Design your bike (i.e. draw it on paper) and give it a name.

Step Three:
Decide on its wholesale price.

Step Four:
Now copy your design onto a transparency, and include its name and cost.

Step Five:
Prepare a five-minute SALES presentation on your amazing bicycle.

Step Six:
Give your presentation, using all the skills and language you have acquired from this unit. Remember to ask for questions.

Step Seven:
After everyone has given his/her presentation, decide (in pairs) on which bicycle you would choose if you were the importing company. You may not vote for your own company. Explain your reasons to the class. The winning pair is the one who receives the most votes.

17 PRESENTATION SKILLS

 As we explained at the beginning of this unit we are concentrating on the bare essentials of presentations, language in particular, and not on presentation skills. However, you might like to consider some of the following factors.
Discuss the following. Work in groups or as a class.

1) Body language
What is it? How does it differ from culture to culture? Mention some things you may have noticed about various cultures, e.g. eye contact, facial expressions, gestures.

2) Appearance
How important is the way we look? How much should we smile? Is posture important?

3) Visual aids
What's their role? How many slides, transparencies etc. should be shown during a presentation? How much information should be in a slide or on a transparency? How should videos be used in presentations? How should we use hand-outs?

4) The spoken word
How loud should we speak? How can we change our voice to make the presentation more interesting? Should we use written English when speaking? Should we use jargon?

5) Purpose
Is it important to know exactly who we are speaking to? If so, how can we adapt our language to suit them? Why are we talking in the first place? Should we be giving the audience something to think about or simply give them information?

18  IT'S NOT WHAT YOU SAY...

In this interview you will hear a language trainer talking about presentation skills and presentations in general.

From pages 156-157, exercise 8, How effective do you think you are as a presenter?
Our suggestion:

		YES	NO
1	Before you actually planned a presentation would you decide on your basic objective(s)?	1	0
2	Would you analyze your audience beforehand?	1	0
3	Would your presentation include a preview and a review?	1	0
4	Would you try to make your introduction and ending as sensational as possible?	0	1
5	Would you make sure that your visual aids were clear, simple, easy to read and useful?	1	0
6	Would you try and be as enthusiastic as possible?	1	0
7	Would you rehearse thoroughly?	1	0
8	Would you rely a great deal on your notes?	0	1
9	Would your notes only contain key words or phrases?	1	0
10	Would you check out the seating, AV equipment, lighting, etc. beforehand?	1	0
11	Would you maintain eye-contact with your audience?	1	0
12	Would you use your normal voice?	0	1
13	Would you be aware of your own body language?	1	0
14	Would you read directly from notes?	0	1
15	Would you care about what clothes you had on?	1	0
16	Would you use humour?	1	0
17	Would you be worried if your audience looked bored?	1	0
18	Would you be constantly worried about making language mistakes?	0	1
19	Would you feel safer talking from behind something, e.g. a table?	0	1
20	Would you feel that what you were saying was far more important than how you said it?	1	0

9

No Problem!

The language of
dealing with difficulties

This unit deals with a wide range

of difficulties, tricky situations,

misunderstandings and complaints.

Obviously, such a selection

demands an equally wide range

of phrases and language.

1 SNAPSHOTS

Listen and repeat. You can also enact the situations.

– There's a slight change in the schedule.

– I'd like to make a change in my reservation.

– Could you help me, please?

– I don't like to complain but my room is very cold.

– Excuse me, there's
  some mistake. This
  is not my order.
– Oh, I'm very sorry.

– I'll see to it right
  away.
– I'd appreciate that.

– Thank you very much indeed for your help.

. . . .

WISE WORDS ON PROBLEMS

It isn't that they can't see the solution. It is that they can't see the problem.
G.K. Chesterton.

In my experience, the worst thing you can do to an important problem is discuss it.
Simon Gray

2 CROSS-CULTURAL CONSIDERATIONS

Unsuitable names are not the only reason why certain products fail to sell well in a new market. There can be many other cultural differences which can influence sales effectiveness. Read the following cases (they're all true) and try and work out why the problems arose.

❏ Instant coffee manufacturers have not done very well in France.

❏ Why doesn't an advert like this work in Arab countries ?

❏ Air New Zealand dropped their advertisements, featuring a kiwi, as well as the slogan "Kiwi Airways". How come?

❏ Many foreign companies have avoided packing goods in fours for the Japanese market. Why?

❏ Why is advertising solely in Arabic in Dubai practically useless?

❏ Refrigerators did not sell well in Japan until their noise level was decreased.

3 🎙️ THE PROBLEM WITH LANGUAGE

Read the text and do the exercises.

A Turkish company, intent on breaking into the UK biscuit market, were surprised when their product, **Bum Biscuits** never made it. A Taiwan company were equally put out when their refreshing toothpaste **Darkie** never caught on. A brand of tinned fish from South America, with the brand name of **Grated Fanny**, never
5 even made it to the shelves. Another South American company had very little success with their product which was sold under the **Bimbo Bread** label.

What's the problem?

Well, as you may have realized, it all hangs on the choice of name. None of the above-mentioned brand names did anything to encourage customer interest for
10 reasons of negative association.

So, here's a little resumé* of a few foreign products which definitely did not sell in Britain in the 60s, 70s and 80s because of their names.

Even North America has come up with a few mind-blowing* names for the Anglo-Saxon market. (Oscar Wilde did say that the two cultures were separated by
15 a common language.) A US company had no joy with their dog food called **Jerky Bits**. Neither did a Canadian company who tried innocently to sell their low-fat milk under the name of **Homo-milk.**

Europeans, too, have managed to choose a few unfortunate brand names over the years, among them being **Moron** wine from Italy, **I'm So Sorry Please**
20 **Forgive Me** chocolate from Switzerland and **Lucky Cow** cheese from Germany.

Two of the most unforgettable product names quite clearly come from France. Namely, **Pschitt**, (as the old joke goes: "The P is silent, as in Pschitt") – a fizzy orange drink, and **Cock**, a perfumed deodorant. Brave names indeed!

But only one courageous* brand name seems to have paid off* and that's the
25 perfume, **Poison**. Mind you, the manufacturers do not expect the customer to drink it.

Nordic countries have traditionally been fairly careful when selecting a name for English-speaking markets. Nevertheless, we were fairly amused to hear that the Finnish product, **Superpiss**, a cleaning fluid* for car windscreens, had been
30 ridiculed* on a British comedy programme. Another Nordic product with an even sillier-sounding name is **SorBits**, a brand of chewing gum. Can you imagine asking someone if they have any sore bits*?

But our all-time, number-one, silly name award goes to an Amsterdam firm who were amazed to hear that their highly popular sugar, sweetly named as **Donkee**
35 **Basterd Suker,** was not going down* at all well with the average English speaker.

Why's that? – we wonder.

Explanation of words:

resumé	summary	**fluid**	liquid
mind-blowing	amazing	**to ridicule**	to make fun of
courageous	brave	**sore bits**	painful parts
paid off	succeeded	**to go down with**	to be accepted by

Now you will see again the unfortunate brand names that appeared in the text. Try and work out what the problem is by selecting the appropriate explanations, i.e. write the appropriate letter before each product.

☐ 1 Bum (biscuits)

☐ 2 Darkie (toothpaste)

☐ 3 Grated Fanny (tinned fish)

☐ 4 Bimbo Bread

☐ 5 Jerky Bits (dog food)

☐ 6 Homo-milk (low-fat milk)

☐ 7 Moron (wine)

☐ 8 Lucky Cow (cheese)

☐ 9 I'm So Sorry, Please ... (chocolate)

☐ 10 Pschitt (drink)

☐ 11 Cock (deodorant)

☐ 12 Superpiss (cleaning fluid)

☐ 13 SorBits (chewing gum)

☐ 14 Donkee Basterd Suker (sugar)

EXPLANATIONS

A means a person's behind
B part of the word is heavy slang for urine
C sounds fine in Dutch
D little pieces that move in strange ways
E sounds as if it's absolutely impossible to drink
F sounds racist
G sounds like someone being rude
   to a fortunate woman
H contains a slang word for vagina
   (UK) or backside (US)
I slang for penis
J a drink for idiots?
K sounds painful
L takes too long to say
M sounds as if it's made especially
   for gay people
N sounds like basic food for fools

4 GET READY

Would you manage in the following situations? If you have difficulties turn to Unit 9 of your Phrase Book.

1   Mr Schmitt is ill and cannot attend the conference you are organizing.
     How would you inform people? (What words would you use?)

     _____

2   You'd like to change your flight ticket. You go to a travel agent's.
     How would you explain?

     _____

3   You want to make sure that your flight is confirmed. You phone up and ask.
     What would you say?

     _____

4   You're working in a hotel. A resident complains that his/her room is too cold.
     What do you say?

     _____

5   You go to an information desk in a large department store. You want to make
     a complaint. How do you begin?

     _____

6   Someone has just helped you a lot. How would you thank him/her?

     _____

7   You're in a restaurant. The waiter/waitress brings you the wrong food.
     What do you say?

     _____

8   You're a waiter/waitress. A customer has received the wrong order.
     How would you apologize?

     _____

9   You're at a conference. You need a photocopier immediately.
     What do you say to the conference officer?

     _____

10   The lecture in Room 9 scheduled for 10 o'clock is, in fact, at 9 o'clock in
     Room 10. How would you inform the participants?

     _____

PHRASE PRACTICE (4)

You will hear nine introductory phrases. Repeat each phrase and then continue in your own way.

1 **(at a conference)**
Before we begin I would like to announce that ... *the canteen is open from one to two every day.*

2 **(at a travel agent's)**
I'd like to make a change in my reservation ...

3 **(at the reception desk)**
I was told that you could possibly help me.

4 **(at the reception desk)**
I'd just like to make sure that ...

5 **(at the airport, airline officer)**
Just a moment, please. I'll have a look on the computer.

6 **(at the information desk)**
I'm very sorry but I can't help you. Please contact ...

7 **(in a department store)**
I don't like to complain but ...

8 **(in a restaurant)**
Excuse me, there's some mistake ...

9 **(anywhere you like)**
Sorry about ...

5 CHANGES IN TRAVEL ARRANGEMENTS

Fill in the spaces with words taken from the following list:

a change	a complaint	a book	change	look
reservation	book	cancel	idea	record
a mistake	work out	a look	mistake	complain

Customer: Good morning. I'd like to make _____ in my _____. I would like to _____ my flight to Oslo. Instead, I'd like to _____ a return flight to Amsterdam.

Travel agent: Just a moment, please. I'll have to have _____ on the computer. I'm sorry. We have no _____ of your reservation to Oslo. There seems to be _____ somewhere. Let's see what we can _____ , shall we?

6 CHANGES IN TRAVEL RESERVATIONS

Act out the following short conversation in pairs. Study sections 9.2 and 9.6 of your Phrase Book first.

Travel agent

Customer

Greet customer.

Offer assistance.

Explain that you will take care of it.

Greet him/her.

Explain that you want to make some kind of change in your travel arrangements.

Thank him/her.

7 CHANGES IN SCHEDULE

Work in pairs and act out the following situation. But first study sections 9.1 – 9.8 and 9.10 of your Phrase Book. The situation takes place at a conference.

Conference Officer

Lecturer

Inform the lecturer that the schedule is changed.

Explain first that there's a room change.

Confirm. Then explain that there's also a time change.

Apologize.

Confirm.

Apologize again.

Ask what the change is.

Make sure you get the information right.

Complain.

Accept apology. Then check the time change again.

Thank him/her.

8 INQUIRING AND DEALING WITH PROBLEMS

 Enact the following situation with your partner. Study sections 9.3 – 9.6 and 9.8 of your Phrase Book. The situation involves someone who wants to trace a package and an information officer who is trying to help.

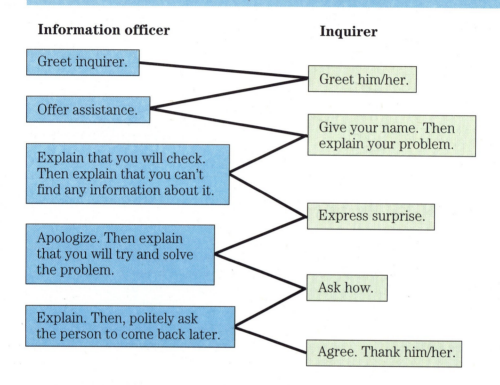

Information officer

- Greet inquirer.
- Offer assistance.
- Explain that you will check. Then explain that you can't find any information about it.
- Apologize. Then explain that you will try and solve the problem.
- Explain. Then, politely ask the person to come back later.

Inquirer

- Greet him/her.
- Give your name. Then explain your problem.
- Express surprise.
- Ask how.
- Agree. Thank him/her.

When clearing out her filing cabinets Samuel Goldwyn's secretary wanted to destroy some of the old files to make room for the more recent ones. "Go ahead," the movie mogul replied, "but make sure you take copies first."

9 CAN'T COMPLAIN

 How do you feel when you make or receive a complaint? Which of the following apply to you? Mark with a cross.

When making a complaint, I feel:

- ☐ aggressive
- ☐ nervous
- ☐ angry
- ☐ upset
- ☐ embarrassed
- ☐ hesitant
- ☐ apologetic

When receiving a complaint, I feel:

- ☐ frustrated
- ☐ guilty
- ☐ offended
- ☐ grateful
- ☐ sympathetic
- ☐ panicky
- ☐ helpless
- ☐ bored

When making a complaint, which of the following reactions irritate you the most? Mark your top three and discuss them with a partner.

- ☐ No apology.
- ☐ Not listening.
- ☐ Blaming you.
- ☐ Blaming the whole thing on someone else.
- ☐ Lack of interest.
- ☐ Being made to wait.
- ☐ Being treated like a trouble-maker.
- ☐ Something else, what?

10 PROBLEMS IN PUBLIC PLACES

Now you should be able to complain or deal with a complaint politely. Choose one of the following situations and act it out in front of the class.

● Situation one:
You're parking your car, unaware that there is a "No Parking" sign above you. A police officer arrives and asks you to wind down your window. What now?

● Situation two:
You're in a restaurant. You have a fly in your soup. What now?

● Situation three:
You're dining in a restaurant. You order turkey but the waiter/waitress brings you chicken instead. You point out the mistake but he/she insists that you are wrong. What now?

11 COMPLAINTS

Work in pairs and act out the following situation. Study sections 9.6 – 9.8 and 9.10 of your Phrase Book. The situation occurs at a hotel reception.

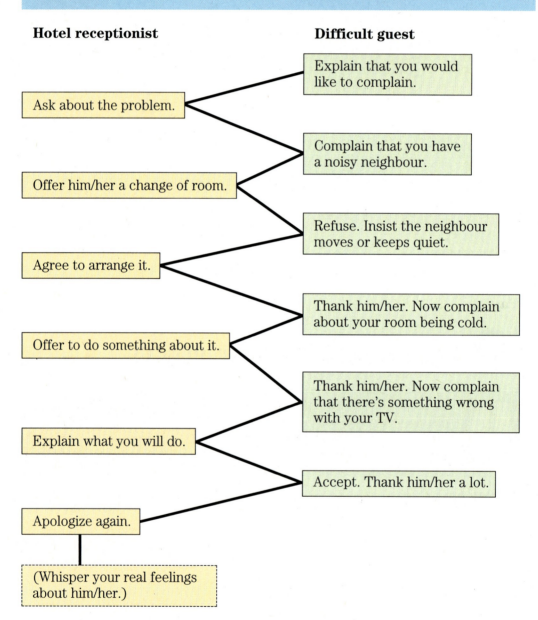

Hotel receptionist

Difficult guest

Explain that you would like to complain.

Ask about the problem.

Complain that you have a noisy neighbour.

Offer him/her a change of room.

Refuse. Insist the neighbour moves or keeps quiet.

Agree to arrange it.

Thank him/her. Now complain about your room being cold.

Offer to do something about it.

Thank him/her. Now complain that there's something wrong with your TV.

Explain what you will do.

Accept. Thank him/her a lot.

Apologize again.

(Whisper your real feelings about him/her.)

12 COMPLAINTS BY PHONE

 Complaints over the phone are commonplace in international communication, particularly in the business sector. Choose one or more of the following role plays. Remember to sit back to back to help create an atmosphere of being on the telephone.

Role play 1 – UPSIDE DOWN

Partner A: Client
A magazine has printed your expensive four-colour ad upside-down. Demand an explanation and compensation.

(**Partner B**: on page 186.)

Role play 2 – WRONG ADDRESSES

Partner A: Client
Your direct sales letters have been sent to the wrong addresses. Refuse to pay for distribution and insist that the letters are sent to the correct addresses immediately. The letters should have been sent to British wholesalers, not to end-users. Why did this happen?

(**Partner B**: on page 186.)

Role play 3 – INVISIBLE AD

Partner A: Client
You were amazed to notice that your expensive full-page four-colour ad never appeared on the back page of Sunday's newspaper. What on earth happened? Demand satisfaction. Refuse to listen to the ad agency's explanations. Threaten to cancel your expensive campaign with them.

(**Partner B**: on page 186.)

13 COMPLAINING IN A RESTAURANT

Enact the following situation, using the phrases from sections 9.6 – 9.10 of your Phrase Book.

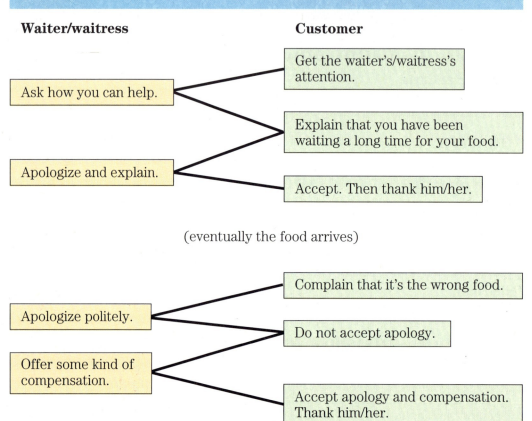

Waiter/waitress

Ask how you can help.

Apologize and explain.

Customer

Get the waiter's/waitress's attention.

Explain that you have been waiting a long time for your food.

Accept. Then thank him/her.

(eventually the food arrives)

Apologize politely.

Offer some kind of compensation.

Complain that it's the wrong food.

Do not accept apology.

Accept apology and compensation. Thank him/her.

14 THE COUNTERFEIT NOTE

 For groups of three people.

Situation:	A shoe shop. A customer walks in and decides on a pair of shoes. Choose a role and act out the following situation.
Roles:	1) shoe salesman/saleswoman 2) customer 3) florist

Customer: Yes, I'll take these. They're perfect.
Salesman: Right. That'll be 40 pounds, please.
Customer: There you go.
Salesman: Oh, a 50-pound note. I'm sorry. I don't have any change. I'll have to go next door to the florist's. I'll be right back.

Florist: Hello.
Salesman: Hi! Can you change this 50-pound note, please?
Florist: Sure. There you are – five ten-pound notes. OK?
Salesman: Thanks.

(He/She returns to the shoe shop.)

Salesman: There – ten pounds change and your shoes.
Customer: Thank you very much.

(Two hours later, the florist comes running into the shoe shop.)

Florist: Hey! That 50-pound note you gave me was a forgery.
Salesman: Counterfeit money?
Florist: Yes. I just went to the bank.
Salesman: Oh, no. Here – take this good 50-pound note. I'm really very sorry.

Now, together, try and work out how much money the poor shoe salesman lost in all the transactions. Compare your decision with other groups and explain how you came to it.

Our answer is in the key.

15 QUITE A PROBLEM

PLEASE NOTE
This activity can be performed by individuals working alone, but, ideally, it forms the basis of a group activity. For groups of four to twenty people. We recommend you choose a chairperson before you start.

You will find 20 clues on pages 184 and 185.

PROBLEM

Each of you has some information on certain Nordic marketing managers. Their names are Jan, Pia, Marja and Kennet. They come from four different countries: Denmark, Sweden, Norway and Finland. Each marketing manager has four product groups: menswear, womenswear, sportswear and underwear.

Your company (i.e. group) is interested in finding out how successful each marketing manager was last year, i.e. who was first in underwear, second in menswear, etc. You would also like to know their nationality, i.e. what country Pia is from, etc.

THE ONLY THING YOU KNOW FOR SURE IS THAT EACH ONE OF THEM CAME FIRST IN ONE PRODUCT GROUP. NOTHING ELSE IS CERTAIN.

The only way of solving the problem is by sharing all the information you have in your group. Everybody has different information. Some of it is useful, some of it is not.

RULES

You may not show your information to anyone else. You MAY, however, read it out. (In fact, you should read it out.)

The meeting should definitely be informal even if you do have a chairperson. Information-sharing is the most important thing here.

Step one:
Decide in your group who gets which simulation clue(s). There are 20 altogether. Photocopy pages 184 and 185, cut out the clues and distribute them.
If you have four people, obviously everyone gets five each. If you have five people, each gets four, etc. You should now also choose your chairperson.

Step two: START

If there are other groups in the class, you might like to compete with them and try to be the first group to get the RIGHT information.
If you are working in one group, time yourselves.
(If you are working alone, it usually takes about 15 minutes.)

Step three:

Use this table to help you gather the information.

Marketing Manager:		Position in product group:			
name	nationality	menswear	womenswear	sportswear	underwear
PIA					
KENNET					
JAN					
MARJA					

DRAW THIS TABLE ON A BOARD SO YOU CAN FILL IN THE MISSING INFORMATION TOGETHER.

Step four:

Read out your simulation clue(s) to the rest of your group. You should all make sure you understand the information correctly. DO NOT HIDE ANY INFORMATION. Discuss together what may or may not be important.

Step five:

Make sure that your table makes sense, i.e. check your information. Let the rest of the class know as soon as you are ready.
IMPORTANT: Even if you are not first, carry on; other groups may have made the wrong decisions.

AUTHORS' NOTE

We have decided not to put the correct solution in the book as some people just might be tempted to have a look. You should be able to check the information together to see if it fits the table.

COPY AND CUT

Simulation clue one:
Everyone was surprised that the Danish manager slipped to second place in menswear as it has always been a secure area for him/her.

Simulation clue two:
Jan was host for the meeting.

Simulation clue three:
Pia said that she would host the next meeting in Copenhagen.

Simulation clue four:
The Swedish manager was embarrassed by his/her coming last in menswear yet again.

Simulation clue five:
The Danish manager explained his/her coming first in womenswear (over the Norwegian) by winning a huge contract with airports.

Simulation clue six:
Pia was the big winner at cards.

Simulation clue seven:
Marja was the only manager who brought her spouse with her.

Simulation clue eight:
The Finnish manager had to leave the meeting early. Before leaving, he/she had a bet with the Swedish manager that he/she would not finish behind him/her in womenswear next year.

Simulation clue nine:
Kennet had a bad cold.

Simulation clue ten:
The Norwegian manager was urged to get out of the cellar in sportswear.

Simulation clue eleven:
Marja is very competitive.

Simulation clue twelve:
The Finnish manager had to pay off a hundred Finnmark bet to the Swedish manager, because the Swede was one place ahead in underwear.

Simulation clue thirteen:
The Finnish manager came first in menswear for the very first time.

Simulation clue fourteen:
Kennet was congratulated on climbing to first place in underwear.

Simulation clue fifteen:
The Danish manager was, as usual, third in sportswear.

Simulation clue sixteen:
Everyone was teasing the Finnish manager, who came last in underwear.

Simulation clue seventeen:
Jan was delighted because at last he had managed to overtake Marja in sportswear.

Simulation clue eighteen:
Pia finished once again ahead of Kennet in menswear.

Simulation clue nineteen:
Marja told Kennet that she had never ever visited Norway but would very much like to.

Simulation clue twenty:
Jan insisted that everybody spoke English because he couldn't stand the way the Danish manager spoke Swedish.

From page 179, exercise 12, Complaints by phone.

1B – UPSIDE DOWN

Partner B: Magazine
You have accidentally printed a four-colour ad upside-down in your magazine. You get a call from the ad company demanding an explanation and compensation. Apologize but explain that compensation is impossible because "accidents do happen".

....

2B – WRONG ADDRESSES

Partner B: Direct mail company
Oops! You have sent some direct mailings to the wrong addresses. You had understood that you should send the letters to private homes in Britain, not to British wholesalers. Refuse to pay the full costs but be prepared to pay half of the costs.

....

3B – INVISIBLE AD

Partner B: Ad agency
A four-colour, full-page ad was not printed in last Sunday's newspaper. Some kind of mix-up between the newspaper and yourselves. However, it was not really your fault. Try to explain to the client and keep your campaign with them. You'd better come up with something good, and quick.

U N I T

10

Your Attention, Please!

The language of conferences

A working knowledge of English
is considered essential for people
representing their companies,
universities or countries at
international conferences. As with
formal meetings, the language of
conferences involves a great deal of
formal procedure and stylized
language.

1  SNAPSHOTS

Listen and repeat. You can also enact the situations.

– It's my honour as the chairperson to welcome you all to this conference.

– It's my great pleasure to introduce our first speaker this afternoon.

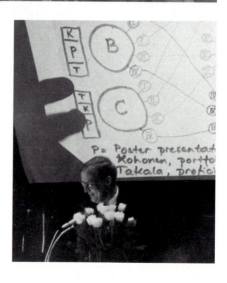

– I'd like to thank the speaker for her very interesting talk.

– The task of our group was to decide on the forms of presentation.

– We'd like to
underline the
following points.

– Do you have any information on
sightseeing tours?

– Who do I see to
arrange a VCR for
my talk?

WISE WORDS ON CONFERENCES

A conference should consist of three people, two of whom should be absent.

A diplomat is someone who can tell you to go to hell in such a way that you look
forward to the trip.

2 CROSS-CULTURAL CONSIDERATIONS

Knowing something beforehand about the culture you're going to visit can sometimes prevent embarrassing moments. The art of giving gifts can also be a pretty difficult task sometimes. In each of the following there is ONE unsuitable gift or custom. Which one and why?

1 **For a French female client/colleague**
   a) perfume
   b) flowers
   c) chocolate
   d) a book

2 **For a German client/colleague**
   a) white roses
   b) yellow tulips
   c) red roses
   d) blue tulips

3 **For a Brazilian client/colleague**
   a) a cup
   b) a knife
   c) a plate
   d) alcohol

4 **For a client/colleague in the Middle East**
   a) give a gift in public
   b) give a gift in private
   c) give a gift every time you meet
   d) no gift whatsoever

5 **For an Argentinian**
   a) a handkerchief
   b) a scarf
   c) a hat
   d) a flag

6 **For a Chinese**
   a) a spoon
   b) a clock
   c) a piece of jewelry
   d) a bag

7 **For a Saudi**
   a) food
   b) clothes
   c) books
   d) toys

8 **For a South Korean**
   a) give a gift in public
   b) give a gift in private
   c) give a gift every time you meet
   d) no gift whatsoever

3 CONFER

Read the text and do the exercises.

LANGUAGE LEARNING FOR EUROPEAN CITIZENSHIP

IGEP

KONGRESSHUSET AB CONGRESS HOUSE

Why hold conferences? Many an important matter can be dealt with by an individual without consulting anyone else. Many more are solved by letter, memo, fax or phone call or even by a straightforward conversation between two people.

Nevertheless, the number of conferences being held in the world suggests that
5 somehow they function as one of the best communication devices* around. If a conference is run smoothly and people come away from it feeling happy and informed it means that someone, somewhere, has put a great deal into its preparation.

How successful a delegate is depends to a large extent on his or her command
10 of language and knowledge of meeting technique and terminology. At large conferences, committee chairmen and vice chairmen are appointed in advance so they can get acquainted with the agenda, related documentation and the list of participants.

Delegates often have to be prepared to serve on committees and in working
15 parties or to serve in advisory capacities. And committees are often set up while a conference is in session.

The principal work at a conference is performed by the committee chairman and secretariat*, with the latter being responsible for the smooth running of the programme. The secretary of the meeting has a variety of duties, including keeping
20 the minutes throughout the meeting.

Although simultaneous interpretation is sometimes provided, the chairman is strongly advised to have a working knowledge of the official language of the conference. And English would definitely seem to be the most favoured conference language in Europe. It is also the chairman's responsibility to open the proceed-
25 ings*. He or she may call on a certain participant who has been asked to make a speech or he may declare the discussion open. He or she usually leads the discussion and gives the floor to delegates who have indicated a desire to express their views. Theoretically at least, it's his or her job to keep the meeting in order.

If a question cannot be resolved, the chairman may propose the formation of a special committee and take the nominations for committee membership. If voting is necessary, the chairman usually decides on how it should be carried out. It may be done by secret ballot or the Chair may ask for a show of hands. Voting is seldom
30 carried out at committee sessions. It is usually only considered necessary for electing officers or officials.

Working together in groups is a common feature of many an international conference. And, as any experienced conference participant will know, knowing how to write a simple but comprehensive* report is a much-valued skill.
35 A report invariably* contains results of committee work, a summary of discussions and recommendations, as well as conclusions or statements.
A committee can issue an interim report while its work is still underway.

Another vital* aspect of international conferences is social interaction* or, for want of a better term, having a good time. And it's here that communication and
40 inter-cultural skills come into effect*. Very often the most memorable moments come from those unofficial interludes*.

Many international conferences culminate* in a banquet. And apart from offering you the ideal opportunity of tasting the local delicacies*, it also demands a certain degree of familiarity with table manners or standard, international
45 etiquette.
We'll drink to that.

Explanation of words:

devices	means
secretariat	the people (body) that take care of the running of an international organization
proceedings	official activities
comprehensive	thorough
invariably	more often than not
vital	extremely important
social interaction	communicating socially
to come into effect	to come into use
an interlude	a break or a period of time
to culminate	to reach the highest point
delicacies	something rather special to eat

In case you found this text rather difficult to read, we would like to point out that we deliberately included as much conference terminology as possible. We could have explained a great deal more words for you but we thought, this time, you might like to work out the rest of the difficult terms by yourself. So, here's a chance for you to test your understanding.

A **Match the words from the text with the correct definitions, i.e. write in the appropriate number.**

WORDS		DEFINITION
a) delegate	_____	1 going on
b) vice-chairman	_____	2 a suggestion
c) advisory capacity	_____	3 to show you want to
d) documentation	_____	4 beforehand
e) underway	_____	5 official papers
f) in advance	_____	6 second only to the chairman
g) a working knowledge	_____	7 temporary
h) to indicate a desire	_____	8 to find a solution
i) to resolve	_____	9 a good enough understanding and use of something
j) a recommendation	_____	10 an official representative
k) interim	_____	11 a situation where speeches are put into your own language as they happen
l) simultaneous interpretation	_____	12 a position which enables others to consult you

B **Select the correct alternative from the following and underline it.**

1 The conference was **given / done / held / run** in Jamaica.
2 The chairman was **made / decided / voted / appointed** in advance.
3 It's important for people to **get acquainted with / be responsible for / call on / indicate a desire to** the agenda.
4 It's the chairman's responsibility to **spoil / control / dominate / lead** the discussion.
5 Committees are **formed / made / issued / nominated** for different reasons.
6 Delegates are often **set up / called on / performed on / demanded on** to make a speech.
7 As soon as a conference is officially opened it's **in service / set up / given the floor / in session.**
8 If no voting takes place publicly during a conference there may be **working knowledge / an advisory capacity / simultaneous interpretation / a secret ballot.**
9 A good **resolve / command / desire / summary** of language is often necessary at a conference.
10 Very often delegates have to serve **on / in / at / for** a committee.

4 GET READY

Would you manage in the following situations? If you have difficulties turn to Unit 10 of your Phrase Book.

1   You're at a travel agent's. You want to make a flight reservation. What do you say?

   _____

2   You're at a conference. You want to register. What do you say?

   _____

3   You have to introduce a guest speaker. How would you begin?

   _____

4   You're a conference officer. You see someone who seems to need help. What do you say?

   _____

5   You're at a conference. You need some help. You go to the information desk. What do you say?

   _____

6   You wish to ask a lecturer a question at the end of a presentation. How do you begin?

   _____

7   You're a presenter. Someone in the audience has asked a good question. How might you begin your answer?

   _____

8   You have to thank a guest speaker for his/her talk. How do you begin?

   _____

PHRASE PRACTICE (4)

Open your Phrase Book (10.1 – 10.13). Respond to the following ten phrases. Later, you will hear the same phrases again with suitable responses.

5 MAKING TRAVEL ARRANGEMENTS

This is designed for people who have to make their own travel arrangements. Work in pairs and act out the following situation. Study section 10.1 of your Phrase Book. You might also find sections 2.14 – 2.15 of some assistance. Before you start, the traveller should decide where he/she would like to go and his/her travel dates. The travel agent should take notes during the conversation.

Traveller **Travel agent**

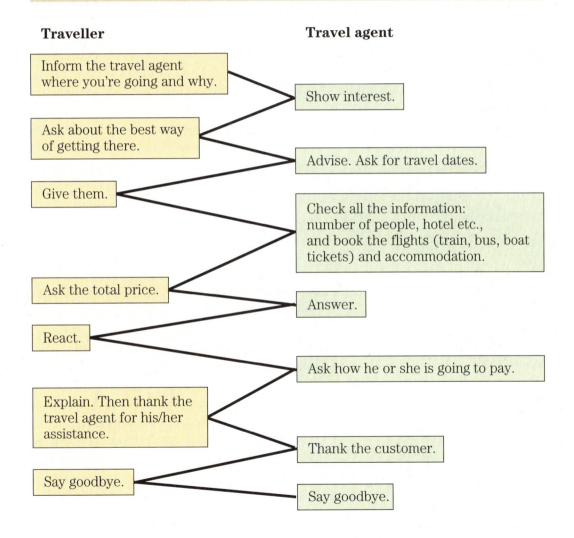

Traveller	Travel agent
Inform the travel agent where you're going and why.	Show interest.
Ask about the best way of getting there.	Advise. Ask for travel dates.
Give them.	Check all the information: number of people, hotel etc., and book the flights (train, bus, boat tickets) and accommodation.
Ask the total price.	Answer.
React.	Ask how he or she is going to pay.
Explain. Then thank the travel agent for his/her assistance.	Thank the customer.
Say goodbye.	Say goodbye.

Jet lag

Many conference participants have to adjust to time differences, particularly if they are attending a conference on another continent. Jet lag is caused by a disturbance of biological cycles. Major influences on body clocks include light and dark, food, stimulants and social interaction.

How to reduce the effects of jet lag:

1 Avoid food and drink containing caffeine such as coffee, coke, chocolate, etc. for the first few days.

2 Limit alcohol consumption until you have rested from travelling. Drink lots of water instead.

3 Have high protein breakfasts and high carbohydrate evening meals. Proteins give you four to five hours of energy. Carbohydrates give you only about an hour's worth of energy, after which you start feeling tired.

4 Do not take any naps during the day. This will help your body clock adjust to the new cycle.

5 Get to bed relatively early.

INFO

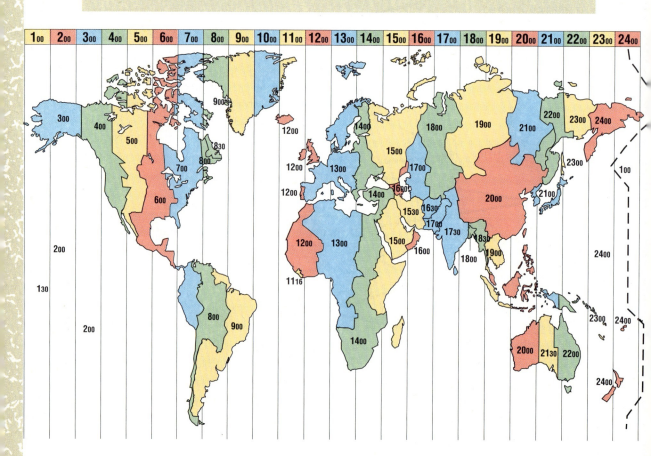

6 CALL FOR PAPERS

 Conferences are usually advertised long before they actually take place and invariably include a call for papers. Look at the one below. Choose one of the three topics (or make up your own) and imagine you would like to present a short paper at a conference. In order to do that you must first send off a proposal. Write about five lines, outlining what you are going to talk about. Keep it short and simple.

CALL FOR PAPERS

Topic one: **A unified Europe – dream or nightmare?**
Topic two: **How open is the new Europe to the rest of the world?**
Topic three: **What exactly is a European?**
Topic four: **A topic of your choice**

Name of proposer: _____

Title: _____

Organization: _____

Address: _____

Phone: _____   Fax: _____

Title of presentation: _____

_____

Outline: _____

_____

_____

_____

_____

_____

_____

---

7 CONFERENCE REGISTRATION

Work in pairs and act out the following conversation. Study sections 10.2 and 10.3 of your Phrase Book.

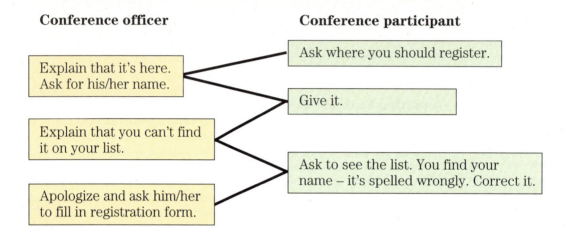

Conference officer

Explain that it's here. Ask for his/her name.

Explain that you can't find it on your list.

Apologize and ask him/her to fill in registration form.

Conference participant

Ask where you should register.

Give it.

Ask to see the list. You find your name – it's spelled wrongly. Correct it.

8 OPENING A CONFERENCE

Act out the following short situation in front of the class. Make up an interesting name for the conference. Study sections 10.4 and 10.5 of your Phrase Book.

Chairperson

Open the conference and introduce the first speaker.

Guest speaker

Thank the chairman and start your presentation.

When introducing a guest speaker, give some background about the person's career and qualifications. Make sure you pronounce the speaker's name correctly. Don't go on too long. Don't bring yourself into the introduction. You usually finish your introduction by saying the person's name.

9 A HELPING HAND

Act out the following mini role play with your partner. Before you start, study sections 10.6 - 10.8 of your Phrase Book.

Person A: conference officer
Offer to help the person. Do the best you can.

Person B: a conference participant
You want
a) complete tourist information, together with a free map,
b) a complete list of all accommodation in the area, together with prices (you don't like your present accommodation),
c) complete timetables of buses and trains leaving the location,
d) a list of the best restaurants to go to,
e) something very difficult (make it up yourself).

Act it out in front of the class, if you wish.

Language hints

You will find out how to introduce the speaker in section 10.5 and how to thank the speaker in section 10.13 of your Phrase Book. But how do you thank someone for introducing you?

Here are a few examples:
– Thank you very much, (name of person).
– Thank you very much for those kind words of introduction.
– Quite an introduction (informal – you can't believe you're that good).

But what do you say after that? Perhaps the following will be of help:
– Let me begin / Allow me to begin by saying / explaining / pointing out, etc.
– I'd like to express my appreciation for having this opportunity of addressing you all here today.
– First of all, I'd just like to say how happy I am to be here today.
– I haven't done this kind of thing before (in English), so I hope you will bear with me.

Now you're ready to start your lecture, talk or whatever.

10 UFOs

Work with the entire class. Before you start, study the phrases in sections 10.11 – 10.13 of your Phrase Book. The presenter has been talking about UFOs. We suggest you choose a brave presenter, with some ideas about flying saucers.

Presenter: **Members of the audience**

(Person 1)
Thank the speaker.
Ask for questions from the audience.

(Person 2)
Refer to something he/she said about communicating with people from another planet.

Respond.

(Person 3)
Ask politely if the speaker has ever seen a UFO in real life.

Respond.

(Person 4)
Ask politely if the speaker is from another planet.

Respond.

(Person 5)
Thank the speaker again.

11 ENGLISH AT CONFERENCES

 How do you feel about international groups using English as a lingua franca at conferences? Do you feel that native speakers have an unfair advantage over non-native speakers of English?

Consider the following:

1. More often than not, you know more about the native English speaker's culture than he or she does about yours.

2. You have an advantage because you are using a foreign language. People show more empathy towards you, respect even.

3. Differences in non-verbal communication (body language, etc.) often lead to misunderstandings or weak communication.

4. You may have great problems in understanding what's being said some of the time.

5. You may not always be able to say what you really mean.

6. Native English speakers may underestimate you because of your language limitations.

7. You may be more used to British English than American English (or vice versa) and uncomfortable hearing the latter (or the former).

SIETAR International's XVIII Annual Congress

Strategies for Cross-Cultural Communications in the New Information Age: Continuity, Change and Innovation

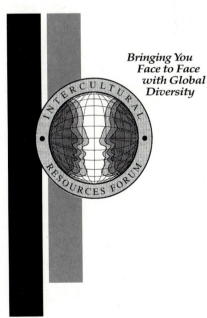

Bringing You Face to Face with Global Diversity

12 THE LANGUAGE OF REPORTING

On this page you will see an example of a group report, taken from a conference on an environmental matter. Read it through, paying special attention to the words in bold.

Group E – report
The objective of group E was to think of as many ways as possible of increasing public awareness of the problem.

the aim

From the outset our group wanted to define the alternatives open to us. These were:
– direct mail
– newspaper ads
– newspaper articles.

the beginning

The discussion then focused on money.
Although budgets varied in different countries, we agreed on a standard investment. **This led to** the problem of funding. **It was agreed that** all members should submit their final budgets by the end of this month.

points discussed

A number of points on which there was general agreement emerged from our discussion:
– sharing information
– sharing materials
– measuring the effect and effectiveness of campaigns
– a follow-up campaign.

points of agreement

We also stressed the necessity of establishing a long-term network for future awareness projects.

other important points

The group's conclusions led us to make the following proposals. Namely that
– a permanent committee **be established**
– an official 'head of awareness' **be appointed** so as to ensure communication and cooperation
– a central fund **be set up** to safeguard financial viability.

proposals

Lastly, the discussion turned to whether or not there were any more cost-effective means of increasing awareness. **All in all,** it was an extremely fruitful discussion.

end of main body of report

As far as group E is concerned, we're ready to put forward a plan of action which centres on newspaper ads (enclosure 1) and newspaper articles (enclosure 2).

further proposals

GROUP WORK AT CONFERENCES

 Working in groups is a common feature of conference participation. Before you start this activity please study sections 10.9 and 10.10 of your Phrase Book. We also presume that you have already studied "The language of reporting" on the opposite page.

Step one:
Organize yourselves into groups. We suggest between three to five people per group depending on the size of the class. (An ideal situation would be three groups of three or four groups of four, etc.)

Step two:
Each group should choose its own issue to discuss from the ones provided. Please feel free to discuss your own issues if you wish. Suggested social issues:

- **Smoking at work**
- **Prohibiting tobacco advertising**
  (TV, radio, magazines, motor sports etc.)
- **Military service**
- **Abortion**

- **The death penalty**
- **The cost of alcohol**
- **Daycare centres for very young children**
- **Looking after elderly people**
- **Unemployment**

Step three:
Introduce yourselves and select a chairman and a secretary.

Step four:
In fact, you will all be secretaries since you should take short notes on what you discuss, decide and recommend. Before you start the discussion make sure you are familiar with the language used in "The language of reporting". This will help you make your own report.

Step five:
Now you are ready to begin your discussion. Try and include the following elements: 1) the aim, 2) the beginning, 3) points discussed, 4) points of agreement, 5) other important points, 6) proposals, 7) end of main body of report, 8) further proposals. IMPORTANT: Everyone should take very brief notes during the discussion in preparation for step six. Try and decide on how long the discussions should last. We suggest about 10 – 15 minutes.

Step six:
You have completed your discussion. Now, FORM NEW GROUPS so that each person from your group is now sitting in another group. It's important that nobody from your original group is with you. This may be a little tricky but your teacher should be able to help you.

Step seven:
You are now sitting in new groups. Now check through your own notes as well as the language in bold in the example "The language of reporting".

Step eight:
Take turns in presenting your group report to the other members of your new group. The others can ask questions and try and help you remember.

13 A WINNING VENUE

 For the whole class.

The choice of venue for a conference depends on many considerations:

– prices	– experience, interpreters etc.
– social conditions	– exoticism
– political climate	– transport, within and to the country/centre
– facilities	– climate, cultural events
– night life	– accommodation
– security	– the venue and even the menu

Imagine that you have to compete to get your country/city accepted as the location for an international conference. The simulation comprises two sides
   a) the promoters
   b) the conference committee.

Step one: GET READY

Decide on the city/country being promoted. Now divide the class into two: 'promoters' and the 'conference committee'.

PROMOTERS:

It's your job to sell your city/country as the venue for next year's conference. Divide yourselves into pairs, threes or small groups.

1   Make a list of all the advantages of holding a conference in your city/country, e.g. security – extremely good. Tight controls. Very little crime. No terrorist organizations operating inside the community, etc.
2   Make a list of the disadvantages, e.g security weak, street crimes commonplace. Terrorist organizations on every street corner, etc.

POINTS TO LOOK OUT FOR:
Remember, the committee members are from other cultures, not yours.
Be careful and take nothing for granted.

CONFERENCE COMMITTEE:

Divide yourselves into pairs, threes or small groups. Make a list, based on the considerations in the box on the opposite page. Decide on the main points you're looking out for.

POINTS TO LOOK OUT FOR:
Observe the way the promoters behave. Pay special attention to their command of English, their manners, body language, etc. What kind of people are they? Remember you are the customer, not them. Would they be good hosts – friendly? How effective are they at selling their country/city?
Even though you may actually know a lot about this city/country, pretend that you DO NOT. In other words, do not let them take things for granted. YOU ARE, AFTER ALL, FROM ANOTHER CULTURE, NOT THEIRS.

Step two: THE PROMOTION ITSELF

The promotion takes place at a conference in session. What kind of promotion would you expect? Formal, informal?
Should it be a presentation or a kind of discussion? Discuss this and decide among yourselves.

Our recommendations:
Alternative one:
A presentation. In groups of four: two promoters, two committee members. (Can be more or less, of course.)
Alternative two:
A discussion. In groups of four: two promoters, two committee members. (Can be more or less.)
Alternative three*:
A combination of alternatives one and two: i.e., a short presentation, followed by a discussion.
* ALTERNATIVE THREE WOULD GIVE YOU AN OPPORTUNITY TO PRACTISE MOST OF THE PHRASES AND LANGUAGE FROM UNITS 4, 5, 7, 8 AND 10.

Step three: FOLLOW-UP

The committee should now decide on whether or not the promotion succeeded. Each group should explain their experiences and the result of the negotiation to the rest of the class.

14 PREPARATION, PARTICIPATION AND COMMUNICATION

Attending conferences can be extremely demanding and rewarding. Listen to what the following people have to say about effective participation at conferences.

SIETAR INTERNATIONAL DAILY BULLETIN
MONDAY, MAY 11, 1992

PROGRAM CHANGES

Cancelled Workshops:
Monday   CS 3   (Ancel);
          CS 18   (Applewhite)

Program Correction:
CS 1 (Carter) HAS NOT BEEN CANCELLED.
CS 108 (Kramer) "Utilizing the Innovation Diffusion Game in Intercultural Training" has been moved to Tuesday Simulation Night at 8:00 pm.

Room Changes:
CS 76 has been moved to Room 162.

Change in Session Title:
CS 63 (Shaak) New Title "Training the Entire Family for Intercultural Assignments"

Title Correction:
Judith Katz Ed. D. "Cultural Diversity: More than Valuing Differences" (Plenary Speaker)

Program Additions
"Network Meeting for Black Delegates" Monday May 11th in Port Antonio, 11:30-2:30 pm. Contact Mutale Chandra Room 579

"Re-Evaluation Counseling Gather-In" lead by Barbara J. Love, Monday May 11th in the Negril Room 4-5:00 pm.
Organizer: L.G. Shanklin-Flowers Room 362

Dialog/Focus Group addressing the Conflicts in Los Angeles,
Monday at   00 pm in the Port Antonio Room.
              What do We Do?"

11

Thanks for the Information

The language of fairs

This unit concentrates on basic
phrases and situations that might
well occur in any kind of fair. It also
brings you into contact with some
practical considerations associated
with trade fairs.

1 SNAPSHOTS

– Could you give me some idea about the size of your company?

– Excuse me, what company did you say you worked for?

– Do you have any brochures I could have?

– Is this model available in different sizes?

– If you'd just give me your name and address, I'll make sure you get all the information as soon as possible.

– Thanks a lot for the information.
– Nice talking to you. I look forward to hearing from you soon.

WISE WORDS ON FAIRS

If you explain so clearly that nobody can misunderstand, somebody will.

2 CROSS-CULTURAL CONSIDERATIONS

Little points to keep in mind

Austrians	Do not make the mistake of calling Austrians Germans.
Belgians	There's a high regard for privacy.
The British	Remember that the Scottish are Scottish and the Welsh are Welsh. Only the English are English.
Danes	Taxi drivers are not usually tipped.
The Dutch	You can be fairly direct with them in business matters.
Finns	Small talk not too popular.
The French	The French really do regard their culture as second to none.
Germans	They have a positive attitude towards anyone trying to speak German.
Icelanders	Remember that Icelandic is Europe's oldest living language.
The Irish	It's not a good idea to be too pro-British.
Italians	There are big differences between the north and the south.
Norwegians	Like to be referred to as Norwegians, not Scandinavians.
Poles	Remember, Catholicism is still a vital part of their society.
The Portuguese	They usually have a siesta between noon and 3.00 p.m.
Spaniards	A siesta is usually held between 1.30 and 4.00 p.m.
Swedes	It's worthwhile proving that you know the differences between Swedes, Norwegians, Danes and Finns.
The Swiss	Four languages: Swiss-German, Swiss-French, Swiss-Italian and Swiss-Romansch.
Turks	Sometimes their hospitality can be overwhelming.

3 LEAVE YOUR CLOTHES HERE!

Read the text and do the exercises.

One of the unavoidable aspects of travelling to fairs is staying in a hotel. And very often it's in the hotel that you have to enter into some detailed conversation in a foreign language. But it's not only the spoken language that has to be considered; there's usually plenty of written information that has to be interpreted. And English
5 would seem to be just about the most preferred foreign language used in notices, signs or safety warnings in hotels.

I have witnessed many a humorous notice in European hotels.

A hotel notice in Finland, displayed in four languages, kindly requested in English that WAITERS be COLLECTED FROM HERE. They had in fact meant
10 TRAYS and not WAITERS. But people queued anyway, so no problems arose.

Another notice in another Finnish hotel read as follows: TO STOP THE DRIP, TURN COCK* TO RIGHT. I toyed with the idea but thought better of it.

Hotels provide an ideal setting for 'Global English'. Most of my travels have comprised European and North American destinations and my eyes have been
15 opened on more than one occasion by incredible 'Inklish'. The following list, however, represents an unashamed collection of 'Hotel English from around the world' compiled from Richard Lederer's book *Anguished English*.

If you can't see the problem, please don't worry; it only proves that Global English really does work. The main problem areas are printed for you in capital
20 letters.

Please to bathe INSIDE the tub.

1 Japanese hotel

The lift is being fixed for the next day. During that time we regret that you will be UNBEARABLE.

2 Romanian hotel

Do not enter the lift BACKWARDS, and only when LIT UP.

3 German hotel

Visitors are EXPECTED to complain at the office between the hours of 9 and 10 A.M. daily.

4 Greek hotel

The FLATTENING of underwear WITH PLEASURE is the job of the chambermaid.

5 Yugoslavian hotel

You are welcome to visit the CEMETERY*
where famous Russian and Soviet composers,
artists and writers ARE BURIED DAILY
except Thursdays.

6 Russian hotel

Our wines leave you nothing to HOPE FOR.

7 Swiss hotel

A new swimming pool is rapidly
taking shape since the contractors have
THROWN IN the bulk of their workers.

8 East African hotel

Because of the IMPROPRIETY*
of entertaining guests in the bedroom,
it is suggested that the
LOBBY BE USED FOR THIS PURPOSE.

9 Swiss hotel

Ladies,
LEAVE YOUR CLOTHES HERE
and spend the afternoon having
A GOOD TIME.

10 Italian hotel laundry
(where else?)

Take one of our
horse-driven city tours
– we guarantee no
MISCARRIAGES.

12 Czech hotel

Would you
like to ride on
YOUR OWN
ASS?

11 Thai hotel

Special today
- NO icecream.

13 Swiss hotel

Ladies are requested not to
HAVE CHILDREN in the bar.

14 Norwegian hotel

The manager has personally
PASSED all the water served here.

15 Brazilian hotel

You are invited to
TAKE ADVANTAGE OF
the chambermaid.

16 Japanese hotel

As you can see, Global English is as entertaining as it is varied. Of course,
the most important thing is that we get the message across. That really is the
main point, isn't it?

Well, I used to think so until I visited Morocco a few years ago. There, I
25 happened upon a sign outside a carpet shop which read as follows: ENGLISH
SPEECHING, ALSO GERMANS. On entering the shop I decided to use French.

P.W.

Explanation of words:

cock	a kind of tap; can also mean penis
cemetery	graveyard
impropriety	bad behaviour

Match the drawings with the examples given in the text.

4 GET READY

. . . .

 Would you manage in the following situations? If you have difficulties turn to Unit 11 of your Phrase Book.

How would you begin

1   if you wanted to confirm something?

    _____

2   if you wanted some information and you wanted to sound polite?

    _____

3   if you wanted to explain that you were absolutely certain about something?

    _____

4   if someone asked you a tricky question?

    _____

How would you respond

5   if someone said something you didn't understand?

    _____

6   if someone asked you: "Does this thing really work?" (You are sure it works well.)

    _____

7   if someone asked you: "Is it possible to use this thing underwater?"
     How would you answer in the following situations?
     a) You are pretty sure it would.

    _____

    b) You are pretty sure it wouldn't.

    _____

    c) You are unsure but maybe it would.

    _____

    d) You are unsure but you don't think so.

    _____

8   if someone asked you: "What is this made of?"

_____

9   if someone asked you: "Excuse me, may I touch this?" What would you say in
     the following situations?
     a) It's allowed.

_____

     b) It's not allowed.

_____

10   You are talking to someone at your stand at a fair. You are not sure who this
     person is. How do you find out his/her identity?

_____

 PHRASE PRACTICE (4)

....

> **You are a representative of a mobile telephone company. You are
> discussing the model given below. You will be asked twelve questions.
> Respond, using some of the phrases given in 11.7 – 11.17.**

NOKIA MOBILE PHONES TODAY

* **Europe's largest and the world's
  second-largest cellular mobile
  telephone manufacturer.**
* **Sales 3.4 billion FIM/
  750 million USD.**
* **Personnel 3 200.**
* **Worldwide production, logistics
  and marketing network.**
* **Sales in 70 countries, global
  R & D approach.**

DIMEN-SIONS	Standard battery	Extended battery
Height	172 mm	172 mm
Width	62 mm	62 mm
Depth	37 mm	46 mm
Volume	339 cc	401 cc
Weight	475 g	560 g

5 A FAIR LETTER?

Fill in the following sentences with appropriate words from the list below:

Dear Per,

Here is the information I promised you about the .... in Holland. As you

can see, the .... offers a variety of ....

.... and even an ....

.... Altogether, there is nearly 300,000 square metres of ....

.... Our stand is located in ....5.

We're particularly pleased with it because it has two ....

.... as well as a .... for negotiations.

In case you're thinking of visiting us I'm enclosing an ....

.... so you won't have to pay to get in. The ....

for the .... is 25 Guilders.

Look forward to seeing you in Amsterdam.
Yours sincerely,   *Peter Shuster*

exhibition area	**exhibition halls**	**fair**
admission fee	**general public**	**hall**
conference room	**invitation card**	**open-air**
exhibition storeys	**exhibition space**	**display area**

6 FAIRS, PLEASE

 There are many reasons why fairs can prove useful to companies or organizations. Work in groups and decide how useful a fair is as regards the following:

	Very useful	Fairly useful	Useless
1 Getting orders			
2 Meeting key people			
3 Keeping on good terms with existing clients/partners			
4 Getting new clients/partners			
5 Supporting local agents			
6 Introducing new products			
7 Getting new ideas			
8 Spying on competitors			
9 Selling products there and then			
10 Having a kind of holiday			

When a typist altered something in a letter that had been dictated, the boss took it as a serious offence. "I don't pay you to correct my work. Just type it exactly as I say it. Don't add anything and don't take anything out."
The next letter that was put in front of the boss to sign went something like this:
"Right then, er, Dear Mr Smythe, spell that with a 'y'– that's him trying to be posh. In response to your letter of, of well, you look up the date. We can give you a price of ... Paul, what kind of price can we give this Smythe guy? OK ... If he accepts it we'd better make sure we get payment up front because I really don't trust him. Where's my coffee? Yours etc."

7 UNDERSTANDING STANDS

Having an attractive stand may be important but it's clearly not enough if you really want to attract new clients. Obviously a great deal depends on the way your staff behave. But what other considerations are there? How would you react to the following situations and how appealing are they? Discuss this with your partner.

Appeal value

You approach a stand where you see three or four representatives smiling at everyone who is passing, trying desperately to get their attention. Suddenly one of them steps out in front of you and says: *Can I have your attention, please, just for one minute?*

□

You approach a stand where two or three formal-looking representatives are standing rather stiffly with their hands in front of them and serious looks on their faces. You are not sure what their products are.

□

You approach a stand represented by three or four very good-looking people of the opposite sex, promoting products you are not particularly interested in.

□

You approach a stand which advertises a free salad and a drink if you fill in a questionnaire. You are feeling rather hungry.

□

You approach a stand, manned, you presume, by people dressed up as robots. However, you cannot be 100% sure that they are not real robots. You are definitely not interested in their products.

□

You approach an empty stand where only a rather sad-looking representative is sitting alone reading one of his own brochures. However, you have heard that the company might have some interesting products.

□

Now number them 1 – 6 in terms of appeal. Then compare your rankings with those of others.

Now go on and list four things that you believe attract people to a stand and four things that do not. Then compare your views with the rest of the class.

8 LOOKING AT PRODUCTS

**Work in pairs. Act out the following conversation.
Study sections 11.13 – 11.15 of your Phrase Book.**

Visitor

Representative

Ask for permission to touch, pick up or try out a product.

Ask for permission to take it home with you.

Offer assistance.

Grant him/her permission.

Refuse him/her permission.

9 ASKING ABOUT A COMPANY

**Work in pairs and act out the following conversation.
Before you start decide on the product range, e.g. umbrellas,
soft drinks, ski equipment, etc. Study sections 11.2 – 11. 5 of
your Phrase Book.**

Visitor

Representative

Introduce yourself.

Ask about the size of the company.

Ask about what countries they operate in.

Ask about their product range.

Ask something specific about one of their products.

Thank him/her.

Introduce yourself and offer assistance.

Explain.

Explain.

Explain.

Explain.

Accept his/her thanks.

10 WHAT IS IT?

 Asking about and describing products is obviously very common at fairs. Study the following with your partner and then follow the instructions below.

a) DIMENSIONS

Question	Answer		
How long ...?	It's ... long.	It's ... in length.	The length is ...
How wide ...?	It's ... wide.	It's ... in width.	The width is ...
How high ...?	It's ... high.	It's ... in height.	The height is ...
How big is it?			

b) WEIGHT

Question	Answer
How heavy is it?	It weighs about ...
How much does it weigh?	

c) MATERIAL

Question	Answer
What's it made of?	It's made of plastic, metal, wood, etc.
	It's plastic, metallic, wooden, etc.

d) SHAPE

Question	Answer
What shape is it?	It's flat, round, square, spherical, triangular, conical, cubic, oval, rectangular, pointed, T-shaped, Y-shaped, banana-shaped, etc.

INSTRUCTIONS

One of you is a representative at a stand, the other an interested visitor. The visitor should ask the representative about his/her company's latest product, using the words above to help.

The representative should first think of a product but not tell the visitor what it is. Your job is to answer the visitor's questions as honestly as possible.

The visitor should try and find out what this company's latest product is by asking about its size, shape, weight, etc.

You can guess what it is whenever you like. If you guess right, one point.
If you guess wrong, no points.

Change roles and continue.

11 NEGOTIATING A FAIR PRICE

Work in pairs. Read through the lists of services offered at a fair. Then act out the following conversation on the telephone. Sit back to back. The fair organizer fills in the prices beforehand.

The basic price including the following services is
_____
– erection of stand
– water
– insurance
– cleaning
– electricity
– compressed air
– dismantling of stand

Extra services wanted by fair participant

	Prices
– carpeting	_____
– furniture	_____
– photography	_____
– telephone	_____
– coffee-maker	_____
– refrigerator	_____
– advertising space in fair brochure	_____

Fair organizer

Fair participant

Ask about the basic price and the services offered.

Explain services included in the price.

React. Then ask for some extra services.

Give him/her a price for such extra services.

Try and get a reduction.

Offer him/her something free.

Accept. Thank him/her.

Thank him/her for calling.

Say goodbye.

Now change roles and repeat the conversation.

12 AT THE STAND

Work in pairs and act out the following conversation. You're discussing the phone in the picture on page 215. Please feel free to discuss a product of your own choice if you prefer. Study sections 11.5 – 11.12 of your Phrase Book.

Visitor   **Representative**

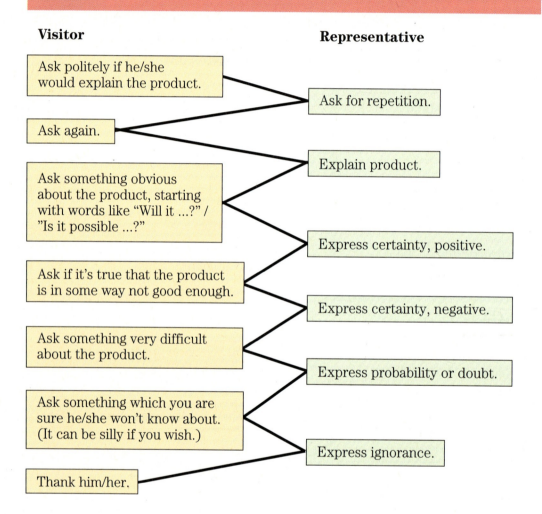

Ask politely if he/she would explain the product.

Ask for repetition.

Ask again.

Explain product.

Ask something obvious about the product, starting with words like "Will it ...?" / "Is it possible ...?"

Express certainty, positive.

Ask if it's true that the product is in some way not good enough.

Express certainty, negative.

Ask something very difficult about the product.

Express probability or doubt.

Ask something which you are sure he/she won't know about. (It can be silly if you wish.)

Express ignorance.

Thank him/her.

13 ORGANIZING A FAIR

Organizing a fair can be a nightmare. Here's a small example of the kinds of problems facing fair organizers. The following represents the present plan for one hall in an exhibition area, Hall Z.

wall ━━━━━   open ----------

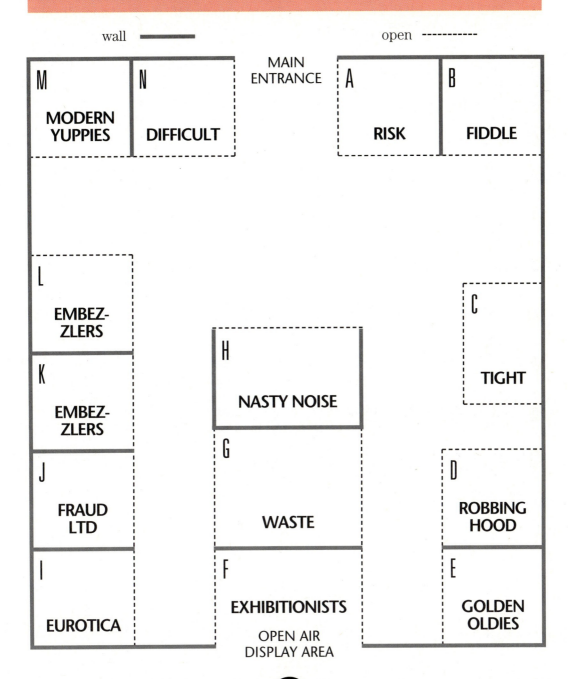

The fair is only two weeks away but there are all kinds of problems. Together with the rest of the group, attempt to solve the problems and keep the fair participants happy.

Problems:

1. FIDDLE and RISK are competitors. There is no way they can be opposite or next to each other.

2. FRAUD Ltd has a live elephant on display. They absolutely need an open-air display area.

3. ROBBING HOOD insists on having a corner space.

4. EUROTICA would like to have three sides of its stand open to the public.

5. EMBEZZLERS would still like to have two stands but not right next to each other. They are demanding two stands directly opposite each other.

6. To save costs TIGHT would like to share their stand with someone. Is this possible?

7. DIFFICULT refuses to be located anywhere near the main entrance. Anywhere else is fine but not there.

8. EXHIBITIONISTS Inc want to be facing directly opposite the main entrance, otherwise they won't come.

9. WASTE are bringing a swimming pool with them. No problem with the water but they insist on having three walls so their fashion models don't get cold.

10. GOLDEN OLDIES will expect to occupy the same stand as last year and the year before – stand 'E'. You already promised it to them.

11. NASTY NOISE cannot be put next to or opposite GOLDEN OLDIES because NASTY NOISE's new marketing director left GOLDEN OLDIES to join them, causing lots of bad feeling.

12. MODERN YUPPIES went bankrupt so they won't be coming at all.

Now working in groups of three or four, try to work out a new plan for the fair participants. Use the blank plan below to help you. Try and give each company a suitable stand. When you're ready, present your suggestion to the whole class. Be prepared to explain your reasons. As you might imagine, there are many possible alternatives, so you won't find a solution in the book.

M   N

A   B

L

C

K

H

J

G

D

I

F

E

14 PHRAZY!

Listen to this impossible story based on some of the phrases covered in WORKING ENGLISH.

Well, what day would suit you best?

Good morning. Can I help you?

Could I have your name, please?

How are things with you?

I disagree entirely.

Look forward to meeting you then.

Are we all agreed on that?

Could we put it to a vote?

Well, I really must be going.

I declare this meeting closed.

KEY AND TAPESCRIPTS

Unit 1 Introducing

Exercise 1 Responses

(Recorded twice; first, phrases only; then phrases with suitable responses.)
1 How about lunch tomorrow? *Fine.* 2 How're things? *Not so bad.* 3 Could you give me a hand, please? *Of course.* 4 Thanks for your help. *You're welcome.* 5 I just got fired. *I'm sorry to hear that.* 6 All right if I smoke? *Go ahead.* 7 Cigarette? *No, thanks.* 8 Say hello to Maria for me. *I will.* 9 It was very nice meeting you. *You too.* 10 Have a nice weekend. *You too.* 11 Look forward to seeing you in London. *Me too.*

Exercise 10 Get Ready

The following are only examples.
1 Pleased to meet you. 2 How do you do? 3 You're welcome. 4 Pardon? (Would you mind repeating that, please?) 5 Well done! 6 Hard luck. 7 Excuse me. 8 Excuse me. 9 Sure. / I'd rather not, if you don't mind. 10 Here. 11 I'd like to introduce my colleague to you ... 12 Hello. How are you? 13 a) Say hello to ... for me. b) Please give my regards to ... 14 I'm very sorry but I'm afraid it's not permitted. 15 I hope you don't mind my asking but I wonder if it would be possible to ... 16 I'd like to propose a toast to ... 17 Sorry I'm late. 18 a) Congratulations. b) Congratulations (to men only) c) Many happy returns. 19 Please accept my deepest condolences. 20 I was wondering if you would like to join me for dinner tonight. 21 I'd very much like to but I'm afraid I can't. 22 I'd be delighted to.

Unit 2 Nice to Meet You

3 The Fax of Life

1 Paul Westlake. 2 He should send a VHS video. 3 A VHS video. 4 This page and a price list. 5 Five.

Exercise 4 Get Ready

The following are only examples.
1a Excuse me, are you Mr Stein? 1b Let me introduce myself. I'm ... Pleased to meet you. 2 Hello ... How are things with you? 3 ..., I'd like you to meet ... 4 Mr / Ms ..., please allow me to introduce you to .... 5a Well, perhaps we can arrange to meet later on tonight. 5b OK, ... it is then. (See you later.) 6 Well, I'm afraid I have to be going now. I have another engagement.

Exercise 4 Phrase Practice.

Tapescript:
1 Receptionist: Good morning. Can I help you? /
2 Receptionist: Could I have your name again, please? /
3 Receptionist: Would you spell that for me, please? /
4 Client: Hello. Did you get my fax? /
5 Client: OK. Well, what day would suit you best? /
6 Client: Where should we meet? /
7 Client: Can we agree on a time? /
8 Client: I'm looking forward to meeting you then. /

Exercise 10 Answerphones

Tapescript:
"Hello, this is Tom Jones / from Williams, Ltd., Birmingham. / Calling at 3 p.m. / on Friday, the 29th of February. / I'm phoning about the price list and contract negotiations / concerning the Delta Project. / We accept your price suggestions. / But can you send us your latest price list, please? / I can be reached on 021-497 632 until seven this evening. / That's on 021-497 632, until seven this evening. / Thanks very much. Bye."

Exercise 15 "Mmm..."

The following are only examples.
1 Really? 2 Sorry to hear that. 3 Oh dear. 4 Of course not. 5 You don't say. 6 Please. Keep going. 7 No. 8 Yes. 9 Go on. 10 What a pity.

Exercise 22 A Warm Reception

Tapescript:
Paul: What's your job?
Receptionist: I'm a receptionist and my job is to welcome the guests, give information of every kind, take reservations and answer the telephone. I have to host more or less the guests until they leave the hotel, give them the bills and keep contact to companies and travel agencies, things like that.
Paul: Do you enjoy your job?
Receptionist: Yes, it's interesting. I learn a lot about people, I get in touch with different kind of people... they're from different countries.
Paul: So you speak two or three languages. How many languages do you speak?
Receptionist: Oh, German of course, then English, French and Spanish.

Paul: Which foreign language do you use the most?

Receptionist: English, of course, yes.

Paul: And what kind of English do you find you have to use? I mean, do you find that you have to talk about everything, the weather... or what kind of things do you find you have to say to people?

Receptionist: Normally only information about the buses, about Berlin, and information about the hotel...

Paul: What about English on the telephone? What kind of things do people want to know in English on the telephone if they phone you?

Receptionist: Normally they want to find out about the rates, about the type of rooms we have, if we have rooms available, or, yes, if they want to make a reservation, how they can find us. That's all, normally.

Paul: Do you have very many people who use English as a second language, meaning that they are not English or Americans?

Receptionist: Yes. For example Japanese people are coming very strongly to Berlin. They normally use English as we normally don't speak Japanese. And people from the eastern countries like Russia, they normally use English too.

Paul: Do you find that it's easy to understand their English or is it a little bit difficult sometimes?

Receptionist: It's difficult, especially with the Japanese people. Yes. Because they normally have very good grammar but they can't talk.

Paul: It's a bit like the opposite of the English speaking other languages; they have no grammar but they still talk... How important is English to people in your kind of job – people who work in reception or in hotels generally?

Receptionist: Speaking English is one of the important... most important points in choosing this job. You can't do this job without speaking English because all the business is in English. The big hotel chains are normally managed from the United States or Asia and they always talk English. So you have to speak English.

Unit 3 On Behalf of Our Company...

3 DEMONstrations

1 The presenter was over-anxious and panicked.

2 The presenter was arrogant and unable to accept criticism.

Exercise 4 Nice to Have You Here

Tapescript:

Hello. I'm glad you could join us. My name is Petra Winheller. I'd like to introduce our company. We are a video company . Here we are first in the secretary department. Here's the telephone exchange. And I would like to show you more of our studio rooms and the copy-street.

First we are here in our Studio Number One. You can see all the technical machines. Here we work for Public Television, for radio stations. We produce and cut the films. This is our main studio. So, would you like, please, follow me in our copy-street where you can see where the copies are made.

_____

Our removal section is divided into three departments: sales department, local moving, European moving and overseas. We start here with the sales people. One is, as it should be, on the road, selling, and two others are in here... Williank, you want to come here just to say hello?

"Hello."

"Hello."

"What are you doing, actually?"

"I'm doing sales promotion, making phone calls, when people want to move they phone us and I arrange..." (fade out)

_____

We give re-location assistance. Re-location assistance means that when people are being sent abroad by their company as an expatriate, we are there to assist the people to get integrated into their new, local environment. We help them to find housing, we help them with the move, we help them with the children going to school and we also help them with all kinds of administrational and logistic things that need to be arranged like going to the alien police, get yourself registered, bank accounts, driving licences, etc, etc.

That is what we do, and that means you have to support the people who are coming to the Netherlands. As they do not speak Dutch, and the people in the Town Hall only speak Dutch, they need somebody who, first of all, understands the culture, the system, but can translate, us being able to speak different languages and English being our first language, we can therefore give the right support.

_____

I will continue to explain what kind of projects we are supporting here from Germany. We have close connections and relations to certain rainforest countries like Malaysia, Costa Rica and Indonesia. We are in contact with non-governmental organizations in these countries. They are doing the real work in the countries, that means, they are trying to protect their own environment. They have the interest to protect the environment there. So we get all the information from them and trying to be a sort of speaker for them here in Germany and supporting projects in these countries.

Exercise 5 Get Ready
The following are only examples.
1 Excuse me. Can you tell me the way to ... , please? 2 May I help you? 3 I'm looking for ... 4 I'm very sorry but ... is not back from lunch yet. 5 Excuse me, can you tell me how to get to room 1038, please? 6 Could you ask Mr Smith to contact me later, please? 7 On behalf of ... I would like to welcome you all here today. 8 Let's start by looking at ... 9 Excuse me, can you explain that for me, please? 10 Would you mind repeating that for me, please?

Exercise 5 Phrase Practice
Our suggestions:
1b, 2c, 3c, 4b, 5a, 6c, 7a, b and c
Tapescript:
1 Is it very far from here? 2 Who shall I say is here? 3 My name is Williams. I have an appointment with Ms Vogel at 3 o'clock. 4 My name's Lombard. Do you have any messages for me? 5 Glad you could join us today.
6 Sorry to interrupt, but I wonder if you could explain that again for me, please? 7 (very fast and indistinctly) So, ladies and gentlemen, the quark is indiscernible.

Exercise 7 Presenting Your Workplace
A A 2 / B 4 / C 5 / D 3 / E 1 / F 6 / G 7
B 1b, 2d, 3c

Exercise 12 Taking Down Messages
Tapescript:
1 Hello, my name is Jim Porter. I can't find Mr Robinson's fax anywhere. Could you ask him to fax the information again, please? My fax number is 6780230. I'll say that again, 6780230.
2 Hello, this is Janet Moore's travel agent speaking. Janet Moore's flight has been cancelled. Can she please phone us for re-scheduling at 843710? I'll say the number again: 843710. Thank you.
3 Good morning. This is Professor Klein speaking. I haven't received Professor Casey's

abstract for the conference. Could he please send it to me immediately by E-mail? Thank you.
4 Hello, there. My name's Sally Reynold. I'd like to inform Albert Benson that he should send his article revisions to me by 8 o'clock Wednesday morning. If there are any problems, could Mr Benson please phone me at 349024? That's 349024.

Exercise 16 Describing Processes
A 2 / B 6 / C 5 / D 1 / E 3 / F 4

Unit 4 The Floor Is Yours

3 Furniture
1 old things / 2 held / 3 unimportant / 4 a suggestion / 5 preferred / 6 to leave until later / 7 to propose / 8 to have the right to speak / 9 to say what you think / 10 a person who supports women's rights / 11 a person in charge of a meeting / 12 a person who doesn't easily approve of changes in tradition

Exercise 4 Get Ready
The following are only examples.
1 Ladies and gentlemen, I declare the meeting open. 2 May I read the minutes? 3 Has everyone seen the agenda? 4 Mr / Ms ..., would you like to say something about this? 5 Could we stick to the agenda, please? 6 Could we move on to the next point, please? 7 Let's put it to the vote. 8 Mr Chairman, could I have the floor, please? 9 I'd like to make a proposal. 10 Seconded!

Exercise 4 Phrase Practice
– Ladies and gentlemen, I declare the meeting open.
– The most important points seem to be....(fade out)
– May I read the minutes?
– Has everyone seen the agenda?
– Mr Smith, would you like to say something about this?
– Mr Chairman, could I have the floor, please?
– We seem to be losing sight of the main point.
– We can't all speak at the same time.
– Could we move on to item three on the agenda?
– Will Ms Brown please report to the information desk.
– Excuse me a moment.
– Where can I phone from?
– With the Chair's permission, I move that...
– Would anyone like to second the motion?

– Perhaps we should take a formal vote on this.
– Those **for** the motion, please?
– It would seem we have a consensus.
– Is there any other business?

Exercise 6 The Stylized Language of Formal Meetings
the minutes / item / agenda / seconded / motion / unanimously / casting vote / adjourned

Exercise 11 Interrupting
Our suggestion: 4 Sorry to interrupt, but ... 6 Might I make a point here? 10 Could I come in here for a second?

Exercise 13 Putting it All Together
Tapescript:

Chairman: Let's get this meeting underway, shall we?

Person 2: What we have to do this morning is discuss the refugee problem in this country.

Person 3: Mr Chairman, could I have the floor, please?

Chairman: Very well, The floor is yours, Colin.

Person 3: Thank you, Mr Chairman. As I see it, we should definitely take more refugees into this country.

Person 4: I'm sorry but I totally disagree.

Chairman: Order, please! Perhaps we can begin more compromisingly.

Person 2: If I may make a suggestion, Mr Chairman, why don't we consider how many more refugees we could take?

Person 3: I agree with that.

Person 4: No, sorry. I don't think that's a very good idea.

Person 2: Let me put it another way, then. How about if we discuss how many refugees we already have here?

Person 3: Fine with me.

Person 4: OK. I could agree to that.

Chairman: Good. Then, let's get the discussion underway. (fade out)
(fade in)

Chairman: So, can I have a proposal, please, from someone?

Person 2: Yes. I would like to propose the motion that we are in favour of receiving more refugees.

Chairman: Would anyone like to second the motion?

Person 3: Seconded!

Chairman: Seconded by Mr Freeman. Now I think we should take a vote on it. Those for the motion please? – two. Those against? – one.

The motion is carried by two votes to one. I declare this meeting closed. Thank you very much, everyone.

Unit 5 What Do You Think?

3 Word in Your Ear
A 1 In fact, 4 Actually, 5 As a matter of fact,
B The following are only examples.
1 I'm afraid it just wouldn't work. 2 I'm afraid it's not ready yet. 3 I'm afraid not. 4 I'm afraid there isn't. 5 I'm afraid that's not possible.
C The following are only examples.
1 Do you think leaving right now could help? 2 What about changing the contract? 3 Why don't you ask him? 4 Wouldn't it be a good opportunity? 5 Would November the 5th be suitable?
D The following are only examples.
1 That would be too little. 2 Money wouldn't be any problem. 3 I'd prefer the other alternative. 4 I wouldn't be able to accept that. 5 KLM would be easier. 6 I wouldn't really be able to say at present.
E
1 That might present us with a slight / a bit of a / a little problem. 2 We would need some / a little more time to think it over. 3 We have run into slight / some difficulties. 4 Obviously, slight / some changes will have to be made. 5 There seems to have been a slight misunderstanding.
F
1 That's not very suitable. 2 This is not very useful. 3 I'm not very happy about that suggestion. 4 In my opinion, that's not a very clever thing to say. 5 It's not a very sensitive proposal.

Exercise 4 Get Ready
The following are only examples.
1 Let's get started, shall we? 2 I'd like to bring up the point about ... 3 Let me give you an example. 4 What's your opinion? 5 I totally agree. 6 I'm sorry, but I disagree entirely. 7 If I may make a suggestion, ... 8 All right. 9 No, I don't think that's a good idea. 10 Well, it's rather difficult to say at present. 11 Let's call it a day, shall we?

Exercise 4 Phrase Practice
– Let me start by...
– I'd like to bring up the point about...
– I must add that...
– But on the whole...
– What do you think about...?

– It seems to me that ...
– I can see what you mean but...
– I hope you don't mind me asking, but...
– How about...?
– Perhaps we can finish by...

Exercise 6 Language Choice

The following are only examples.
Stating purpose: I suppose we all know why we're all here.
Introducing a point: I'd like to bring up the question of ...
Asking for opinions: What do you think?
Suggesting something: Why don't we ...?
Supporting: I think you're right.
Disagreeing: I'm sorry, but I don't agree with you.
Closing: If there's nothing else, I suggest that we finish.

Exercise 8 Intonation

Tapescript:
1 (excited) How do you feel about it? 2 (bored) No, I don't agree at all. 3 (angry) If I may make a suggestion. 4 (excited) Yes, I suppose we could. 5 (angry) Well, it's rather difficult to say at present.

Exercise 9 Direct or Diplomatic?

Our suggestions:
1 direct 2 diplomatic 3 diplomatic
4 diplomatic 5 diplomatic 6 direct

Exercise 13 Mini-meeting

Tapescript:
Person 1: Let's get started, shall we? Abortion – right or wrong?
Person 2: Well, first I'd like to bring up the question of the age of the foetus. I mean, if the foetus is younger than three months you can't really consider it to be more than a worm - it's not human yet, is it?
Person 3: Mm. It seems to me that it's very difficult indeed to know how conscious a child is in the womb, no matter how old he might be.
Person 1: I totally agree.
Person 2: Well, I really can't agree with you on that. According to all the scientific studies, foetuses are not aware of themselves until a fairly late stage.
Person 3: I can't help feeling that we can't be sure of that fact. Scientific research looks at things from the outside. It can't look into a person's soul.
Person 1: Are you suggesting that we should consider people's souls in this discussion?
Person 3: Um...well, actually. How shall I put

it? Perhaps we can come back to this later. If I may make a suggestion. What I would like to discuss now is how safe it is for the mother to have an abortion after the third month of pregnancy
Person 1: All right.
Person 2: No, I don't think that's a good idea. I think we should discuss the foetus first.
Person 1: Let's discuss both. (fade out)

Exercise 17 Body Language

Tapescript:
Paul: Well, I'm sitting on a stage here in Espoo, here in Finland, talking to Alan Pease who has just given us a five-hour lecture on body language. Alan has written at least four, possibly five, books on the subject and is considered to be an expert in his field.

First question, very simply, is: How relevant is body language for people from different cultures when they come together and try and communicate? How aware should they be of body language?
Alan: Well, it's critical, Paul, because studies have shown that face to face, regardless of what culture they come from, between 60 to 80% of the message that is said face to face is done with signals, gestures, movements, dress, clothing and appearance - and not what you say or the way you say it. In fact, what you say and the way you say it only accounts for between 25 to 35% of the effect that you have face to face - most of it is what's called body language.
Paul: What kind of things should be people looking out for both from their own body movements and also other people's?
Alan: Well, two things, Paul. First is, you need to be able to read whether the other person is being straight with you and being honest with you: whether they're telling the truth or whether they'll likely to be holding back information or maybe telling you what they think you might want to hear rather than the truth. So, you need to be able to read those signals. And secondly, you need to be aware of what signals you might be sending yourself – that – which might accidentally be sending the wrong message. For example, if you have a habit of folding your arms on your chest because, ah, you've got a lower back problem, if the other person doesn't know you have lower back problem they will instinctively get the feeling that you're not being open and honest with them and they'll react as if that were true.
Paul: OK. What about here in the Nordic

countries? Have you noticed that there are any general tendencies as regards body language for people from Sweden, Norway, Finland etc. Do they have anything particular?

Alan: Well, they're pretty much the same as most people around the world. With the Finns in particular; they do a lot of hand holding, that is holding their hands in front of their body - what's usually referred to with men as the broken zipper position where their, both hands are crossed in front of their body. Women also tend to do that a lot, particularly when in a public place. That's a defensive-type reaction.

Touching frequency in Scandinavia is not as much as it is in most other countries. And one thing that is different in the Scandinavian region to, say, most of the western world is eye-contact; it's a little longer here than it is, say, in Australia, New Zealand or England. Now, of course, the cultural problem that could result there: if I'm talking to a Finn a Norwegian - Norwegians particularly because they do have long eye contact - as an Australian I feel as though they're staring at me but in fact they're not. So, as a result I will instinctively keep looking away. Now they think that I'm being a bit suspicious because I'm not looking at them, so both of us are likely to make cultural misinterpretations. Now fortunately I'm aware of the cultural difference and so when they meet my gaze I will meet it longer but I still feel uncomfortable because it's not part of my culture.

Paul: I understand you've done a lot of work with Americans or in America , perhaps both. Can you tell us something about that? How seriously do Americans take body language? How do they use that in business and outside of business?

Alan: Well, in America, it's like in Australia and New Zealand. There's virtually no course that you can do in a university or college or any business course, that doesn't have understanding body signals in there as a major part of that training because it makes up, as I've said earlier, 60 to 80%. Now, if a person's not studying and making an effort to learn what the 60 to 80% in human communication through body language is, that means that you're going to be disadvantaged to that extent.

Paul: How aware are you of your own body language? Do you find that you can't move because you're too aware of what you do or how you react to it?

Alan: Yeah, I'm very aware of my own body language signals, particularly when I do a seminar like this one here today because everybody's watching me to see what I'm going to do, so I'm too scared to scratch my nose too in case they read something into it.

Paul: Alan Pease, thank you very much indeed.

Alan: My pleasure.

Unit 6 Be My Guest

3 Understand?!

A 1 order 2 answer 3 suppose 4 say again 5 bring about 6 point out 7 mean 8 involve 9 keep going 10 feed 11 keep up 12 dominate 13 vanish

B Understanding and using a foreign language demands much more than simply a knowledge of words and grammar. Some kind of cultural understanding is necessary if you are to communicate effectively.

Exercise 4 Get Ready

The following are only examples. 1 Hello. Glad you could make it. 2 I'd really like to but I'm afraid I can't. 3 I'd love to. / I'm afraid I can't. 4 I've got some bad news for you, I'm afraid. 5 Sorry to interrupt, but dinner is served. 6 That's great! 7 Could you pass me the salt, please? 8 No, thanks. I'm driving. 9 Good evening. We have a table reservation. 10 Give my best regards to ...

Exercise 4: Phrase Practice

1 I was wondering if you would like to join me for a drink tonight. 2 I'd like to join you tonight but I've already arranged to go somewhere else. 3 I'm so pleased you could come. 4 Guess what! I won the competition. 5 Bad news, I'm afraid. The party's cancelled. 6 Would you like a drink? 7 Could you pass me the salt, please? 8 Give my regards to Tom. 9 Best regards from Frank. 10 Thank you for a lovely evening.

Exercise 14 Party-goers

Friday: John and Carol / Kevin and Jane Saturday: Dave and Anita / Jeff and Christina Sunday: Joe and Linda / Ed and Maggie

Unit 7 To Be Quite Frank...

3 Negotiating

A 1: phase two 2: phase one 3: phase three 4: phase three 5: phase four 6: phase four **B** The following are only examples. 1 I don't think that's such a good idea. 2 I very much doubt if we'll do that. 3 I'm not so sure I agree with you. 4 I'm afraid I couldn't do that. 5 Don't you think it might be a bit of a problem? 6 I absolutely agree with you on that. 7 I'm afraid she's not here at the moment. 8 Would you like some coffee? 9 I must admit that I find that slightly difficult to believe. 10 Excuse me. Could you tell me where the toilet is, please?

Exercise 4 Get Ready
The following are only examples.
1 I would like to propose that ... 2 You have a point there, but ... 3 I don't know about that. 4 Let me add that ... 5 If I've understood you correctly, you're saying that ... 6 I'm afraid there seems to be a slight misunderstanding. 7 Let me put it in another way. 8 Let me assure you straight away on that point. 9 Perhaps. But this, after all, is a relatively small point. 10 Is that acceptable as a compromise solution? 11 Yes. I think that would be perfectly acceptable. 12 I'm sorry, I can't go along with that.

Exercise 4 Phrase Practice
– I propose that...
– Well, I agree with you on the whole but...
– Do you really think so?
– There are certain points you should bear in mind.
– Could you expand on that?
– Would I be correct in saying that...?
– I'm afraid there seems to be a slight misunderstanding.
– Perhaps I haven't made myself clear.
– There's no danger of that.
– I particularly want to emphasize the fact that...
– OK. But this is a minor issue.
– That's a very interesting question.
– I wonder if that view is justified in the light of...
– Is that acceptable as a compromise solution?
– That seems to be a reasonable compromise.
– I'm sorry I can't go along with that.
– Well, if I could just sum up the discussion.
– Let me conclude by saying...

Exercise 11 The Deal
Tapescript:
Seller: Well, how about if I make you an offer of 100 tractors at 10,000 ecus each?
Buyer: Mm. Well, I would propose that we take into consideration the fact that we would be prepared to buy so many.
Seller: Are you saying that you would like some kind of discount?

Buyer: Basically, what I'm saying is that if we were to buy say ten tractors, then I think 10,000 ecus per tractor <u>would</u> be reasonable. But we're interested in 100, so I really do feel we should negotiate the price, don't you?
Seller: I agree with you in principle but I am only allowed to offer a price reduction under special circumstances.
Buyer: Let me assure you straight away on that point. If we are satisfied with the first 100 tractors you can be sure that we will order some more in the future.
Seller: Oh, really?
Buyer: Yes. But now I would also like you to consider the delivery date. You see I think we would need the tractors here before mid-summer, in good time for the harvest, you know.
Seller: Ah! Well, I'm very sorry but it just wouldn't be feasible. Mid-summer would be the earliest we could manage.
Buyer: Well, OK. I suppose we could accept that deadline. However, as I mentioned before, how about some modifications to the wheels?
Seller: At an extra cost?
Buyer: No. I was thinking of no extra cost.
Seller: I'm very sorry but I'm afraid that won't work. No. Any modifications would a) have to be funded by you and b) would delay delivery.
Buyer: Well, never mind. I think we could manage without the modifications for the time being. But let's return to my questions about discount.
Seller: Mm.
Buyer: Because of the size of the order and the possibility of future orders I would propose that you give us 10% discount on the deal. I think that sounds reasonable.
Seller: Well, I don't know about that. I can't really say I share your view. I honestly don't think we could offer you that much discount. Our unit price is already the best in the market.
Buyer: Yes. I take your point, but potentially we could be very big clients.
Seller: Yes, I realize that. Ordinarily, I am allowed to offer a client up to 5% discount but in your case I think we could offer you, say... 7%.
Buyer: Well, to be perfectly honest, I really do have to insist on 10% in view of the nature of the deal.
Seller: If we look at it in another light, neither of us should feel that the other party is inflexible. So, how about if we agree on 8%? We're prepared to give you an 8% reduction

provided that you agree to all the other terms we've discussed. Is that acceptable as a compromise solution?

Buyer: Yes. I think that would be perfectly acceptable.

Seller: Great. Well, if I could just summarize the discussion so far. You're taking 100 tractors at a reduced price of... let me see. (calculates) 8% of a million? That's 80,000. Leaving 920,000 ecus.

Buyer: Yes.

Seller: Delivery time; mid-summer and no modifications. Right?

Buyer: That's it. Agreed.

Seller: Fine. Now, I suppose we had better look at the shipping details.

Exercise 16 How to Negotiate

Tapescript:

Paul: Philip O'Connor is an Irishman who lives in England. As a trainer he has had to prepare a great deal of material, particularly in regards to negotiation. In this interview he talks about what he considers to be the eight stages of negotiation.

Philip: The first one, and it's often one which people don't think about in negotiating, is relationship building, that is, getting to know the person you are negotiating with. And this is quite important. It's quite important to know who you are with. It's a stage which can take a short time or a long time. Typically in North America, for example, relationship building may take only ten minutes and can be quite informal "Hi! My name's Jack" and, and so on. So that's a little bit of language for it. If you are negotiating with partners in the Arab world then relationship building could take, uh, three or four weeks, even a month, even two years before you get to the next stage.

After relationship building what many people don't do and what is important is to agree procedure. So that both sides know where they are going and why they are going there. And this is also a good opportunity for using language which will create a climate, a feeling of co-operation, so people in this stage typically will be saying things like "Can we agree to deal with price first and delivery terms later?" And, typically to that kind of question, the other side will say "Yes. That's fine."

So, relationship building, agreeing procedure, then exchanging information. This is often giving a little presentation. If it's two companies, (a) little presentation about what each company is doing and in particular, what their interests in this negotiation are.

And typically, and normally, after this people will have questions. They will need to ask questions to make sure they have understood, particularly if you're using a foreign language it's quite easy not to understand and it's important to feel confident to ask questions.

After this we come to a stage that is very often neglected. and this is particularly important when it's an open situation. This is generating options - throwing around ideas.

So, what is very important at the stage of generating options is to be completely open, to brainstorm, and to put as many ideas on the table as possible and then later, and only later, to evaluate them, to say "Yes. I like that one because..." or "I don't like that one because..." And this, if it's done properly, the research seems to suggest that a better idea will be arrived at in the end rather than people just fixing on, on, on the first idea that comes into their mind. After that, people move into the more typical, I suppose what people think of as negotiating; bidding – putting forward proposals.

So, bidding is putting forward proposals. And from a language point of view this is typically, "Our proposal is..." so that it is absolutely clear that you have moved into a clear stage of putting forward a proposal. This is no longer just an idea but is something that you feel that this is really now what I want to negotiate about. This then, of course, leads into bargaining about this. This is an important of the negotiation but it's not the only part of the negotiation. Very often, if you pick somebody off the street and ask what is negotiating they think of bargaining. They think of trying to get a lower price than the other person. Very often, in our experience, when people work through this model the bargaining phase comes much more easily if they have clarified everything, made everything clearer at an earlier stage.

And then finally we get to the stage of concluding: reaching agreement. And this may seem, uh, very simple. It's not necessarily so simple to reach agreement even if you have gone through the other stages. For example, if you take a country like the United States. It's a country which is very very, keen on, interested in, seeing everything in writing, seeing everything in contract, having everything in words, on paper signed by everybody with lawyers present. That is – an agreement.

So that is a cultural factor, so agreement may not cause many language problems but there can be cultural differences which cause problems. So those are some of the stages that we felt were useful and useful to look at in terms of language that people need to negotiate more successfully and also cultural differences that they need to be aware of in order to do that.

Paul: How do you feel that negotiations and English as a lingua franca work?

Philip: This is a very interesting area. It's an interesting area from two points of view. If we look, if we look for example, at Finnish people negotiating with Italians in, using English as a language to negotiate in and you ask those people what their experience has been if they've also negotiated with let's say British people, in my experience almost always they will say it is easier to negotiate with other people whose first language is not English. So, I think this is something we have to look at very, very carefully, that the English which or lingua franca that people are using is, seems to be an effective tool for negotiating and seems to work quite well.

1 Relationship building 2 Agreeing on procedure 3 Exchanging information 4 Asking questions 5 Generating options 6 Bidding: putting forward proposals 7 Bargaining 8 Concluding

Unit 8 Clearly and Simply

2 Cross-cultural Considerations
1 a / 2 b / 3 a / 4 b / 5 a / 6 a / 7 b / 8 a

3 One Man's Meat Is Another Man's Poison
1 a / 2 a / 3 c / 4 b / 5 c

Exercise 4 Get Ready
The following are only examples.
1 All right, everyone. 2 Good morning, ladies and gentlemen. (Welcome to ...) 3 I'm here to talk about ... 4 I'd now like to draw your attention to ... 5 OK. So much for ... 6 Now I'd like to move on to ... 7 Please, allow me to digress for a while. 8 I'd like to finish by ...

Exercise 4 Phrase Practice
Tapescript:
1 get attention 2 start your presentation 3 explain your purpose 4 draw attention to a point 5 finish a point 6 start another point 7 digress 8 end your presentation

Exercise 7 The Bare Essentials
The Introduction
1 take 2 welcoming 3 for 4 as 5 objective

6 Then, 7 lastly 8 only too delighted 9 at The Main Body

Due to rumours in some European countries there has been some speculation. **So**, the situation is a little unsteady at present. However, **thanks to** the stability of the Deutschmark, **a result of** wise investment, no long-term trend is forecast **as there was** no change whatsoever in German interest rates.

Exercise 9 Presentation
3 / 5 / 2 / 4 / 6 / 1

Exercise 10 Presenting Information
1 a percentage bar chart 2 a multiple bar chart 3 a simple line graph 4 a pie chart 5 a simple bar chart 6 a multiple line graph 7 a table

Exercise 11 Speed and Degree
SPEED: A 1 / B 3 / C 2 / D 4
DEGREE: A 3 / B 2 / C 4 / D 1

Exercise 12 Describing Contents

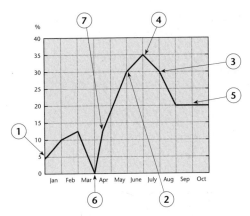

Exercise 13 Talking of Figures
1 doubled 2 trebled 3 six-fold 4 reduced

Exercise 14 Ups and Downs
Tapescript:
Presenter: Well, everyone, I'm now going to show you our sales figures for the first ten months of the year. In January sales figures stood at 5%. That's 5% of the total market. And, as you can see, things seemed to be going quite well until the beginning of March when sales suddenly dropped from about 12% to zero. The reason for this was, of course, our failure to get our new products ready in time. Anyway, as soon as they were ready figures started to rise rapidly. From April onwards

sales began to recover very nicely and reached 30% by the end of May, peaking at a record 35% at the end of June. Early July saw our market share beginning to decrease, dropping quite sharply to only 20% by the end of August. But, happily things levelled out in September and October, so there's no cause for alarm. If you look at the ten months it's quite evident that spring and early summer would seem to be the best time to sell our products, although we might be able to improve our competitiveness in winter if we get our products ready in time. Right, well, thank you for your attention. Any questions, anyone?

Person: Yes. What about November and December?

Presenter: Yes. I thought someone might ask that. Er..(fade)

Exercise 18:
It's Not What You Say...

Tapescript:

My name is Paul Westlake and I'm a language trainer. And among other things, I specialize in presentation skills.

I think that I'd like to begin by talking about preparing for presentations, which is a very important part of presentations.

First of all I think it's important to develop objectives as to why you are giving the presentation; is your goal to give information? or are you there to entertain them? or to support them? That's very important because it will shape what you say and how you say it.

And secondly, I think it's important to analyze your audience: who are you talking to? That way you'll avoid talking below them or talking above their heads, as they say, talking down to them. So, know who you are talking to, that's very important.

Thirdly, if you're planning to give out handouts, I think it's important to know that you shouldn't put too much information in handouts, or too little. And then also important to think when you're gonna give the handouts out – at the beginning or the end of your lecture? If you give them out at the beginning then people tend to read through it and don't listen to you, for example.

And then, lastly, for the preparation of presentations, I think it's very important to practise in front of a mirror. Some people practise with a friend. Doesn't really matter but the more you practise, I think, the more you notice the weaknesses in your presentation. So practice makes perfect, as they say.

When you actually get to the place where you are going to give the presentation, I think it's very important to make sure all the basics are right, I mean, by checking out the place, making sure that the wires are plugged in if you're using a TV or something... So all the audio-visual equipment should be in place. And check out the seating arrangements and that the lights are right. Check out the atmosphere generally. And then, of course, you can always explore some new possibilities... Maybe you can see that perhaps you'll be able to walk around the audience if you rearrange a few chairs, for example.

Okay. And then the presentation itself. I think it's very important to be alert during the presentation. What I mean is (that) to be very aware of what you say and how you say it. And then, of course, eye contact with the audience – you can't look at everybody straight in the eyes for the whole time, it's impossible, but you can keep looking at people, moving your eyes around and that gives people the idea of a kind of a personal or a conversational presentation, not a cold, distant one.

And then, of course, your voice. And this is true for any culture, I think, in any language: it's important to have a clear, strong voice so that everybody can hear you and that they hear every word. Then, of course, particularly if there are people in the audience who are not native speakers of your language, it's important not to talk too fast or to use words which are too difficult. So, basically, keep your voice clear.

And then, of course, with presentations, the question of visual aids. There are lots of things available, but I think the secret of using visual aids effectively is the KISS principle, as they say. KISS, K-I-S-S, which means, "keep it simple, stupid." Then, in other words, don't use audio-visuals, visual aids, too much. A lot of people tend to talk at their visual aids and not at their audience. So, if you're using a flip chart or a white board, it's very difficult to maintain eye contact with your audience, for example. If you're using things like cassette players or videos, although they have their value definitely, you must make sure that the audience can actually hear what's going on or see what's going on. And that has to be checked out beforehand, of course.

Okay. Another important aspect is, when using visual aids, is to ask why you are using them, really. And the way I see it, there are three main reasons. One is to emphasize something. The second one would be to help explain a point. And thirdly, I think, also sometimes just to make something easier to remember.

Okay. Well, to return to presentations themselves, it's very important to structure your presentation. How you do that is very much up to you and depends on the culture, for example. But I think it's a very good idea to structure your beginning – some kind of logical introduction – and very often people like to explain what it is they are going to talk about. That depends, of course, on the nature of the presentation – sometimes it's nice to surprise people.

And then, at the end of the presentation, I think it's important to end strongly – either with a story or a thought or maybe an anecdote, a joke or maybe something like a proposition, anything, really, as long as you leave them with some kind of idea.

And then, after the presentation, well, it's question time, even if people are rather reluctant to ask you questions. Nevertheless, there are certain considerations to keep in mind. For example, I think it's very important indeed to anticipate the kind of questions people might ask you. And therefore, one technique is to practise the answers beforehand. That way you come across as being somebody who knows more than just the presentation you've given. Another thing is that, if somebody asks you a question, it's important to look at that person and to really listen to the question, not to just think that "the worst is over, I can say anything now" – it's very important.

Then also, I think it's important to keep the same voice as you used during the presentation. There's no reason why suddenly they should change from hearing John Wayne to Mickey Mouse, if you see what I mean, so just keep the same voice as you used during the presentation. And then, if somebody asks you a question, I think it's polite and correct to repeat that question – for two reasons. One; so that everybody understood the question; and b) it gives you a little time to actually come up with an answer.

And then, lastly, for questions, I think it's important still to maintain eye contact and to keep the audience in touch with you.

Okay. And then the last word, I think, about presentations is about the fact how to be a good presenter. I think the answer is, "you don't have to be an entertainer to be a good presenter." I think the most important thing is to be yourself, but more so.

Unit 9 No Problem!

3 The Problem with Language
1 A / 2 F / 3 H / 4 N / 5 D / 6 M / 7 J / 8 G / 9 L / 10 E / 11 I / 12 B / 13 K / 14 C

Exercise 4 Get Ready
These are only examples.
1 Apologies from Mr Schmitt. Unfortunately he won't be able to participate. 2 I'd like to change my flight. 3 I'd just like to make sure that my flight reservation has been confirmed. 4 We'll take care of it right away. 5 Excuse me but I really feel I have to complain. 6 Thank you very much for your help. 7 Excuse me, this is not what I ordered. 8 Sorry about the mistake. 9 Could you help me, please? I'd like to do some photocopying. 10 There's been a mistake in the schedule. The lecture in Room 9 ...

Exercise 4 Phrase Practice
1 (at a conference) Before we begin I would like to announce that... (*the canteen is open from one to two every day*) 2 (at a travel agent's) I'd like to make a change in my reservation... 3 (at a reception desk) I was told that you could help me... 4 (at a reception desk) I'd just like to make sure that... 5 (an airline official at the airport) Just a moment, please. I'll have a look on the computer... 6 (at the information desk) I'm very sorry but I can't help you. Please contact... 7 (in a department store) I don't like to complain but... 8 (in a restaurant) Excuse me, there's some mistake... 9 (anywhere you like) Sorry about...

Exercise 5 Changes in Travel Arrangements
Customer: Good morning. I'd like to make a change in my reservation. I would like to cancel my flight to Oslo. Instead, I'd like to book a return flight to Amsterdam.
Travel agent: Just a moment, please. I'll have to have a look on the computer. I'm sorry. We have no record of your reservation to Oslo. There seems to be a mistake somewhere. Let's see what we can work out, shall we?

Exercise 14 The Counterfeit Note
50 pounds! Explanation: the value of the shoes (£40) plus the 10 extra pounds he had to give back to the florist. Feel free to disagree with our suggestion!

Unit 10
Your Attention, Please!

2 Cross-cultural Considerations

1 a: perfume. Don't give perfume to a French client/colleague. It's considered too intimate.
2 c: red roses. Don't give red roses to a German client/colleague. They are reserved for lovers or spouses only. 3 b: a knife. Never give a South American a knife. It suggests cutting off a relationship. 4 b: Don't give a gift in private in the Middle East. Someone might think it's a bribe. 5 a: a handkerchief. Don't give South Americans handkerchiefs. They are associated with tears. 6 b: a clock. Avoid giving clocks to Chinese people. The Chinese word for clock sounds very much like the word for funeral.
7 a: food. Giving food or drink to your Saudi hosts would suggest that they haven't given or aren't giving you enough to eat or drink.
8 a: Don't give a South Korean a gift in public. In most Asian countries, giving and receiving gifts is a delicate art, so keep it low key.

3 Confer
A
a 10 / b 6 / c 12 / d 5 / e 1 / f 4 / g 9 / h 3 / i 8 / j 2 / k 7 / l 11
B
1 held / 2 appointed / 3 get acquainted with / 4 lead / 5 formed / 6 called on / 7 in session / 8 a secret ballot / 9 command / 10 on

Exercise 4 Get Ready
These are only examples.
1 I'd like to book a flight, please. 2 Can you tell me where I register, please? 3 It's my pleasure to introduce ... 4 May I be of assistance?
5 I wonder if you could help me? 6 I was wondering if I could ask something about ...
7 That's a good question. 8 Thank you. I'm sure you've given us a lot to think about.

Exercise 4 Phrase Practice
(Recorded twice; first, phrases only; then phrases with suitable responses.)
1 Can you tell me where we register, please? *Here.* 2 Excuse me, you've spelled my name wrong. *Oh, I'm so sorry.* 3 May I be of assistance? *Yes, please.* 4 I wonder if you can help me? *Yes, of course.* 5 Where's the lecture being held? *Over there, in room five.*
6 Where can I get a map of the area? *At the information desk over there.* 7 I was wondering if I could ask you something. *Sure.*

Go ahead. 8 I'm not sure if I understood your question. *Well, let me put it in another way.*
9 Maybe it would be better if we had a word afterwards. *OK.* 10 Would anyone like to ask a question? *Yes, I would.*

Exercise 14
Preparation, Participation and Communication.
Paul: What do you think is important that people understand about conferences before they go to an international one? What considerations should they keep in mind?
Bengt: First I think you have to realize what it is all about. What it is all about. Why are we travelling from various places to a certain spot to sit together? What will come out of it? What is my personal aspiration? What do I want to get out of this, to bring home to my work, to my colleagues? And I think you have to consider that before you enter an international conference.
Paul: But what about the practical considerations? I mean, what about travel and hotels and things?
Bengt: Yes. In some international conferences the conference centre takes care of all the practical arrangements. If it's not, you have to consider yourself (as) a travel agent and have to make all bookings and arrangements so you are there when you are supposed to be there. Could take some time if you are not used to it.
Paul: What about listening to other people? Have you thought about what makes it easier to listen to some people who use English as a lingua franca or a second language than others? Have you given that any thought?
Bengt: I mean, a language is one of the elements when you communicate. Another thing, you have to use your body and your imagination. And I think that is very important, even if you have (a) perfect English and you are not giving anything else... I don't think you communicate so very well and the opposite could work as well. You have to be flexible both with your language and the way you behave and the way you approach a conference; because if you should survive (a) one week of a lot of new contacts, with a lot of new food and a lot of drinks and a lot of information, I think you have to have some kind of flexibility.

Reg: Your colleagues spoke about congresses. /Yes./ What do you mean?
Widar: The moving industry is very much depending on establishing contacts with other moving companies in the world and the

meeting place are the congresses that are being organized by moving organizations in various places, countries, all over the world and several times a year. It's a very, very important meeting place for movers all over the world. We have about five to six different congresses every year, international congresses where moving companies like ours are attending. I was only one and a half month ago in Florida. There were 1,200 movers present, a big congress.

Reg: With that number of people there, how do you make that sort of contact with the right person?

Widar: No, you can't really... First of all you can't meet all, that's clear, and you have to make a selection of people and companies you want to and then you use the internal communication system in the hotel and say "I want to meet you down at the lobby at eight o'clock tomorrow", for instance. Or you find out other ways and it's just the smoothing you have to do during the cocktail parties and the receptions and so forth and you exchange your visiting cards and there are many ways... Then there are other smaller type congresses with only two hundred people - easier to get in touch with (the) more colleagues...

Kate: How important is social networking in conferences?

Delegate: I think it's extremely important, I think it's getting to be more important all the time. There's such an explosion of information available to us that I think no one person, no matter how diligent they are, can keep up with all of the publications being made around the world and so this is a way of being exposed in a fairly painless way to different approaches to the work. And so if I can network with those people I can maybe make suggestions on their work and they can surely make suggestions that I can use in my own work.

Kate: And what about when you attend social gatherings at a conference, a banquet or..., do you like to talk shop or are you there purely to enjoy yourself?

Delegate: I think there's a little bit of both... And I'm the type of person who enjoys myself most when I'm talking shop, so I have trouble separating those two things. I guess part of that would vary as a function of how I know the people... If it's someone that I've met before we'd probably have shared experiences and I'd like having the opportunity to socialize with those people. But I'm also the type of person who's sort of uncomfortable if I'm around a lot

of people I don't know anyone already and so it's always very safe to talk about work.

Kate: Thank you.

Delegate: You're welcome.

Unit 11 Thanks for the Information

3 Leave Your Clothes Here!
A 8 / B 1 / C 14 / D 11 / E 2 / F 6 / G 5

Exercise 4 Get Ready
These are only examples.
1 I'd just like to make sure that ... 2 I wonder if you could tell me ... 3 Yes. Definitely. / No. Definitely not. 4 I can't tell you off-hand, I'm afraid. 5 Sorry? What did you say? 6 I'm absolutely sure it does. 7 a: I should think so. 7 b: Probably not. 7 c: Well, it's possible, I suppose. 7 d: I doubt it. 8 I must admit, I don't know. 9 a: Sure. 9 b: I'm afraid you can't. 10 Excuse me, but I didn't quite catch your name.

Exercise 4 Phrase Practice
1 Excuse me, could you spare me a moment, please? 2 I wonder if you could give me some idea about the size of your company? 3 What exactly is your product range? 4 Is this model available in different colours? 5 Can you use it under water? 6 Can you use it in extreme temperatures? 7 Sorry, could you say that again, please? 8 Excuse me, may I test it? 9 How much does it cost? 10 Do you have any brochures I could have? 11 Could you send me some more information later, please? 12 Nice talking to you. Thank you so much.

Exercise 5 A Fair Letter?
Here is the information I promised you about the <u>fair</u> in Holland. As you can see, the <u>exhibition area</u> offers a variety of <u>exhibition halls</u> and even an <u>open air display area</u>. Altogether, there is nearly 300,000 square meters of <u>exhibition space</u>. Our stand is located in <u>hall</u> 5. We're particularly pleased with it because it has two <u>exhibition storeys</u> as well as a <u>conference room</u> for negotiations. In case you're thinking of visiting us I'm enclosing an <u>invitation card</u> so you won't have to pay to get in. The <u>admission fee</u> for the <u>general public</u> is 25 Guilders.

Exercise 14 Phrazy
Tapescript:
Receptionist: Central Hospital. Good morning. Can I help you?

Ruok: Yes. Could I speak to someone, please?
Receptionist: Um. With whom would you like to speak?
Ruok: Anyone at all. It doesn't matter.
Receptionist: Ah! Who shall I say is calling?
Ruok: Pardon?
Receptionist: Could I have your name, please?
Ruok: No. I'm afraid that's not possible.
Receptionist: Why's that?
Ruok: Well, it's my name and I'm not giving it to anyone.
Receptionist: I see. Well, if I don't know your name and you don't know who you want to talk to it's very difficult to help you.
Ruok: Really?
Receptionist: Yes.
Ruok: Oh, well, in that case. My name is Ruok.
Receptionist: I'm sorry. I wonder if you would repeat that for me, please?
Ruok: Oh, well, in that case. My name is Ruok.
Receptionist: Um. Could you spell it for me, please?
Ruok: Yes, of course. I could.
Receptionist: Well?
Ruok: Well what?
Receptionist: How do you spell your name please?
Ruok: R ... U ... O ... K.
Receptionist: R ..U.. O.. K?
Ruok: Yes, I'm fine, thanks.
Receptionist: (realizing she's got a right one here) Oh. Good. Now then, how can I help you. Mr Ruok?
Ruok: I would like to make an appointment.
Receptionist: With which doctor?
Ruok: No, I don't want a witch-doctor, thank you. Um (thinks) Do you have a psychiatric doctor there?
Receptionist: Dr Watt.
Ruok: (as if explaining) A pyschiatric doctor.
Receptionist: Yes - Dr Watt. Hold the line please. I'll put you through to him.
Dr Watt: Watt.
Receptionist: Hello, Doctor Watt. There's a Mr Ruok, on the line. He sounds a little strange. I think you had better talk to him.
Dr Watt: OK. Put him through. Hello, Mr Ruok?
Ruok: You have changed your voice, Ms Receptionist! Are you trying to be funny?
Dr Watt: No. This is Dr Watt speaking.
Ruok: Ah! Dr Watt. Why didn't you say so? Yes! Would it be possible to make an appointment with you?
Dr Watt: Um. Let me see. What day would be the most convenient?

Ruok: How about Sunday?
Dr Watt: Sorry. I don't work on Sundays.
Ruok: I'm very glad to hear that. I couldn't come either.
Dr Watt: Yes. Well, what day would suit you best?
Ruok: How about today?
Dr Watt: Mmm. What time?
Ruok: Three minutes past three?
Dr Watt: Suits me fine. Oh no. Wait a minute. I've got something else then.
Ruok: How about four minutes to four?
Dr Watt: Possible.
Ruok: Good. So, just to confirm. We're meeting in your surgery today at four minutes to four?
Dr Watt: Yes. Let's leave it like that.
Ruok: Look forward to meeting you then.
Dr Watt: Yes. Thanks for calling.

Narrator: A few hours later

Dr Watt: Come in. Ah! Mr Ruok? Pleased to meet you. Seat?
Ruok: I know that.
Dr Watt: Pardon?
Ruok: I can see it's a seat.
Dr Watt: Well, would you like to have a seat?
Ruok: No, thanks. I have nine of them at home.
Dr Watt: Would you like to sit down?
Ruok: Certainly not. I can't stand sitting.
Dr Watt: Fine. OK. Well, how can I help you?
Ruok: In any way you wish. I really don't mind.
Dr Watt: Well, what seems to be the trouble?
Ruok: (pause) Dr Evans. I take everything (dramatic pause) literally.
Dr Watt: Pardon me?
Ruok: What did you do?
Dr Watt: I beg your pardon?
Ruok: Why? What have you done wrong?
Dr Watt: Oh I see.
Ruok: Yes, I can see that you can see. But the question is what's wrong with me?
Dr Watt: Mr Ruok.
Ruok: That's correct.
Dr Watt: You are suffering from what we doctors call...'Phrasiness'.
Ruok: Are you trying to say I'm phrazy?
Dr Watt: I'm afraid so. When did all this start?
Ruok: Let me think. It must have been about a year ago. I had bought a copy of Working English and was on my way to work when I met an aquaintance. (fade out)

Narrator: This is where we find out how it all started.
Tom: Hello, Mickey. Good to see you again.

Ruok: Nice to see you again. How's it going?
Tom: Fine. You?
Ruok: Very well, thank you. How are you keeping?
Tom: Fine, as I said.
Ruok: Good. Well. How are things with you?
Tom: Not so bad.
Ruok: Great! Things are pretty good with me, too. You?
Tom: (tring to develop the conversation) It's been some time.
Ruok: Yes. How are you, by the way?
Tom: (gasp).
Ruok: Oh, I'm sorry. I can't quite remember your name.
Tom: Tom.
Ruok: Oh yes, of course; Tom! Well, how are things with you, Tom?
Tom: (groan) Sorry. I... um... really must be off now.
Ruok: Oh, look at the time. Well, I'd better be going, too.
Tom: Yes.
Ruok: Well, I really must be getting along. I can't stay any longer. But it's been marvellous running into you like this.
Tom: Absolutely.
Ruok: I must be getting along. Be seeing you!
Tom: Mm. Bye!
Ruok: OK. See you then! See you later! (fade out) See you around sometime, I hope...

Ruok: And that was the first time I noticed that people were looking at me in a strange way.
Dr Watt: Very interesting, Mr Ruok.
Ruok: Isn't it?
Dr Watt: And the next time?
Ruok: That was when I was a chairperson in a formal meeting I had great difficulties.
Dr Watt: Really?
Ruok: Yes. Well, I had been managing quite well until the end of the meeting.
Dr Watt: Then what happened?
Ruok: Well, we were going through the last item (fade) on the agenda and...

Ruok: Right. Well, perhaps we should take a formal vote on this. Could we put it to a vote? Yes? OK. Can we please move to vote on this? In other words, let's put it to a vote.
(grumble grumble)
Ruok: Those for the motion, please? Will those in favour of the motion raise their right hands? (pause) Six. Those against? None. Any abstentions? None. The motion has been carried by six votes to none. Are we all agreed on that?
(noises of approval)
Ruok: Good. The motion has been passed unanimously and the decision was unanimous.
voice: I beg your pardon.
voice: What's wrong with you?
Ruok: Yes, well it looks as if we're basically in agreement on this. Can I take it everyone's in favour?
voice: Get on with it!
Ruok: Is there any other business?
voice: No!
voice: Absolutely not!
Ruok: Any further points?
voice: Oh God!
Ruok: Is there anything else to discuss?
(People get up and leave, complaining)
Ruok: In that case, if nobody has any further business, I think we can conclude the meeting for today.
(Everyone has gone)
Ruok: (desperately) I declare this meeting closed.

Ruok: That was when I really noticed that I was in trouble. However, I still couldn't understand what I was doing wrong.
Dr Watt: When did you realize that?
Ruok: During some negotiations at work with some foreign clients. We had been negotiating for about three hours (fade) and things seemed to be going quite well when...
Client 1: Well, I agree with you on the whole but what about payments?
Ruok: What about them?
Client 2: Would twice a year be reasonable?
Ruok: Well, personally I think that isn't often enough.
Client 1: I respect your opinion, of course; however, I think twice a year really is enough.
Ruok: I feel I must disagree because I'm not sure I agree with you, you see. Four times a year would be reasonable.
Client 2: Well, I don't know about that. Don't you think twice a year is a fair deal, all things considered?
Client 1: Yes. I mean, you're getting quite a good deal.
Ruok: I'm sorry, but I totally disagree with you. (pause) No. I really can't agree with you on that.
Client 1: Really? (a bit shocked)
Ruok: Yes. I disagree entirely. Under no circumstances could I agree to that. What you're saying is just not feasible. To be frank, it's just plain silly.
Client 2: Is that so? (offended)

Ruok: Well, on the other hand, perhaps we could reach a compromise.

Client 1: We could? (amazed)

Ruok: How about three times a year? But only for the first two years. Then we could renegotiate.

Client 2: I'm in favour of that.

Client 1: Yes. We would have no objections to that. To meet you halfway on this, I think we could agree to your condition. After all, it's in both our interests.

Ruok: I totally agree because that's exactly my opinion. I think you're right and I agree with you completely.

Client 1: Good. (worried)

Ruok: Exactly. It is good because we are in complete agreement. I agree with you totally and you agree with me absolutely. We are in absolute and total agreement.

Client 2: (trying to calm things down) Yes. We <u>do</u> seem to have found a reasonable compromise.

Ruok: I couldn't agree more. Even if I tried (fade) . The reason is that I agree with you - both of you...

(Fade in)

Ruok: That was when I became aware that I was repeating myself. And saying the same thing twice or even more.

Dr Watt: That's typical of Phrasiness, all right.

Ruok: What am I going to do, doctor? Am I going to be phrazy for the rest of my life?

Dr Watt: Well, Mr Ruok...

Ruok: No, I'm not, Doctor Watt.

Dr Watt: Ah. (pressing on) There's nothing to worry about. It will go away after a while. Just relax and slowly you will find that you will start using and understanding phrases correctly.

Ruok: Are you sure, doctor?

Dr Watt: Absolutely. No doubt about it. Nothing to worry about.

Ruok: Oh, thank God for that. Oh! One more thing.

Dr Watt: Yes?

Ruok: Is it contagious?

Dr Watt: Contagious?

Ruok: Mm. Can other people catch Phrasiness from me?

Dr Watt: I understand what contagious means, Mr Ruok. I AM a doctor, you know.

Ruok: Yes. I heard about that.

Dr Watt: The answer is no. No way. Definitely not.

Ruok: I'm happy to hear that. Well, thank you very much, doctor.

Dr Watt: You're welcome. Glad to be of help.

Ruok: Right. Well, it's been nice talking to you.

Dr Watt: Yes. You too. Nice meeting you.

Ruok: Absolutely. Time to make a move, I suppose.

Dr Watt: Right... Well, it's time you were off, then. I don't want to keep you any longer than is necessary.

Ruok: Yes indeed. And I don't want to take up any more of your valuable time.

Dr Watt: Nice to have met you, Mr Ruok.

Ruok: You, too, doctor. Goodb...

Dr Watt: After all, time's money.

Ruok: Mmmm.

Dr Watt: And money doesn't grow on trees

Ruok: Yes. Well, I really must be going. You see,...

Dr Watt: Oh, don't let me keep you, please. People come in and out of here all the time. I'm used to saying goodbye to people.

Ruok: Dr Watt, I really must be off.

Dr Watt: (saddened) Bye, bye, then.

Ruok: Bye.

Dr Watt: Well, you're off then. See you again some time.

Ruok: Yes. (getting exasperated)

(Ruok starts to leave, moving out the door)

Dr Watt: (shouts) See you around!

(Ruok is walking away briskly)

Ruok: You too! (trying to get away)

Dr Watt: Goodbye!

(Dr Watt is pursuing his patient)

Dr Watt: Take care!

Dr Watt: So long !

Dr Watt: Bye for now!

Ruok: Mm (more a groan than anything else).

Dr Watt: Auf Wiedersehen as they say in Germany. (manic)

(Ruok is running, trying to escape the phrasey doctor.We fade out, hearing Dr Watt screaming...)

Dr Watt: Au revoir as they say in France! Ciao!.
Adios!
Da svidanija!
Cheerio!
Farewell!

ENGLISCH-DEUTSCHES WÖRTERVERZEICHNIS

* = Das Endungs-r wird gesprochen, wenn das folgende Wort mit einem Vokal beginnt.

Am.	= amerikanisches Englisch	*j-n*	= jemanden
		sl.	= slang
Brit.	= britisches Englisch	*s.o.*	= someone
		s.th.	= something
etw.	= etwas	*tel.:*	= Telefon
j-m	= jemandem	*vulg.*	= vulgar

A

ability [ə'biliti]   Fähigkeit
able ['eibl]   fähig
abortion [ə'bɔ:ʃn]   Abtreibung
abroad [ə'brɔ:d]   im/ins Ausland
absence ['æbsəns]   Abwesenheit
absent ['æbsənt]   nicht anwesend
absolutely ['æbsəlu:tli]   absolut, völlig
abstention [əb'stenʃn]   Stimmenthaltung
acceptance   Annahme
 [ək'septəns]
accidentally   zufällig
 [æksi'dentəli]
accommodation   Unterkunft
 [ə,kɔmə'deiʃn]
according to [ə'kɔ:diŋ]   entsprechend
accordingly [ə'kɔ:diŋli]   entsprechend
account [ə'kaunt]   Beschreibung,
                                 Bericht; Konto
accountant   Buchprüfer(in);
 [ə'kauntənt]   Steuerberater(in)
accounting   Buchhaltung,
 [ə'kauntiŋ]   -führung
accounts manager   Leiter(in) der
 [ə'kaunts ,mænidʒə*]   Rechnungsstelle
accurate ['ækjurit]   richtig
achieve [ə'tʃi:v]   erreichen
acquaintance   Bekannte(r)
 [ə'kweintəns]
acquainted: become   kennenlernen
acquainted with
 [ə'kweintid]
acquire [ə'kwaiə*]   sich aneignen,
                                 erwerben
actual ['æktʃuəl]   eigentlich
actually ['æktʃuəli]   tatsächlich
ad [æd]   Anzeige, Inserat
adapt [ə'dæpt]   anpassen
add [æd]   hinzufügen

adequate ['ædikwət]   angemessen
adjourn [ə'dʒə:n]   vertagen
adjust to [ə'dʒʌst]   sich gewöhnen an
admission [əd'miʃn]   Eintritt
advance: in advance   vorher
 [əd'va:ns]
advanced [əd'va:nst]   fortgeschritten
advantage   Vorteil
 [əd'va:ntidʒ]
 take advantage of   ausnutzen; (sexuell)
 [əd'va:ntidʒ]   mißbrauchen
advent ['ædvənt]   Aufkommen
advertise ['ædvətaiz]   anbieten
advertisement   Anzeige
 [æd'və:tismənt]
advertising   Werbung
 ['ædvətaiziŋ]
advisor [əd'vaizə*]   Berater(in)
advisory [əd'vaizəri]   beratend
affirmative   bejahend
 [ə'fə:mətiv]
agency ['eidʒənsi]   Vertretung
agenda [ə'dʒendə]   Tagesordnung
agitated ['ædʒiteitid]   aufgeregt
agreeable [ə'gri:əbl]   angenehm
agreement [ə'gri:mənt]   Einwilligung
ahead [ə'hed]   vorn; voraus;
                                 bevorstehend
aim [eim]   Ziel
 aim at   darauf abzielen
aircraft ['ɛəkrɑ:ft]   Flugzeug
all-encompassing   allumfassend
 [ɔ:lin'kʌmpəsiŋ]
allow [ə'lau]   gestatten
alter ['ɔ:ltə*]   (ab)ändern
alternative   Alternative
 [ɔ:l'tə:nətiv]
alternatively   oder (aber)
 [ɔ:l'tə:nətivli]
amazing [ə'meiziŋ]   erstaunlich
amount [ə'maunt]   Betrag
ample ['æmpl]   reichlich
amused [ə'mju:zd]   amüsiert
ancient ['einʃənt]   alt
anecdote ['ænikdəut]   Anekdote
anguished ['æŋgwiʃt]   qualvoll
announce [ə'nauns]   bekanntgeben
answerphone   Anrufbeantworter
 ['ɑ:nsəfəun]
anthropologist   Anthropologe
 [,ænθrə'pɔlədʒist]
anticipate [æn'tisipeit]   voraussehen
apart from [ə'pɑ:t]   außer
apologetic   zurückhaltend
 [ə,pɔlə'dʒetik]
appealing [ə'pi:liŋ]   ansprechend
appear [ə'piə*]   erscheinen

appearance [əˈpiərəns]	Aussehen
application [ˌæpliˈkeiʃn]	Bewerbung
apply [əˈplai]	anwenden, verwenden; (for) sich bewerben
apply oneself to [əˈplai]	sich Mühe geben mit
appoint [əˈpɔint]	ernennen
appointment [əˈpɔintmənt]	Termin
appreciate [əˌpriːʃieit]	zu schätzen wissen
appreciation [əˌpriːʃiˈeiʃn]	Dankbarkeit
approach [əˈprəutʃ]	Annäherungsversuch; Vorstoß; ansprechen; zugehen auf
appropriate [əˈprəupriət]	angemessen
approximate [əˈprɔksimət]	ungefähr
approximately [əˈprɔksimitli]	ungefähr
archive [ˈɑːkaiv]	Archiv
argue [ˈɑːgjuː]	streiten
argument [ˈɑːgjumənt]	Argument
arise, arose, arisen [əˈraiz, əˈrəuz, əˈrizən]	entstehen; sich erheben
arrangement [əˈreindʒmənt]	Vereinbarung
arrangements	Pläne
arrow [ˈærəu]	Pfeil
as if	als ob
as to	bezüglich
aspect [ˈæspekt]	Aspekt
ass [æs]	Esel; Am. sl. Arsch
assembly [əˈsembli]	Versammlung
assessment [əˈsesmənt]	Auswertung
assistance [əˈsistəns]	Hilfe
associate [əˈsəuʃiət]	Partner(in)
associated with [əˈsəuʃieit]	in Verbindung mit
association [əˌsəuʃiˈeiʃn]	Gedankenverbindung, Assoziation
assume [əˈsjuːm]	annehmen
atmosphere [ˈætməsfiə*]	Atmosphäre
Att = attention [əˈtenʃn]	zu Händen von, z. Hd.
attempt [əˈtempt]	Versuch
attend [əˈtend]	teilnehmen an
attend to [əˈtend]	sich widmen
attention [əˈtenʃn]	Aufmerksamkeit
pay attention to	achten auf
attentive [əˈtentiv]	aufmerksam
attitude [ˈætitjuːd]	Einstellung

attract [əˈtrækt]	anziehen
attractive [əˈtræktiv]	attraktiv
audience [ˈɔːdiəns]	Publikum, Zuhörer
author [ˈɔːθə*]	Autor
authorities [ɔːˈθɔritiz]	Behörden
available: be available [əˈveiləbl]	zur Verfügung stehen; erreichbar sein
aversion [əˈvəːʃn]	Abneigung
avoid [əˈvɔid]	vermeiden
award [əˈwɔːd]	gewähren, zusprechen; Preis
aware: be aware [əˈwɛə*]	sich bewußt sein
awareness [əˈwɛənis]	Bewußtsein
awkwardness [ˈɔːkwədnis]	Peinlichkeit
axis [ˈæksis]	Achse

B

back-pack [ˈbækpæk]	Rucksack
background [ˈbækgraund]	Hintergrund
bake [beik]	backen
ballot [ˈbælət]	Wahl; Abstimmung
ban [bæn]	verbieten
bankrupt: go bankrupt [ˈbæŋkrʌpt]	Bankrott machen
banquet [ˈbæŋkwit]	Bankett
bar chart [ˈbɑːtʃɑːt]	Balkendiagramm
bare [bɛə*]	bloß, nackt
bargaining [ˈbɑːginiŋ]	Handeln
bartender [ˈbɑːˌtendə*]	Barkeeper
basic [ˈbeisik]	wesentlich
basis [ˈbeisis]	Basis; Haupt-, wesentlich
bear hug [ˈbɛə hʌg]	kräftige Umarmung
bear with [bɛə*]	Nachsicht haben mit
beat [biːt]	schlagen
beckon [ˈbekən]	zu sich winken
behalf: on behalf of [biˈhɑːf]	im Namen (von)
benefit [ˈbenifit]	Nutzen, Vorteil; profitieren
bet [bet]	Wette
beware [biˈwɛə*]	Vorsicht!
bewildered [biˈwildəd]	verwirrt
bid [bid]	bieten
bill [bil]	Rechnung
bimbo [ˈbimbəu]	"Puppe", "Hase"
blade [bleid]	Klinge
blame s.o. [bleim]	j-m die Schuld geben
blank [blæŋk]	leer

block [blɔk]	blockieren		**cause** [kɔ:z]	verursachen
bluntly ['blʌntli]	unverblümt		**caution** ['kɔ:ʃn]	Vorsicht
board [bɔ:d]	Aufsichtsrat		**cc = cubic centimetre**	Kubikzentimeter
body ['bɔdi]	Körper		['kju:bik 'senti,mi:tə]	
body language	Körpersprache		**cellar** ['selə*]	Keller
['bɔdi ,læŋgwidʒ]			**cellular mobile**	Funktelefon
boil [bɔil]	kochen		**telephone** ['seljulə	
bonus: (Christmas)	(Weihnachts-)		'məubail 'telifəun]	
bonus	Gratifikation		**cemetery** ['semitri]	Friedhof
['bəunəs]			**certainty** ['sə:tənti]	Gewißheit
bottom out ['bɔtəm]	die Talsohle erreichen		**chair** *(a meeting)*	den Vorsitz haben bei
brand [brænd]	Marke		[tʃɛə*]	
breakdown	Zusammenbruch;		**chair = chairman,**	
['breikdaun]	Aufschlüsselung,		**chairwoman**	
	Übersicht		**chairman** ['tʃɛəmən]	Vorsitzender
brewer ['bru:ə*]	Brauer		**chairwoman**	Vorsitzende
brief [bri:f]	kurz;		['tʃɛəwumən]	
	Kurzdarstellung		**challenge** ['tʃælindʒ]	Herausforderung,
briefly ['bri:fli]	kurz, knapp			Aufgabe
broaden ['brɔ:dn]	erweitern		**challenger**	Herausforderer
brochure ['brəuʃə*]	Prospekt, Broschüre		['tʃælindʒə*]	
bubble ['bʌbl]	Blase;		**chambermaid**	Zimmermädchen
	sprudeln		['tʃeimbəmeid]	
bulk [bʌlk]	Großteil		**chance** [tʃa:ns]	zufällig
bum [bʌm]	Hintern		**chant** [tʃa:nt]	im Chor ausrufen
burgle ['bə:gl]	einbrechen		**charge** [tʃa:dʒ]	berechnen
bury ['beri]	beerdigen		**charge: be in charge of**	verantwortlich sein
buzz off [bʌz]	abhauen		[tʃa:dʒ]	für, leiten
			chart [tʃa:t]	Schaubild
			chassis ['ʃæsi]	Chassis
C			**chauvinistic**	chauvinistisch
			[,ʃəuvi'nistik]	
			chef [ʃef]	Koch
cabinet ['kæbinit]	Kabinett		**cherry** ['tʃeri]	Kirsche
caffeine ['kæfi:n]	Koffein		**chop** [tʃɔp]	hacken
call for [kɔ:l]	verlangen		**cinnamon** ['sinəmən]	Zimt
calm [ka:m]	still		**circulate** ['sə:kjuleit]	in Umlauf bringen
can [kæn]	Dose, Büchse		**circumstances**	Umstände
cancel ['kænsl]	annullieren		['sə:kəmstənsiz]	
candidate ['kændidət]	Kandidat(in)		**under the**	unter den gegebenen
canteen [kæn'ti:n]	Kantine		**circumstances**	Umständen
capacity [kə'pæsiti]	Funktion		**claim** [kleim]	für sich in Anspruch
car body ['ka: ,bɔdi]	Karosserie			nehmen
carbohydrate	Kohlenhydrat		**clap** [klæp]	klatschen
[,ka:bəu'haidreit]			**clarification**	Klarstellung
career [kə'riə*]	Karriere		[klærifi'keiʃn]	
carpet ['ka:pit]	Teppich		**clarify** ['klærifai]	klarstellen
carpeting ['ka:pitiŋ]	Teppichboden		**clarity** ['klæriti]	Klarheit
carrier ['kæriə*]	Bote, Botin;		**classify** ['klæsifai]	einstufen
	Spediteur		**clerk** [kla:k]	Büroangestellte(r),
carry: the motion is	der Antrag ist			Sachbearbeiter(in)
carried ['kærid]	angenommen		**client** ['klaiənt]	Kunde, Kundin
carry out	ausführen		**climate** ['klaimit]	Klima
cashier [kæ'ʃiə*]	Kassierer(in)		**clinch** [klintʃ]	zum Abschluß
casting vote	ausschlaggebende			bringen, perfekt
['ka:stiŋ vəut]	Stimme			machen
casual ['kæʒjuəl]	zwanglos		**clockwise** ['klɔkwaiz]	im Uhrzeigersinn

clue [klu:]	Anhaltspunkt	
cock [kɔk]	(Wasser)Hahn;	
	sl. Schwanz (Penis)	
coherent [kəu'hiərənt]	zusammenhängend	
column ['kɔləm]	Spalte	
combination	Kombination	
[kɔmbi'neiʃn]		
come up with	vorbringen	
[kʌm 'ʌp wið]		
command [kə'mɑ:nd]	Beherrschung	
commercial [kə'mə:ʃl]	Handels-, Wirtschafts-	
committed [kə'mitid]	engagiert	
committee [kə'miti]	Komitee, Ausschuß	
commonplace	alltäglich, an der	
['kɔmənpleis]	Tagesordnung	
communicate	mitteilen;	
[kə'mju:nikeit]	sich verständigen	
communication	Kommunikation,	
[kə,mju:ni'keiʃn]	Verständigung	
communicative	kommunikativ	
[kə'mju:nikətiv]		
community	Gemeinde	
[kə'mju:niti]		
commute [kə'mju:t]	pendeln	
compensation	Entschädigung	
[,kɔmpen'seiʃn]		
compete [kəm'pi:t]	konkurrieren	
competitive	wettbewerbsfähig	
[kəm'petitiv]		
competitor	Konkurrent	
[kəm'petitə*]		
complain	sich beklagen,	
[kəm'plein]	sich beschweren	
complaint [kəm'pleint]	Beschwerde	
complete [kəm'pli:t]	vollständig;	
	beenden	
completely	völlig	
[kəm'pli:tli]		
compliment	Kompliment, Lob	
['kɔmplimənt]		
component	Bestandteil	
[kəm'pəunənt]		
composer	Komponist	
[kəm'pəuzə*]		
comprehensive	umfassend	
[,kɔmpri'hensiv]		
compressed air	Druckluft	
[kəm'prest 'ɛə*]		
comprise [kəm'praiz]	umfassen	
concentrate on	das Interesse	
['kɔnsəntreit]	richten auf	
concept ['kɔnsept]	Idee, Vorstellung	
concerned: as far as	was ... anbetrifft	
... is concerned		
[kən'sə:nd]		
concise [kən'sais]	kurz und prägnant	
conclude [kən'klu:d]	beschließen	

conclusion [kən'klu:ʒn]	Schluß	
concrete ['kɔŋkri:t]	konkret	
conditions [kən'diʃnz]	Bedingungen	
confer [kən'fə:*]	konferieren	
confident ['kɔnfidənt]	vertrauensvoll	
confirm [kən'fə:m]	bestätigen	
confirmation	Bestätigung	
[,kɔnfə'meiʃn]		
confused [kən'fju:zd]	verwirrt	
conical ['kɔnikl]	konisch,	
	spitz zulaufend	
conscience ['kɔnʃəns]	Gewissen	
conscientious	gewissenhaft	
[,kɔnʃi'enʃəs]		
consensus [kən'sensəs]	Konsens, Einigkeit	
consequence	Konsequenz, Folge	
['kɔnsikwəns]		
be of no consequence	unerheblich sein	
['kɔnsikwəns]		
consider [kən'sidə*]	ansehen, betrachten;	
	überlegen, bedenken	
consideration	Überlegung	
[kən,sidə'reiʃn]		
consist of [kən'sist]	bestehen aus	
constantly ['kɔnstəntli]	dauernd	
consult [kən'sʌlt]	konsultieren	
consume [kən'sju:m]	verzehren	
consumption	Konsum	
[kən'sʌmpʃn]		
contact ['kɔntækt]	sich in Verbindung	
	setzen mit	
contain [kən'tein]	enthalten	
contemplative	besinnlich	
[kən'templətiv]		
continent ['kɔntinənt]	Kontinent	
continental:		
continental	kleines Frühstück	
breakfast		
['kɔnti,nentl]		
contract ['kɔntrækt]	Vertrag	
contractor	Bauunternehmer	
[kən'træktə*]		
convenient	passend, günstig	
[kən'vi:njənt]		
conventional	(allgemein) üblich	
[kən'venʃənəl]		
convey [kən'vei]	vermitteln	
convincing [kən'vinsiŋ]	überzeugend	
cooperation	Zusammenarbeit	
[kəu,ɔpə'reiʃn]		
cord [kɔ:d]	Schnur	
cordial ['kɔ:diəl]	herzlich	
core [kɔ:*]	Kerngehäuse	
corridor ['kɔridɔ:*]	Gang	
cost-effective	rentabel	
['kɔsti,fektiv]		
counterfeit	gefälscht	
['kauntəfit]		

courageous [kə'reidʒəs]	mutig		deliver [di'livə*]	liefern
courtesy ['kə:tisi]	Höflichkeit		delivery [di'livəri]	Lieferung
cover sheet ['kʌvə ʃi:t]	Deckblatt		demand [di'ma:nd]	erfordern; Nachfrage
create [kri'eit]	machen		meet the demand	die Nachfrage befriedigen
creature ['kri:tʃə*]	Wesen			
crime [kraim]	Verbrechen		demon ['di:mən]	Teufel
cross [krɔs]	Kreuz		demonstrate ['demənstreit]	veranschaulichen
cross-cultural ['krɔs,kʌltʃərəl]	interkulturell		demonstration [,demən'streiʃn]	Vorführung
crossed: keep one's fingers crossed [krɔst]	die Daumen drücken		departure [di'pa:tʃə*]	Abfahrt
			depend on [di'pend]	abhängen von
crossing ['krɔsiŋ]	Überfahrt		depth [depθ]	Tiefe
crowded ['kraudid]	überfüllt		description [di'skripʃn]	Beschreibung
crucial ['kru:ʃl]	entscheidend			
cubic ['kju:bik]	würfelförmig		design [di'zain]	konstruieren
culminate ['kʌlmineit]	gipfeln		desire [di'zaiə*]	Wunsch
current ['kʌrənt]	aktuell; laufend		desperate ['despərit]	verzweifelt
curve [kə:v]	Kurve		despite [di'spait]	trotz
custom ['kʌstəm]	Brauch		destination [,desti'neiʃn]	Ziel
cutlery ['kʌtləri]	Besteck			
cycle ['saikl]	Zyklus, Kreislauf		destroy [di'strɔi]	vernichten
			detail ['di:teil]	Detail, einzelner Punkt
			detailed ['di:teild]	eingehend
D			develop [di'veləp]	entwickeln
			development [di'veləpmənt]	Entwicklung
daily ['deili]	täglich		device [di'vais]	Mittel
dam [dæm]	Damm		dictate [dik'teit]	diktieren
dash [dæʃ]	rennen, stürzen; Schuß		digress [dai'gres]	abschweifen
			dilemma [di'lemə]	Dilemma
daughter-in-law ['dɔ:tərinlɔ:]	Schwiegertochter		dim [dim]	dämpfen
deal [di:l]	Handel		dimension [di'menʃn]	Dimension, (Aus)Maß
a big deal	eine große Sache		diner ['dainə*]	Speisende(r)
deal with [di:l]	sich befassen mit		dip [dip]	eintauchen
debate [di'beit]	Debatte		disadvantage [,disəd'va:ntidʒ]	Nachteil
declare [di'klɛə*]	erklären			
decline [di'klain]	ablehnen		disagreeable [,disə'griəbl]	unangenehm
decrease [di'kri:s]	abnehmen			
dedicate to ['dedikeit]	widmen		disagreement [,disə'gri:mənt]	Uneinigkeit
dedicated ['dedikeitid]	engagiert			
defeat: be defeated [di'fi:tid]	abgelehnt werden		disbelief [,disbi'li:f]	Ungläubigkeit
			discount ['diskaunt]	Rabatt
defer [di'fə:*]	aufschieben		discover [di'skʌvə*]	entdecken
define [di'fain]	definieren		discreet [di'skri:t]	diskret
definitely ['definitli]	auf jeden Fall		disgusting [dis'gʌstiŋ]	ekelhaft
definition [,defi'niʃn]	Definition		dish [diʃ]	Gericht
degree [di'gri:]	Grad		dismantle [dis'mæntl]	abbauen
delay [di'lei]	Verspätung		display [di'splei]	Ausstellung
delegate ['deligit]	Konferenzteilnehmer(in)		on display [di'splei]	aufgestellt
			dispute [di'spju:t]	Streit
deliberately [di'libəritli]	absichtlich		distribute [di'stribju:t]	verteilen
delicacy ['delikəsi]	Delikatesse, Leckerbissen		distribution [,distri'bju:ʃn]	Vertrieb

disturbance [di'stə:bəns]	Störung
divide [di'vaid]	teilen
documentation [ˌdɔkjumen'teiʃn]	Dokumentation
dogmatic [dɔg'mætik]	dogmatisch
domestic [də'mestik]	der privaten Haushalte
dominate ['dɔmineit]	beherrschen
dot [dɔt]	Pünktchen
dozens of ['dʌznz]	Dutzende von
drip [drip]	Tropfen
due to [dju:]	wegen
duty ['dju:ti]	Pflicht
dwarf [dwɔ:f]	Zwerg

E

eager ['i:gə*]	eifrig
earphones ['iəfəunz]	Kopfhörer
ease [i:z]	(Wohl)Behagen
eavesdrop ['i:vzdrɔp]	heimlich lauschen
edge [edʒ]	Kante
edgewise: not get a word in edgewise ['edʒwaiz]	kaum zu Wort kommen
editorial [ˌedi'tɔ:riəl]	Verlags-
effect [i'fekt]	Wirkung
come into effect	zum Tragen kommen
something to that effect	etwas in diesem Sinne
effective [i'fektiv]	effektiv
effectiveness [i'fektivnis]	Effektivität
efficient [i'fiʃənt]	effizient
elderly ['eldəli]	älter
elect [i'lekt]	wählen
embarrassed [im'bærəst]	verlegen
embarrassing [im'bærəsiŋ]	peinlich
embarrassment [im'bærəsmənt]	Verlegenheit
embezzler [im'bezlə*]	Veruntreuer(in)
embrace [im'breis]	umarmen
emerge [i'mə:dʒ]	hervorgehen aus
emergency landing [i'mə:dʒənsi ˌlændiŋ]	Notlandung
empathetic [ˌempə'θetik]	einfühlsam
emphasis ['emfəsis]	Schwergewicht
employee [ˌemplɔi'i:]	Angestellte(r)
enable [in'eibl]	ermöglichen
enact [in'ækt]	spielen

enclose [in'kləuz]	beilegen
enclosure [in'kləuʒə*]	Anlage
encourage [in'kʌridʒ]	fördern
end-user ['end ˌju:zə*]	Endverbraucher
engaged [in'geidʒd]	beschäftigt; tel.: besetzt
engaged to [in'geidʒd]	verlobt mit
engagement [in'geidʒmənt]	Verabredung
engineer [ˌendʒi'niə*]	Ingenieur(in)
enquire [in'kwaiə*]	fragen
ensure [in'ʃuə*]	gewährleisten
entail [in'teil]	mit sich bringen, zur Folge haben
enter: enter into conversation with ['entə*]	ein Gespräch beginnen mit
enthusiastic [in,θju:zi'æstik]	begeistert
entire [in'taiə*]	gesamt
environment [in'vairənmənt]	Umwelt
environmental [in,vairən'mentl]	Umwelt-
equal ['i:kwəl]	gleich
equality [i'kwɔliti]	Gleichberechtigung
equip: be equipped with [i'kwipt]	verfügen über
equipment [i'kwipmənt]	Ausstattung
erection [i'rekʃn]	Aufbau
error ['erə*]	Fehler
essential [i'senʃl]	entscheidend
the bare essentials	das Allernotwendigste
establish [i'stæbliʃ]	schaffen, bilden
estimated ['estimeitid]	geschätzt
evasion [i'veiʒn]	Hinterziehung
even if ['i:vn if]	wenn auch
event: in the event of [i'vent]	im Falle
eventually [i'ventʃuəli]	schließlich
evident ['evidənt]	offensichtlich
exactly [ig'zæktli]	genau
exceptional(ly) [ik'sepʃənəl]	außergewöhnlich
excited [ik'saitid]	aufgeregt
exclusive [ik'sklu:siv]	Allein-
executive [ig'zekjutiv]	leitende(r) Angestellte(r)
executive director [ig'zekjutiv di'rektə*]	geschäftsführende(r) Direktor(in)
exhibition [ˌeksi'biʃn]	Ausstellung
expect [ik'spekt]	erwarten
expenses [ik'spensiz]	Kosten
experience [ik'spiəriəns]	Erfahrung

expertise [ˌekspə'tiːz]	Sachkenntnis
explanation [ˌeksplə'neiʃn]	Erklärung
explode [ik'spləud]	(heraus)platzen
express [ik'spres]	ausdrücken
expression [ik'spreʃn]	Ausdruck
facial expression [ˌfeiʃl ik'spreʃn]	Gesichtsausdruck
extended [ik'stendid]	erweitert, vergrößert
extent [ik'stent]	Ausmaß
to a large extent [ik'stent]	weitgehend
extract ['ekstrækt]	Auszug
extremely [ik'striːmli]	äußerst
extrovert ['ekstrəvəːt]	extrovertiert

F

facilities [fə'silitiz]	Einrichtungen
fact: in fact [fækt]	tatsächlich
fade away [feid]	nachlassen
fair [fɛə*]	Messe
fairly ['fɛəli]	ziemlich, recht
fake [feik]	vortäuschen
familiar: be familiar with [fə'miliə*]	können, beherrschen
familiarity [fə,mili'æriti]	Vertrautheit
fanny ['fæni]	*Am. sl.* Po; *Brit. vulg.* Möse
fault [fɔːlt]	Fehler
faux pas [fəu'paː]	Fauxpas, Schnitzer
favoured ['feivəd]	beliebt
feasible ['fiːzəbl]	durchführbar
feature ['fiːtʃə*]	Merkmal; darstellen
fee [fiː]	Gebühr, Honorar
feed [fiːd]	eingeben
fiancé [fi'aːnsei]	Verlobter
fiddle ['fidl]	*sl.* Gaunerei
fiddle with	herumspielen mit
figure: put a figure on ['figə*]	zahlenmäßig festlegen
file [fail]	Akte
filing cabinet ['failiŋ ˌkæbinit]	Aktenschrank
filthy ['filθi]	schmutzig, dreckig
final ['fainəl]	Schluß-
finale [fi'naːli]	Finale
finally ['fainəli]	zum Schluß
finance [fai'næns]	finanzieren
financial [fai'nænʃl]	finanziell
financial director [fai'nænʃl di'rektə*]	Leiter(in) der Finanzabteilung
finish: finish ahead of s.o. ['finiʃ]	vor j-m liegen

finish behind s.o.	hinter j-m liegen
firm [fəːm]	fest
fit [fit]	passen in
fizz [fiz]	Fizz (*Mixgetränk*)
fizzy ['fizi]	sprudelnd
flatten ['flætn]	plattdrücken
flexibility [ˌfleksə'biliti]	Flexibilität
flexible ['fleksəbl]	flexibel
flight [flait]	Flug
floor [flɔː*]	(Fuß)Boden; Stockwerk
florist's ['florists]	Blumengeschäft
flow [fləu]	fließen
flowery ['flauəri]	blumig
fluent ['fluːənt]	fließend
fluid ['fluːid]	Flüssigkeit
fly [flai]	Fliege
focal point ['fəukəl pɔint]	Mittelpunkt
focus on ['fəukəs]	sich konzentrieren auf
fold [fəuld]	Falte
-fold [fəuld]	-fach
follow-up ['fɔləuʌp]	Nachfolgeaktivitäten
fore: to the fore [fɔː*]	in den Vordergrund
forecast ['fɔːkaːst]	voraussagen
forgery ['fɔːdʒəri]	Fälschung
fork [fɔːk]	Gabel
formality [fɔː'mæliti]	Formalität
format ['fɔːmæt]	Aufbau
formation [fɔː'meiʃn]	Bildung
former: the former ['fɔːmə*]	der/die/das erstere
fortunately ['fɔːtʃənitli]	glücklicherweise, zum Glück
franchise ['fræntʃaiz]	Wahlrecht
frank [fræŋk]	offen
fraud [frɔːd]	Betrug
frenzy ['frenzi]	Raserei
frequent ['friːkwənt]	üblich
frequently ['friːkwəntli]	häufig
frog [frɔg]	Frosch
front: up front [ʌp 'frʌnt]	im voraus
frown [fraun]	Stirnrunzeln
frustrated [frʌ'streitid]	frustriert
fry [frai]	braten
function ['fʌŋkʃn]	fungieren
fund [fʌnd]	Fonds
fundamental [ˌfʌndə'mentl]	grundlegend
funding ['fʌndiŋ]	Finanzierung
furniture: piece of furniture ['fəːnitʃə*]	Möbelstück
further ['fəːðə*]	weitere

G

gap [gæp] — Kluft
general outline — allgemeiner Entwurf
[,dʒenərəl 'autlain]
generate ['dʒenəreit] — führen zu; erzeugen
genius ['dʒi:niəs] — Genie
gently ['dʒentli] — behutsam
gesture ['dʒestʃə*] — Geste
giant ['dʒaiənt] — riesig, Riesen-
gift [gift] — Geschenk
gifted ['giftid] — begabt
glimpse [glimps] — Einblick
global ['gləubl] — global
goal [gəul] — Ziel
gossip ['gɔsip] — Klatsch
governmental — Regierungs-
[,gʌvən'mentl]
gracious ['greiʃəs] — wohlwollend
grading ['greidiŋ] — Benotung
gradual ['grædʒuəl] — allmählich
graduate student — Hochschulabsolvent
['grædʒuit 'stju:dənt]
grant [grɑ:nt] — bewilligen, gewähren
granted: take s.th. for — etw. für selbstver-
granted ['grɑ:ntid] — ständlich halten
graph [grɑ:f] — Schaubild
grate [greit] — raspeln
graveyard ['greivjɑ:d] — Friedhof
ground [graund] — Grundlage
guarantee — Garantie;
[,gærən'ti:] — garantieren
guts [gʌts] — Mumm, Power
gymnasium — Turnhalle
[dʒim'neiziəm]

H

halo ['heiləu] — Heiligenschein
hand: on the other — andererseits
hand
handkerchief — Taschentuch
['hæŋkətʃif]
hand-out ['hændaut] — Handzettel, Presse-,
Reklamezettel
hang up [hæŋ 'ʌp] — tel.: auflegen,
aufhängen
hang-gliding — Drachenfliegen
['hæŋ,glaidiŋ]
hanger ['hæŋə*] — Kleiderbügel
harbour ['hɑ:bə*] — Hafen
harmless ['hɑ:mlis] — harmlos
health [helθ] — Gesundheit
heat [hi:t] — Hitze
hedgehog ['hedʒhɔg] — Igel

height [hait] — Höhe
hence [hens] — daher
hesitant ['hezitənt] — zögernd
hesitate ['heziteit] — zögern
hesitation [,hezi'teiʃn] — Zögern
highly ['haili] — höchst, äußerst
hijack ['haidʒæk] — entführen
hint [hint] — Hinweis
hit on [hit] — finden
honey ['hʌni] — Honig
horizontal [,hɔri'zɔntl] — waagerecht
hors d'oeuvre — Vorspeise
[ɔ:'də:vrə]
hospitality — Gastfreundschaft
[,hɔspi'tæliti]
host [həust] — Gastgeber
host: a host of [həust] — eine Fülle von
hostess ['həustis] — Gastgeberin
household ['haushəuld] — Haushalt
housing ['hauziŋ] — Wohnungssituation
hug [hʌg] — umarmen
huge ['hju:dʒ] — riesig, gewaltig
humble ['hʌmbl] — bescheiden
humidifier — Befeuchter
[hju:'midifaiə*]
humility [hju:'militi] — Bescheidenheit
hunting ['hʌntiŋ] — das Jagen
hydro-electric — hydroelektrisch
[,haidrəui'lektrik]
hydro-electricity — durch Wasserkraft
[,haidrəuilek'trisiti] — erzeugte Energie

I

i.e. = that is — d. h.
ideal [ai'diəl] — ideal
identification: means — Ausweispapiere
of identification
[ai,dentifi'keiʃn]
identify oneself — seinen Namen
[ai'dentifai] — nennen
identity [ai'dentiti] — Identität
idle ['aidl] — faul
ignorance ['ignərəns] — Unkenntnis
illegal [i'li:gl] — illegal
imaginary — erdacht
[i'mædʒinəri]
immediately — sofort
[i'mi:diətli]
impatient [im'peiʃənt] — ungeduldig
imply [im'plai] — beinhalten,
implizieren
impractical — undurchführbar
[im'præktikəl]
impression [im'preʃn] — Eindruck

impropriety [ˌimprə'praiəti]	Unanständigkeit
include [in'klu:d]	mit einbeziehen; einschließen
increase [in'kri:s]	zunehmen, (an)wachsen, steigen;
['iŋkri:s]	Zuwachs, Erhöhung
increasingly [in'kri:siŋli]	immer häufiger
incredible [in'kredəbl]	unglaublich
indicate ['indikeit]	hinweisen
indigestion [ˌindi'dʒestʃn]	Magenverstimmung
indirectness [ˌindi'rektnəs]	Indirektheit
inevitable [in'evitəbl]	unvermeidlich
inflexibility [inˌfleksə'biliti]	mangelnde Flexibilität
influence ['influəns]	beeinflussen
inform [in'fɔ:m]	informieren
informative [in'fɔ:mətiv]	lehrreich
ingenuity [ˌindʒi'nju:iti]	Einfallsreichtum
innocently ['inəsntli]	in aller Unschuld
inquire [in'kwaiə*]	sich erkundigen
insensitive [in'sensitiv]	gefühllos
insert [in'sə:t]	inserieren
insight ['insait]	Einblick
insignificant [ˌinsig'nifikənt]	geringfügig
insist on [in'sist]	bestehen auf
install [in'stɔ:l]	installieren, (an)legen
instant ['instənt]	sofortig
instant coffee ['instənt ˌkɔfi]	Pulverkaffee
instruct [in'strʌkt]	anweisen
instrumental: be instrumental in [ˌinstrə'mentl]	behilflich sein bei
insurance [in'ʃuərəns]	Versicherung
insurance policy [in'ʃuərəns ˌpɔlisi]	Versicherungspolice
integral ['intigrəl]	wesentlich
intent: be intent on ... [in'tent]	darauf versessen sein zu ...
inter- ['intə*]	zwischen-, untereinander
interaction [ˌintər'ækʃn]	Austausch
interest ['intrist]	Zinsen
interest rate ['intrist reit]	Zinssatz
interim ['intərim]	Zwischen-
interlude ['intəlu:d]	Pause, Unterbrechung

interpersonal skills [ˌintə'pə:sənəl skilz]	zwischenmenschliches Geschick
interpret [in'tə:prit]	auslegen, deuten
interpreter [in'tə:pritə*]	Dolmetscher
interrupt [ˌintə'rʌpt]	unterbrechen
interval ['intəvl]	Pause
introductory [ˌintrə'dʌktəri]	einleitend
invariably [in'vɛəriəbli]	stets
invent [in'vent]	erfinden
invention [in'venʃn]	Erfindung
inventor [in'ventə*]	Erfinder(in)
invest (in) [in'vest]	investieren (in)
investment [in'vestmənt]	Investition
invisible [in'vizəbl]	unsichtbar
invite [in'vait]	einladen
invoice ['invɔis]	Rechnung
involve [in'vɔlv]	erfordern
involved:	
be involved in [in'vɔlvd]	sich befinden in
inwards ['inwədz]	nach innen
iron out ['aiən]	aus dem Wege räumen
irritate ['iriteit]	ärgern
issue ['iʃu:]	herausgeben
item ['aitəm]	Punkt

J

jargon ['dʒɑ:gən]	Jargon, Fachsprache
jealous ['dʒeləs]	eifersüchtig
jerky ['dʒə:ki]	zuckend
jet lag ['dʒetlæg]	Jetlag, Zeitverschiebung
jewelry: piece of jewelry ['dʒu:əlri]	Schmuckstück
joint [dʒɔint]	gemeinsam
journey ['dʒə:ni]	Reise
justify ['dʒʌstifai]	rechtfertigen

K

keen [ki:n]	scharf
be keen on s.th.	begeistert sein von etw.
kettle [ketl]	Teekessel
keyboard ['ki:bɔ:d]	Tastatur

L

label ['leibl]   beschriften; Etikett

ladder ['lædə*]   Leiter
lap [læp]   Schoß
lasting ['lɑːstiŋ]   nachhaltig
latter: the latter   der/die/das letztere
['lætə*]

laundry ['lɔːndri]   Wäscherei
lawn [lɔːn]   Rasen
lawyer ['lɔːjə*]   Rechtsanwalt
leave: take one's   sich verabschieden
leave [liːv]

lecture ['lektʃə*]   Vortrag, Vorlesung
legal(ly) ['liːgəl(i)]   gesetzlich
length [leŋθ]   Länge
lengthy ['leŋθi]   lang(atmig)
level ['levl]   Pegel
 level off/out ['levl]   sich einpendeln
lightning ['laitniŋ]   blitzartig
liken ['laikən]   vergleichen
likewise ['laikwaiz]   ebenso
lily ['lili]   Lilie
limit ['limit]   einschränken
limitation [ˌlimi'teiʃn]   Beschränkung
line of work   Branche
[ˌlain əv 'wəːk]

lingua franca   Lingua franca,
[ˌliŋgwə'fræŋkə]   Verkehrssprache
linguistic [liŋ'gwistik]   linguistisch
liquor ['likə*]   Spirituosen
lit up [lit 'ʌp]   blau, sternhagelvoll
load [ləud]   Ladung
lobby ['lɔbi]   Hotelhalle
local resident   Ortsansässige(r)
[ˌləukl 'rezidənt]

location [ləu'keiʃn]   Platz, Stelle, Ort
logistics [ləu'dʒistiks]   Logistik
long-term ['lɔŋtəːm]   langfristig
look out for   aufpassen auf
[luk 'aut fɔː*]

loosely ['luːsli]   grob
loss [lɔs]   Verlust
lottery ['lɔtəri]   Lotto
low-fat ['ləufæt]   fettarm

M

main [mein]   Haupt-, hauptsächlich

 main body   Hauptteil
maintain [mein'tein]   aufrechterhalten
major ['meidʒə*]   größere(-r, -s)
manned [mænd]   bemannt, besetzt

manufacturer   Hersteller
[ˌmænju'fæktʃərə*]
manuscript   Manuskript
['mænjuskript]
map [mæp]   Karte
mark [mɑːk]   bezeichnen
mash [mæʃ]   zerdrücken
masterstroke   Glanzleistung
['mɑːstəstrəuk]
match [mætʃ]   anpassen
means [miːnz]   Mittel
measure ['meʒə*]   abschätzen
mechanic [mi'kænik]   Mechaniker
medication   Medikament
[ˌmedi'keiʃn]
Mediterranean   Mittelmeer-
[ˌmeditə'reiniən]
medium ['miːdiəm]   Medium
membership   Mitgliedschaft
['membəʃip]
memorable   unvergeßlich
['memərəbl]
mention ['menʃn]   erwähnen
mess [mes]   Klemme, Patsche
message ['mesidʒ]   Nachricht
military service   Militärdienst
['militəri 'səːvis]
mind: be caught in   sich über etw.
 two minds over s.th.   unschlüssig sein
['maindz]
mind-blowing   wahnsinnig
['maindbləuiŋ]
minutes ['minits]   Protokoll
miscarriage   Fehlgeburt
[mis'kæridʒ]
misinformation   Fehlinformation
[ˌmisinfə'meiʃn]
mix-up ['miksʌp]   Mißverständnis
mobile telephone   Funktelefon
[ˌməubail 'telifəun]
modification   Änderung
[ˌmɔdifi'keiʃn]
moron ['mɔːrɔn]   Trottel
motion ['məuʃn]   Bewegung
move *(a motion)*   einen Antrag stellen
[muːv]
multiple ['mʌltipl]   mehrfach
mutual ['mjuːtʃuəl]   gemeinsam

N

namely ['neimli]   nämlich
nap [næp]   Nickerchen, Schläfchen
napkin ['næpkin]   Serviette

narrate [nɔ'reit]	erzählen	**operate** ['ɔpəreit]	bedienen;
nasty ['nɑ:sti]	schmutzig; eklig; fies		operieren, tätig sein
necessity [ni'sesiti]	Notwendigkeit	**opportunity**	Gelegenheit;
negotiate [ni'gəuʃieit]	verhandeln	[ˌɔpə'tju:niti]	Möglichkeit
negotiation	Verhandlung	**opposed: as opposed**	im Gegensatz zu
[niˌgəuʃi'eiʃn]		**to** [ə'pəuzd]	
negotiator	Unterhändler	**opposite** ['ɔpəzit]	gegenüberliegend
[ni'gəuʃieitə*]		**the opposite sex**	das andere
network with	vernetzt sein mit		Geschlecht
['netwə:k]		**option** ['ɔpʃn]	Wahlmöglichkeit
neutral ['nju:trəl]	neutral	**oral** ['ɔrəl]	mündlich
nevertheless	trotzdem	**-oriented** ['ɔrientid]	-orientiert
[ˌnevəðə'les]		**otherwise: or**	oder auch nicht
nightmare ['naitmɛə*]	Alptraum	**otherwise** ['ʌðəwaiz]	
nod [nɔd]	nicken	**outdated** [aut'deitid]	veraltet, überholt
noisy ['nɔizi]	laut	**outline** ['autlain]	kurz umreißen
nominate ['nɔmineit]	ernennen	**outlook** ['autluk]	Aussichten
nomination	Nominierung	**out-of-date**	veraltet
[ˌnɔmi'neiʃn]		[ˌautəv'deit]	
Nordic ['nɔ:dik]	nordisch	**outset: from the**	von Anfang an
note [nəut]	Notiz; (Geld)Schein	**outset** ['autset]	
noun [naun]	Substantiv	**outstanding**	überragend
nourish ['nʌriʃ]	erhalten, nähren	[ˌaut'stændiŋ]	
nuclear ['nju:kliə*]	Kern-, atomar	**oval** ['əuvl]	oval
nut [nʌt]	Nuß	**oven** ['ʌvn]	Ofen
nutshell: in a	in aller Kürze	**overall** ['əuvərɔ:l]	Gesamt-
nutshell ['nʌtʃel]		**overpowering**	überwältigend
		[əuvə'pauəriŋ]	
		overwhelming	überwältigend
		[əuvə'welmiŋ]	
O		**owing to** ['əuiŋ]	wegen, infolge
		oyster ['ɔistə*]	Auster
object to s.th.	etwas gegen etw.	**oz. = ounce/ounces**	Unze/Unzen
[əb'dʒekt]	haben	[auns] ['aunsiz]	
objection [əb'dʒekʃn]	Einwand		
objective [əb'dʒektiv]	Ziel		
obliged: be obliged	gezwungen sein zu …	**P**	
to … [ə'blaidʒd]			
observation	Beobachtung		
[ˌɔbzə'veiʃn]		**package** ['pækidʒ]	Paket
observe [əb'zə:v]	bemerken	**panicky** ['pæniki]	in Panik
obtain [əb'tein]	erreichen	**paper: present a**	ein Referat halten
obvious ['ɔbviəs]	naheliegend	**paper** ['peipə*]	
obviously ['ɔbviəsli]	offensichtlich	**paragraph** ['pærəgrɑ:f]	(auf)gliedern
occasion [ə'keiʒn]	Gelegenheit, Anlaß	**parent company**	Stammfirma
occasionally	hin und wieder	['pɛərənt ˌkʌmpəni]	
[ə'keiʒənəli]		**partial** ['pɑ:ʃl]	teilweise
occupation [ˌɔkju'peiʃn]	Beruf	**partially** ['pɑ:ʃəli]	teilweise
occupied ['ɔkjupaid]	beschäftigt;	**participant**	Teilnehmer(in)
	tel.: besetzt	[pɑ:'tisipənt]	
occupy ['ɔkjupai]	in Besitz nehmen;	**participate**	sich beteiligen
	besitzen; innehaben	[pɑ:'tisipeit]	
occur [ə'kə:*]	passieren;	**participation**	Teilnahme
	vorkommen	[pɑ:ˌtisi'peiʃn]	
off-putting ['ɔfputiŋ]	entmutigend	**particular: in**	insbesondere
offence [ə'fens]	Vergehen	**particular**	
offend [ə'fend]	beleidigen	[pə'tikjulə*]	

particularly [pə'tikjuləli]	insbesondere	**preferably** ['prefərəbli]	vorzugsweise
pat [pæt]	klopfen, schlagen	**pregnant** ['pregnənt]	schwanger
patient ['peiʃnt]	geduldig	**prejudice** ['predʒudis]	Vorurteil
pause [pɔ:z]	Pause, Unterbrechung	**premises** ['premisiz]	Gelände
peak [pi:k]	einen Höchststand erreichen	**present: at present** ['prezənt]	im Moment
penalty ['penəlti]	Strafe	**presentation** [ˌprezən'teiʃn]	Präsentation
percentage [pə'sentidʒ]	prozentual	**preside (over)** [pri'zaid]	den Vorsitz haben (bei)
perform [pə'fɔ:m]	vorführen; ausführen	**pressure** ['preʃə*]	Druck
performance [pə'fɔ:məns]	Vortrag; Leistung	**prestigious** [pre'stidʒəs]	angesehen, namhaft
permanent ['pə:mənənt]	ständig	**presume** [pri'zju:m]	annehmen
permission [pə'miʃn]	Erlaubnis	**pretend** [pri'tend]	vortäuschen, vorgeben
personnel [ˌpə:sə'nel]	Belegschaft, Personal	**preview** ['pri:vju:]	(Vor)Ausblick
persuade [pə'sweid]	überreden	**previous** ['pri:viəs]	vorherig, früher
phase [feiz]	Phase	**principal** ['prinsipl]	Haupt-
phonetics [fə'netiks]	Phonetik, Lautschrift	**prior** ['praiə*]	vorherig
photocopier ['fəutəˌkɔpiə*]	Fotokopierer	**privacy** ['praivəsi]	Privatsphäre
		pro- [prəu]	pro-
pick-pocket ['pikˌpɔkit]	Taschendiebstahl begehen	**probability** [ˌprɔbə'biliti]	Wahrscheinlichkeit
pictorial [pik'tɔ:riəl]	illustriert	**procedure** [prə'si:dʒə*]	Prozedur, Verfahrensweise
pidgin ['pidʒin]	Pidginenglisch		
pie chart ['paitʃɑ:t]	Kreiseldiagramm	**proceed** [prə'si:d]	fortfahren
pitch [pitʃ]	Tonlage, Stimme	**proceedings** [prə'si:diŋz]	Veranstaltung
plain [plein]	einfach		
plastics ['plæstiks]	Plastik	**process** ['prəuses]	Vorgang
play down [ˌplei 'daun]	herunterspielen	**proclaim** [prə'kleim]	ausrufen
pleasant ['pleznt]	angenehm	**produce** [prə'dju:s]	herstellen
pleasantries ['plezntriz]	Nettigkeiten	**product range** ['prɔdʌkt reindʒ]	Produktbereich
plug [plʌg]	Stecker; Stöpsel	**production line** [prə'dʌkʃn lain]	Fließband
plug in [plʌg]	einstecken, -stöpseln; anschließen	**PR-officer** [pi:'ɑ:r ˌɔfisə]	Öffentlichkeitsreferent
point out [point]	hinweisen auf	**profile** ['prəufail]	Porträt
pointed ['pɔintid]	spitz	**profit** ['prɔfit]	Gewinn
poison ['pɔizn]	Gift	**prohibit** [prə'hibit]	verbieten
polish ['pɔliʃ]	verfeinern	**promote** [prə'məut]	Werbung machen für
pollute [pə'lu:t]	verschmutzen	**be promoted**	befördert werden
pop-up ['pɔpʌp]	automatisch	**promoter** [prə'məutə*]	Befürworter
population [ˌpɔpju'leiʃn]	Bevölkerung	**promotion** [prə'məuʃn]	Werbekampagne
		proposal [prə'pəuzl]	Vorschlag
pork [pɔ:k]	Schweinefleisch	**propose: propose a toast** [prə'pəuz]	einen Trinkspruch aussprechen
port [pɔ:t]	Hafen		
posh [pɔʃ]	(stink)vornehm	**prospective** [prə'spektiv]	zukünftig; potentiell
position [pə'ziʃn]	Stellung		
poster ['pəustə*]	Poster	**proud** [praud]	stolz
postpone [pəust'pəun, pə'spəun]	aufschieben	**proverb** ['prɔvə:b]	Sprichwort
		provide [prə'vaid]	bereitstellen
posture ['pɔstʃə*]	Haltung	**provide with**	versorgen mit
potential [pə'tenʃl]	potentiell, möglich	**pub-crawl** ['pʌbˌkrɔ:l]	Kneipenbummel
potentially [pə'tenʃəli]	potentiell	**publisher** ['pʌbliʃə*]	Verleger
precise [pri'sais]	genau	**pump** [pʌmp]	pumpen

punctual ['pʌŋktʃuəl]   pünktlich
punctuality   Pünktlichkeit
  [pʌŋktʃu'æliti]
purchase ['pəːtʃəs]   kaufen
purchasing officer   Einkäufer, Disponent
  ['pəːtʃəsiŋ ˌofisə*]
purpose ['pəːpəs]   Zweck
put across   übermitteln
  [ˌput ə'krɔs]
put forward   vorlegen
  [ˌput 'fɔːwəd]
put through   *tel.:* durchstellen,
  [ˌput 'θruː]   verbinden

Q

quadruple ['kwɔdrupl]   sich vervierfachen
qualification   Qualifikation
  [ˌkwɔlifi'keiʃn]
quality ['kwɔliti]   von hoher Qualtität
quality control   Qualitätskontrolle
  ['kwɔliti kənˌtrəul]
quantity ['kwɔntiti]   Quantität, Menge
quarrel ['kwɔrəl]   Streit
quarter ['kwɔːtə*]   Viertel
question tag   Frageanhängsel
  ['kwestʃn tæg]
questionnaire   Fragebogen
  [ˌkwestʃə'nɛə*]
queue [kjuː]   sich anstellen
quota ['kwəutə]   Quote

R

R&D = research and   Forschung und
  development   Entwicklung
  [ri'səːtʃ] [di'velɔpmənt]
raisin ['reizn]   Rosine
range: a wide   eine Vielzahl ...
  range of [reindʒ]
  range from ... to ...   sich bewegen
     zwischen ... und ...
rank [ræŋk]   rangmäßig anordnen
rape [reip]   Vergewaltigung
rapid(ly) ['ræpid(li)]   schnell, rapide
rarely ['rɛəli]   selten
rate [reit]   Geschwindigkeit
reason:
  give the reasons for   begründen
  ['riːznz]
reasonable ['riːzənəbl]   vernünftig
reassure [ˌriːə'ʃuə*]   beruhigen
received

pronunciation   englische Standard-
  [ri'siːvd]   aussprache
recently ['riːsntli]   kürzlich
recipe ['resipi]   Rezept
recognize ['rekəgnaiz]   anerkennen, zugeben
recommend   empfehlen
  [ˌrekə'mend]
recommendation   Empfehlung
  [ˌrekəmen'deiʃn]
recondition   überholen
  [ˌriːkən'diʃn]
record ['rekɔːd]   Aufzeichnung, Beleg
rectangular   rechteckig
  [rek'tæŋgjulə*]
redecorate   renovieren
  [riː'dekəreit]
redo [riː'duː]   renovieren
reduce [ri'djuːs]   vermindern
reduction [ri'dʌkʃn]   Nachlaß
refer to [ri'fəː*]   sich beziehen auf
refinery [ri'fainəri]   Raffinerie
refreshing [ri'freʃiŋ]   erfrischend
refrigerator   Kühlschrank
  [ri'fridʒəreitə*]
refugee [ˌrefju'dʒiː]   Flüchtling
refuse [ri'fjuːz]   ablehnen
regard:
  have a high regard   etw. sehr schätzen
  for s.th. [ri'gaːd]
  as regards [ri'gaːdz]   was ... anbetrifft
regardless of   ungeachtet, ohne
  [ri'gaːdlis]   Rücksicht auf
regiment ['redʒimənt]   Regiment
region:
  somewhere in the
  region of ['riːdʒn]   ungefähr
register ['redʒistə*]   sich einschreiben
registration   Einschreibung
  [ˌredʒi'streiʃn]
rehearse [ri'həːs]   proben, einstudieren
reign [rein]   herrschen
reject [ri'dʒekt]   ablehnen
relate to [ri'leit]   betreffen, zutreffen
   auf
relative ['relətiv]   Verwandte(r)
release [ri'liːs]   freilassen, freigeben
relevance ['relivəns]   Relevanz, Bedeutung
reluctant [ri'lʌktənt]   unwillig
rely on [ri'lai]   sich verlassen auf
remain [ri'mein]   bestehenbleiben
remark [ri'maːk]   Äußerung,
   Bemerkung
remote [ri'məut]   entfernt
remove [ri'muːv]   entfernen
renew [ri'njuː]   erneuern
repair [ri'pɛə*]   Reparatur
repetition [ˌrepi'tiʃn]   Wiederholung

rephrase [ri:'freiz]	anders formulieren
replace [ri'pleis]	ersetzen
reply [ri'plai]	antworten
represent [ˌrepri'zent]	darstellen
representative [ˌrepri'zentətiv]	Teilnehmer
request [ri'kwest]	bitten
research [ri'sə:tʃ]	Forschung
resemble [ri'zembl]	ähneln
reservation [ˌrezə'veiʃn]	Reservierung; Bedenken
reserve [ri'zə:v]	reservieren
be reserved for s.o.	j-m vorbehalten sein
reserved [ri'zə:vd]	zurückhaltend
resident ['rezidənt]	Einwohner(in); Anlieger(in)
resist [ri'zist]	sich sträuben
resolve [ri'zɔlv]	klären, regeln; Vorsatz
respect: with respect, ... [ri'spekt]	bei allem Respekt, ...
respected	geschätzt
respond [ri'spɔnd]	antworten
response [ri'spɔns]	Antwort
responsibility [riˌspɔnsə'biliti]	Verantwortung
result: as a result [ri'zʌlt]	folglich
resume ['ri'zju:m]	die Sitzung fortsetzen
resumé ['rezjumei]	Zusammenfassung
retail ['ri:teil]	Einzelhandel
reveal [ri'vi:l]	zeigen
review [ri'vju:]	wiederholen; überprüfen; Rückblick
revive [ri'vaiv]	wiederaufblühen
reward [ri'wɔ:d]	belohnen
ridicule ['ridikju:l]	verspotten
rip up [rip]	zerreißen
rise: give rise to [raiz]	führen zu
risky ['riski]	riskant
rival ['raivəl]	Konkurrent
roar [rɔ:*]	brüllen
rob [rɔb]	rauben
Romansch [rəu'mænʃ]	Romantsch
rough sea [ˌrʌf 'si:]	unruhige See
route [ru:t]	Route, Strecke
rude [ru:d]	unhöflich, grob
rumour ['ru:mə*]	Gerücht
run into [ˌrʌn in'tu]	zufällig treffen

S

safeguard ['seifgɑ:d]	sichern
salary ['sæləri]	Gehalt
sales promotion [ˌseilz prə'məuʃn]	Werbung
satisfaction [ˌsætis'fækʃn]	Befriedigung; Erfüllung (des Vertrags)
saucer ['sɔ:sə*]	Untertasse
scarf [skɑ:f]	Schal; Tuch
schedule ['ʃedju:l]	(Zeit)Plan
scheduled ['ʃedju:ld]	wie geplant
scholar ['skɔlə*]	Wissenschaftler
scholarship ['skɔləʃip]	Stipendium
scientist ['saiəntist]	Wissenschaftler(in)
score [skɔ:*]	Punkte(zahl)
scratch [skrætʃ]	kratzen
scribble ['skribl]	kritzeln
seating ['si:tiŋ]	Sitzgelegenheit
second (a motion) ['sekənd]	(einen Antrag) unterstützen
second: be second to none ['sekənd tu 'nʌn]	unübertroffen sein
be second to	an zweiter Stelle kommen nach
seconder ['sekəndə*]	Befürworter
secretariat [ˌsekri'tɛəriət]	Sekretariat
secretary ['sekrətəri]	Sekretär(in)
secretly ['si:krətli]	insgeheim, im stillen
section ['sekʃn]	Abschnitt
secure [si'kjuə*]	sichern
security [si'kjuəriti]	Sicherheit
select [si'lekt]	auswählen
selection [si'lekʃn]	Wahl
self-assessment [ˌselfə'sesmənt]	Selbsteinschätzung
sensitive ['sensitiv]	sensibel, empfindsam
sentence ['sentəns]	Satz
sequence ['si:kwəns]	die Reihenfolge angeben von
serious ['siəriəs]	ernsthaft
servant ['sə:vənt]	Diener
session ['seʃn]	Sitzung
be in session ['seʃn]	abgehalten werden
set the scene [si:n]	die Ausgangssituation darlegen
set up [ˌset 'ʌp]	gründen; bilden
settle (a time) ['setl]	festlegen
sex [seks]	Geschlecht; Sex(ualität)
sharp [ʃɑ:p]	schnell, scharf
shattering ['ʃætəriŋ]	erschütternd
shelve [ʃelv]	auf Eis legen

shop steward [ˌʃɔp 'stjuəd] — Obmann, Vertrauensmann

shoplift ['ʃɔplift] — Ladendiebstahl begehen

show of hands [ˌʃəu əv 'hændz] — Handheben

shrug (one's) shoulders [ˌʃrʌg 'ʃəuldəz] — mit den Schultern zucken

shy [ʃai] — schüchtern

sight [sait] — Anblick

signal ['signəl] — signalisieren, zu verstehen geben

significant [sig'nifikənt] — bezeichnend

signify ['signifai] — bedeuten, zum Ausdruck bringen

similar to ['similə*] — ähnlich

simmer ['simə*] — köcheln, ziehen lassen

simplify ['simplifai] — vereinfachen

simulation [ˌsimju'leiʃn] — Vortäuschung, Nachahmung

simultaneous interpretation [ˌsiməl'teiniəs inˌtə:pri'teiʃn] — Simultandolmetschen

sincerely [sin'siəli] — aufrichtig

skill [skil] — Technik, Kunst

slap [slæp] — schlagen auf

slick [slik] — clever, gewieft

slide [slaid] — Dia

slightly ['slaitli] — leicht, geringfügig

slip [slip] — abrutschen

slogan ['sləugən] — Slogan

smooth [smu:ð] — geschmeidig

smoothly ['smu:ðli] — leicht

smuggle ['smʌgl] — schmuggeln

snappy ['snæpi] — forsch

snapshot ['snæpʃɔt] — Schnappschuß

socket ['sɔkit] — Steckdose

soften ['sɔfn] — mildern

solar ['səulə*] — Solar-, Sonnen-

solely ['səulli] — nur

solution [sə'lu:ʃn] — Lösung

solve [sɔlv] — (Problem) lösen

somewhat ['sʌmwɔt] — ein wenig

sore [sɔ:*] — wund

source [sɔ:s] — Quelle

spank s.o. [spæŋk] — j-m den Hintern versohlen

specific [spə'sifik] — bestimmt

specification [ˌspesifi'keiʃn] — Spezifizierung, (technische) Beschreibung

specify ['spesifai] — genaue Angaben machen über

spectacles ['spektəklz] — Brille

spectator [spek'teitə*] — Zuschauer

spectator sport [spek'teitə spɔ:t] — Zuschauersport

speculation [ˌspekju'leiʃn] — Spekulation

speed [spi:d] — Geschwindigkeit

spherical ['sferikl] — kugelförmig

spider ['spaidə*] — Spinne

spirits ['spirits] — alkoholische Getränke

split [split] — halbe Flasche

spoil [spɔil] — verderben

spouse [spauz] — Ehepartner(in)

spout [spaut] — (aus)speien, (heraus)spritzen

spring to one's feet [spriŋ] — aufspringen

sprinkle ['spriŋkl] — streuen

sprint [sprint] — rennen

spy [spai] — spionieren

square [skwɛə*] — Kästchen

stability [stə'biliti] — Stabilität

staff [sta:f] — Belegschaft

stage [steidʒ] — Phase, Stadium

stamp [stæmp] — stampfen

stand [stænd] — Stand

standard ['stændəd] — Normal-

stare at [stɛə*] — anstarren

state [steit] — darlegen

statement ['steitmənt] — Aussage

status ['steitəs] — Rang

steady ['stedi] — fest

steam iron ['sti:m ˌaiən] — Dampfbügeleisen

steering wheel ['stiəriŋ wi:l] — Lenkrad

step-by-step [ˌstep bai 'step] — schrittweise

stiff [stif] — steif

stimulant ['stimjulənt] — Anregungsmittel

stir [stə:*] — umrühren

stomp [stɔmp] — trampeln

stone dead [ˌstəun'ded] — mausetot

store [stɔ:*] — speichern

storey ['stɔ:ri] — Geschoß, Stockwerk, Etage

straightforward [ˌstreit'fɔ:wəd] — direkt

streamline ['stri:mlain] — vereinfachen

strengthen ['streŋθn] — festigen

striped [straipt] — gestreift

stroke [strəuk] — Schrägstrich

structure ['strʌktʃə*] — Aufbau, Struktur

stumble ['stʌmbl] — stolpern

stylize ['stailaiz] — stilisieren

sub-committee ['sʌbkəˌmiti]	Unterausschuß
submit [səb'mit]	vorlegen
substance ['sʌbstəns]	Substanz, Materie; das Wesentliche
substantial [səb'stænʃl]	beträchtlich
substitute (for) ['sʌbstitjuːt]	Ersatz (für)
summarize ['sʌməraiz]	zusammenfassen
sum up [ˌsʌm 'ʌp]	zusammenfassen
supersede [ˌsuːpə'siːd]	ablösen
supervisor ['suːpəvaizə*]	Aufseher
supper ['sʌpə*]	Abendessen
supply [sə'plai]	Vorrat; Angebot
surroundings [sə'raundiŋz]	Umgebung
survive [sə'vaiv]	überleben
sustain [sə'stein]	durchhalten
sweatshirt ['swetʃəːt]	Sweatshirt

T

table ['teibl]	Tabelle
table *(matters)* ['teibl]	auf die Tagesordnung setzen lassen
tag [tæg]	Schild
talented ['tæləntid]	talentiert
tap [tæp]	klopfen
tap [tæp]	Wasserhahn
target ['tɑːgit]	Ziel, Soll
task [tɑːsk]	Aufgabe
taxation [tæk'seiʃn]	Besteuerung
tease [tiːz]	aufziehen, verspotten
teetotaller [tiː'təutələ*]	Antialkoholiker(in)
temperature ['tempritʃə*]	Temperatur
temporary ['tempərəri]	vorübergehend
tempt [tempt]	in Versuchung führen, dazu bringen
tend [tend]	neigen zu
tentative ['tentətiv]	vorläufig
term:	
in terms of [təːmz]	was ... betrifft
be on speaking terms	miteinander sprechen
therefore ['ðɛəfɔː*]	also
thorough ['θʌrə]	gründlich
thought-provoking ['θɔːtprəˌvəukiŋ]	nachdenklich stimmend
threaten ['θretn]	drohen

three-dimensional = 3-D [ˌθriːdai'menʃnl]	dreidimensional
throughout [θruː'aut]	überall in
thumb [θʌm]	Daumen
tidy ['taidi]	ordentlich
tie [tai]	binden
tie [tai]	Stimmengleichheit
tight [tait]	streng
tights [taits]	Strumpfhosen
timetable ['taimteibl]	Fahrplan
tin [tin]	Blech
tine [tain]	Zinke
tinned [tind]	in Dosen
tiny talk ['taini tɔːk]	Mini-Kommunikation
tip [tip]	Tip, Ratschlag; Trinkgeld geben
to and fro [frəu]	hin und her
toast [təust]	Toast(brot); Trinkspruch
tolerant ['tɔlərənt]	tolerant
tone [təun]	Ton
tongue [tʌŋ]	Zunge
toothbrush ['tuːθbrʌʃ]	Zahnbürste
toothpaste ['tuːθpeist]	Zahnpasta
top off [ˌtɔp 'ɔf]	abschließen
topic ['tɔpik]	Thema
toss one's head [tɔs]	den Kopf zurückwerfen
tour [tuə*]	Rundgang
trace [treis]	ausfindig machen
trainer ['treinə*]	Ausbilder
training ['treiniŋ]	Ausbildung, Schulung
transaction [træn'zækʃn]	Durchführung; Transaktion
transition [træn'ziʃn]	Übergang
transparency [træns'pærənsi]	Dia
transport ['trænspɔːt]	Transportmöglichkeiten
tray [trei]	Tablett
treble ['trebl]	sich verdreifachen
trend [trend]	Trend, Tendenz
triangular [trai'æŋgjulə*]	dreieckig
tricky ['triki]	heikel, knifflig
troops [truːps]	Truppen
trustworthy ['trʌstˌwəːði]	vertrauenswürdig
tub [tʌb]	Badewanne
tulip ['tjuːlip]	Tulpe
turkey ['təːki]	Truthahn
turn: take turns in [təːnz]	sich abwechseln bei ..., abwechselnd ...
turn down [ˌtəːn 'daun]	ablehnen, ausschlagen
turnover ['təːnəuvə*]	Umsatz

twice [twais]	zweimal	**use: make use of**	verwenden
typical ['tipikl]	typisch	[ju:s]	
ulcer ['ʌlsə*]	Geschwür	**utensils** [ju'tenslz]	Utensilien, Geräte
		utmost ['ʌtməust]	äußerst, höchst

U

unacceptable	nicht akzeptabel
[ˌʌnək'septəbl]	
unanimous	einstimmig
[ju'næniməs]	
unashamed	schamlos
[ˌʌnə'ʃeimd]	
unavoidable	unvermeidlich
[ˌʌnə'vɔidəbl]	
unaware [ˌʌnə'wɛə*]	ohne zu wissen
unbearable	unerträglich
[ʌn'bɛərəbl]	
underestimate	unterschätzen
[ˌʌndər'estimeit]	
undergo [ˌʌndə'gəu]	durchmachen
underwear	Unterwäsche
['ʌndəwɛə*]	
unemployment	Arbeitslosigkeit
[ˌʌnim'plɔimənt]	
unenviable	wenig beneidens-
[ʌn'enviəbl]	wert
unforgettable	unvergeßlich
[ˌʌnfə'getəbl]	
unfortunate	ungeschickt
[ʌn'fɔ:tʃnit]	
unfortunately	leider
[ʌn'fɔ:tʃənitli]	
unified ['ju:nifaid]	vereint
universal	allgemein verbreitet
[ˌju:ni'və:səl]	
unload [ʌn'ləud]	entladen, löschen
unplug [ʌn'plʌg]	herausziehen
unpresentable	nicht präsentabel,
[ˌʌnpri'zentəbl]	unansehnlich
unsteady [ʌn'stedi]	unsicher,
	schwankend
up: be up to s.b.	j-m überlassen sein
up-and-coming	aufstrebend
[ˌʌpən'kʌmiŋ]	
update [ʌp'deit]	auf den neuesten
	Stand bringen,
	aktualisieren
upset [ʌp'set]	verärgert
upside down	auf den Kopf gestellt
[ˌʌpsaid'daun]	
up-to-date [ˌʌptə'deit]	modern
urge [ə:dʒ]	eindringlich
	nahelegen
urine ['juərin]	Urin
usage ['ju:sidʒ]	Gebrauch

V

vague [veig]	vage, undeutlich
value ['vælju:]	schätzen;
	Wert
vanish ['væniʃ]	verschwinden
variety: a variety of	verschiedene ...
[və'raiəti]	
various ['vɛəriəs]	verschiedene
varnish ['va:niʃ]	lackieren
vary ['vɛəri]	unterschiedlich sein
vast [va:st]	enorm
VCR = video cassette	
recorder [ˌvi:si:'a:*]	Videorekorder
vehicle ['vi:ikl]	Vehikel, Mittel
venture ['ventʃə*]	Unternehmen
venue ['venju:]	(Veranstaltungs)Ort
verbal ['və:bəl]	verbal, Wort-
vertical ['və:tikl]	senkrecht
vessel ['vesl]	Gefäß
via ['vaiə]	über
viability [ˌvaiə'biliti]	Realisierbarkeit
vice [vais]	Vize
vice versa	umgekehrt
[ˌvaisi 'və:sə]	
viewable ['vju:əbl]	zu besichtigen
viewpoint ['vju:pɔint]	Standpunkt
village ['vilidʒ]	Dorf
visual aids	Anschauungsmaterial
[ˌviʒuəl 'eidz]	
vital ['vaitl]	lebenswichtig
voice [vɔis]	zum Ausdruck
	bringen
volume ['vɔlju:m]	Volumen
volunteer [ˌvɔlən'tiə*]	Freiwillige(r);
	sich anbieten
vote [vəut]	wählen
voyage ['vɔiidʒ]	Seereise

W

waiter ['weitə*]	Kellner
walkman ['wɔ:kmən]	Walkman
wallet ['wɔlit]	Brieftasche
want: for want of	in Ermangelung
[wɔnt]	
warranty ['wɔrənti]	Garantie
waste [weist]	Verschwendung

wave [weiv]	winken	**wind** [waind]	kurbeln
wear [wɛə*]	(*Kleidung*) tragen	**windscreen**	Windschutzscheibe
weigh [wei]	wiegen	['windskri:n]	
weight [weit]	Gewicht	**withdraw money**	Geld abheben
weird [wiəd]	verrückt	[wið'drɔ:]	
welder ['weldə*]	Schweißer;	**withstand** [wið'stænd]	standhalten
	Schweißbrenner	**witness** ['witnis]	Zeuge sein von,
well-groomed	gepflegt		erleben
[ˌwel'gru:md]		**witty** ['witi]	geistreich, witzig
while:		**works manager**	Betriebs-, Werksleiter
for a while [wail]	für kurze Zeit	['wə:ks ˌmænidʒə*]	
whilst [wailst]	während	**worth** [wə:θ]	wert
whip [wip]	schlagen	**worthwhile:** [ˌwə:θ'wail]	
whisper ['wispə*]	flüstern	be worthwhile	sich lohnen
whistle ['wisl]	pfeifen	**would-be** ['wudbi:]	Möchtegern-
wholesale ['həulseil]	Großhandel	**yawn** [jɔ:n]	gähnen
wholesaler ['həulseilə*]	Großhändler	**yuppie** ['jʌpi]	Yuppie
wide [waid]	weit	**zero** ['ziərəu]	Null
width [widθ]	Weite	**zoom** [zu:m]	sausen lassen

NOTIZEN

ACKNOWLEDGEMENTS

Most of the activities that appear in this book
are the result of years of experimentation and
development. Some are entirely original, others
are modified versions of traditional formulae
for practising oral skills. We sincerely hope that
language trainers will not only benefit from the
activities we have presented but also be
motivated to develop their own.

Acknowledgements are due to the following:

© The signs and notices (on pages 211–212)
are reprinted from Anguished English,
copyright 1987 by Richard Lederer. Used with
the permission of the author and the publisher,
Wyrick & Company, P.O. Box 89, Charleston,
SC 29402, USA.

The pictures on pages four and five are from
the following Finnish films:

Matti Kassila: Tyttö kuun sillalta, 1953
(My Moonlight Love)
Wilho Ilmari: Kuriton sukupolvi, 1938
(The New Generation)
Jukka Virtanen: Pähkähullu Suomi, 1967
(Finland in a Nut's Hell)
Toivo Särkkä: Runon kuningas ja muuttolintu, 1940
(The Poet and the Emigrée)
Ilmari Unho: 13. koputus, 1945
(Knock Thirteen Times)
Aki Kaurismäki: Boheemielämää, 1992
(La vie de bohème)

Thanks to Phill Lewis and Simon Boswell
for help with the brand names in The Problem
with Language. (Working English p.171)
Thanks to Geoffrey Hilton for the idea for
The most amazing bicycle in the world.
(Working English p.164)
Special thanks to TVA, Kauniainen,
for material testing.